QUEERING
ANARCHISM

Addressing and Undressing Power and Desire

QUEERING ANARCHISM

Addressing and Undressing Power and Desire

Edited by C. B. Daring, J. Rogue, Deric Shannon, and Abbey Volcano

AK PRESS

EDINBURGH • OAKLAND • BALTIMORE

Queering Anarchism: Addressing and Undressing Power and Desire
© 2012 Edited by C. B. Daring, J. Rogue, Deric Shannon, and Abbey Volcano

This edition © 2012 AK Press (Oakland, Edinburgh, Baltimore)
ISBN: 978-1-84935-120-1 | eBook ISBN: 978-1-84935-121-8
Library of Congress Control Number: 2012914347

AK Press   AK Press
674-A 23rd Street   PO Box 12766
Oakland, CA 94612   Edinburgh EH8 9YE
USA   Scotland
www.akpress.org   www.akuk.com
akpress@akpress.org   ak@akedin.demon.co.uk

The above addresses would be delighted to provide you with the latest AK Press distribution catalog, which features the several thousand books, pamphlets, zines, audio and video products, and stylish apparel published and/or distributed by AK Press. Alternatively, visit our websites for the complete catalog, latest news, and secure ordering.

Visit us at:
www.akpress.org
www.akuk.com
www.revolutionbythebook.akpress.org

Printed in Canada on acid-free, recycled paper, with union labor.

To all those struggling toward a world without bosses, borders, and boredom.

(dis)Contents

Preface

MARTHA ACKELSBERG

Queering anarchism? What would that mean? Isn't "anarchism" enough of a bogeyman in this country that any effort to "queer" it would only make it appear even more alien and irrelevant to mainstream culture than it already is? Why do it? And why now?

Because—as this anthology makes evident in its multifaceted exploration of the many dimensions of both anarchism and queer— we have only just begun to understand the many possibilities offered by a queered anarchism, both with respect to critiques of existing institutions and practices and with respect to imagining alternatives to them.

It is a true pleasure to see this anthology—so long in the making—become available to the reading public. As the authors note in their introduction, there have been many books written on anarchism, and many others on queer politics and theory. Interest in the *activist* side of anarchism, in particular, seems to have increased in recent years. And—at least within more politically progressive communities—attention to queer activism has also grown. But this volume is, I believe, the first to bring these two traditions—in both their intellectual and activist dimensions—together and into conversation, particularly for "lay," non-academic readers. The project is certainly a timely one, and the outcome of the years of planning demonstrates both the wisdom of the editors' initial goals and the value of the work they stimulated.

The editors' introduction sets the appropriate tone for the volume—highlighting both some of the myths about anarchism and the complexities of the term "queer." I must admit that my enthusiasm for their introduction (and for the work as a whole) is probably connected to the fact that I share their explication of "anarchism"— its destructive as well as its constructive urges, its multi-dimensionality, and the ways it provides a framework for addressing what recent (feminist) scholarship has referred to as "intersectionality."[1]

Although anarchism has often been thought of as synonymous with nihilism or, alternatively, as an extreme version of a kind of libertarianism (à la Robert Nozick[2]), most of the essays in this book locate themselves within the broader tradition of what has been referred to as more collectivist or communitarian anarchism—that which treats individuality and community as mutually constitutive, rather than as in opposition to one another. That tradition—exemplified in the writings of Mikhail Bakunin, Peter Kropotkin, Gustav Landauer, Errico Malatesta, Emma Goldman, and Spanish anarchists—values freedom *and* equality, individuality *and* community, and treats freedom as a *social product*, rather than as a value/goal that is necessarily in tension with community.[3] Such an approach—often difficult even to fathom within the liberal individualist culture of the US—is wonderfully illustrated through the unusual format/framing of a number of the chapters, e.g. "queering the script" in the CRAC collective's graphic presentation on sexuality, or the mixing of personal and analytical materials in Sandra Jeppesen's essay on queering heterosexuality, or in Farhang Rouhani's or Benjamin Shepard's essays on organizing, among others.

More generally, this book offers us, its readers, an eclectic mix of topics, but also of genres, a mix that highlights and manifests the multiple perspectives offered by anarchist approaches, particularly when those approaches, themselves, are "queered." The placement of somewhat more traditional "academic" essays—such as those, for example, by Jamie Heckert, J. Rogue, and Diana Becerra, or by Liat Ben Moshe, Anthony Nocella, and AJ Withers—alongside the contribution of the CRAC collective, or even of what we might term "analytical personal testimony" offered by many of the writers—provides readers with an opportunity to "queer" our own expectations of what constitute serious intellectual interventions. In the process, as both anarchism and queer theory propose, these challenges open us up to further explorations of both theory and practice.

I will not attempt here to explore, or even point toward, the many theoretical and practical questions offered by the essays in this volume. The editors' introduction does a fine job of surveying the broader landscape. But I would note that one of the things I find most valuable is precisely the *range* of topics addressed and the authors' explorations of the language necessary to communicate their views in ways that are both respectful of the complexity of the experiences discussed and, at the same time, committed to clarity. Queer theory, in particular, can often be dense and obscure, seemingly meant to be read (or at least understood) only by those in the academy who are willing to spend long hours reading (and rereading) it. But the essays in this volume communicate complexity without obfuscation, many of them drawing on real-life, concrete organizing experiences to elucidate the challenges to fixed categories and to binary thinking that have traditionally characterized queer theory. At the same time, they highlight the difficulties posed *for* an activism that attempts to move forward without re-inscribing those same binaries in the name of challenging them.

This dimension of both anarchist and queer politics—the (anarchist) insistence that "means must be consistent with ends," that the way to create a new world is to take steps *to* create it, to live the life we want to live—to my mind constitutes both its greatest contribution to the theory and practice of social change *and* the greatest challenge to its instantiation. It is, I think, why (as the editors note) anarchism has *both* destructive and creative dimensions: ideally, the creation of the new *itself* destroys the old forms, by making them irrelevant or *passé*. But, of course, that is only in the ideal world: as many of the essays in this volume (and as the recent experience of the "occupy" movements) attest, the "mere" creating of alternatives is often treated as dangerous and/or threatening by powers that be, and responded to with force and violence. Peaceful prefigurative politics[4]—whether anarchist collectives in revolutionary Spain of the 1930s, the communes of the 60s in the US, or the "free spaces" of food coops, book exchanges, child-care exchanges, or "radical queer spaces"—may well be ignored only until they start being successful, at which point they confront the full force of the economic, religious, sexual, and/or police powers to which they pose a challenge.

How do we begin to talk about these challenges—or the goals to which they aspire? If we use the language of "empowerment"—even in the sense of "power to," rather than of "power over"—we find ourselves, willy-nilly, in the discourse of "power," and, perhaps, in the midst of the very binaries that we are trying to avoid or challenge. How *do* we challenge that binary—or others—without reinscribing it? As Ryan Conrad put it, "How do we, as radical queer and trans folks, push back against the emerging hegemony of rainbow flavored neoliberalism and the funneling of our energy into narrow campaigns that only reinforce the hierarchical systems and institutions we fundamentally oppose? How do we reconcile the contradiction of our anger and fervent criticism of so called equality when presently many of our material lives depend on accessing resources through the very subject of our critique?"

The strength of this volume is not that it provides simple solutions to these questions (if it did, we'd have a handy blueprint for revolution!). Rather, the essays—each in its own way—persistently and consistently ask them and explore the answers. In the process, they queer not only anarchism, but our ways of seeing, and understanding, the connections and mutual reinforcements among structures of political, religious, economic, sexual, and other forms of power and hierarchy in the daily worlds we inhabit.

1   See Kimberlé Crenshaw, "Mapping the Margins: Intersectionality, Identity Politics, and Violence Against Women of Color" in *The Public Nature of Private Violence*, ed. Martha A. Fineman and Roxanne Mykitiuk (New York: Routledge, 1994), 93–118; also Martha A. Ackelsberg, *Free Women of Spain: Anarchism and the Struggle for the Emancipation of Women* (Bloomington: Indiana University Press, 1991; reprinted AK Press, 2004), especially ch. 1; and Kathy Ferguson, *Emma Goldman: Political Thinking in the Streets* (Lanham, MD: Rowman and Littlefield, 2011), especially "Introduction."

2   See Robert Nozick, *Anarchy, State and Utopia* (New York: Basic Books, 1974).

3   See my *Free Women of Spain*, ch. 1; also Kathy Ferguson, *Emma Goldman: Political Thinking in the Streets*; and Colin Ward, *Anarchy in Action* (London: George Allen and Unwin, 1973), among others.

4   Barbara Epstein's *Political Protest and Cultural Revolution: Nonviolent Direct Action in the 1970s and 1980s* (Berkeley: University of California Press, 1993) introduced the term into much radical theorizing; it has since been taken up by many theorists, including in a number of the essays in this book.

Queer Meet Anarchism, Anarchism Meet Queer

C. B. DARING, J. ROGUE, ABBEY VOLCANO, AND DERIC SHANNON

The purpose of this book is an introduction of sorts—an "introduction" in two meanings of the word. Queer politics and anarchism have not been completely disconnected on the ground, but finding texts that draw out these relations can be a difficult task. We think queer politics and anarchism have a lot to offer each other and we're excited by some of the connections being drawn between the two by people in their writing, organizing, struggling, and daily lives. So we want to suggest that an introduction to the overlaps between anarchist and queer politics could be useful at this juncture.

We also mean "introduction" in a different sense of the word. That is, we'd like more of our anarchist comrades to be acquainted with queer politics and we'd like more of our queer friends to be familiar with anarchism, again, because we think these connections can be particularly fruitful. We hope that this collection can be an introduction in the sense of two ideas meeting one another, or perhaps getting to know one another better, as we don't mean to suggest that queers and anarchists are two distinct and separate groups (they're not). Nor do we really want to suggest that queers or anarchists necessarily always have a decent grasp of queer and anarchist politics respectively.

So to be clear, we're not suggesting that this idea is particularly novel. There are already many folks doing this work. If we just look at the last five years or so—from "Bash Back!" to "Black and Pink" to "Queers Without Borders" to name just a few—groups with a variety of theories, practices, and lives have been staking out space within the larger project of queering anarchism. Indeed, people with varying levels of involvement in each of these groups, and more, have contributed to the collection you now hold in your hands.

We put together this volume to help draw out some of the propositions and debates within this overlap. And, importantly, we tried to collect pieces that were not written for an academic audience.

Much of queer theoretical writing is dense and difficult. While we feel that dense and difficult texts have their place, we wanted to provide a collection for a general audience.

That said, we'd like to begin the book with some short introductions of our own. Anarchism is littered with misinformation and distortions, so any text introducing materials on anarchism might include a brief explanation of where the authors are coming from. Similarly, anarchism is admittedly a diverse milieu, not a unified movement, so while the editors of this volume don't have a strict and singular "unity" on the meanings and dimensions of anarchism, we do hope that briefly sketching out what we mean by the term can serve as a method for making sense of the contents of this volume for readers unfamiliar with anarchism. Similarly "queer" is a contested term, used in a number of different ways and requires a bit of unpacking. We don't hope to resolve large debates within anarchist, queer, and anarchist-queer communities about these definitions, meanings, and so on, but rather hope to provide some insight on the pieces in this particular volume and, with any luck, provide a framework for continuing much-needed discussion with this short introduction.

Anarchism

Many volumes have been written throughout history explicating anarchism, and the movement has seen many historical periods of retreat and resurgence. We're living in a resurgence of interest in anarchist ideas right now. It's a common trope that after the Battle of Seattle in 1999—when a loose coalition of environmentalists, trade unionists, anarchists, feminists, and many others shut down the World Trade Organization conference—anarchism has seen a bit of a rebirth, often connected with the anti/alter-globalization movement. Similarly, the Occupy Wall Street Movement was initiated by anarchists, among others, and has had heavy anarchist involvement.[1] And mainstream news media, in both instances, have often demonized anarchists and spread misinformation about us.

This is certainly nothing new. Alexander Berkman, as far back as 1929 in his introduction to anarchism, exclaimed that "Anarchism has many enemies; they won't tell you the truth about it...newspapers and publications—the capitalistic press—are...against it."[2] As such, he started his book with a list of what anarchism is not:

It is not bombs, disorder, or chaos.
It is not robbery and murder.
It is not a war of each against all.
It is not a return to barbarism or to the wild state of man.
Anarchism is the very opposite of all that.
Anarchism means that you should be free; that no one should enslave you, boss you, rob you, or impose on you.[3]

There is a rather long history of anarchism being distorted and many anarchist writers have spent considerable years trying to clear up these misconceptions.

"The Urge to Destroy"

Nevertheless, attempts to paint anarchism in purely peaceful terms miss out on its destructive impulse. By this, of course, we don't mean that anarchists revel in wanton destruction like mainstream media often depict in their caricatures of anarchists. But anarchists do hold a critique of the existing society and attempting to hide or ignore this puts unnecessary limits on anarchism. We might discuss anarchism in terms what it seeks to destroy and negate.

The anarchist analysis of our present society, for example, has always held that capitalist property relations are based on a legalized robbery of sorts. That is, we allow (and our laws defend) a system in which things like housing, food, water—the things that everyone needs access to in order to live dignified lives of their own choosing—are privately owned and sold for profit. Similarly, we allow the means of producing these things, and everything else too, to be owned privately. And when most of us go to work, we make the owners of these things even wealthier through our labor. Anarchists propose to negate this legalized robbery—the system that we call capitalism.

We also live in societies in which we are alienated from the means of decision-making. While we are typically rented by bosses in our working lives, we are ruled by political bosses elsewhere. If we go against the dictates of these political bosses, we can be beaten, kidnapped, caged, or even killed by police. And the decisions that affect our lives are made by politicians that ostensibly "represent" us. Anarchists argue that we should negate political representation—the institution that we call the state.

Anarchism also argues for alterations to our selves, and anarchists in the past have suggested that the process of negating our institutions also involves a process of changing our daily lives and understandings of the world. Italian anarchist Errico Malatesta, for example, wrote that "(b)etween man [sic] and his social environment there is a reciprocal action. Men make society what it is and society makes men what they are, and the result is therefore a kind of vicious circle. To transform society men must be changed, and to transform men, society must be changed."[4] This means fighting against and in some instances unlearning relations of domination including, but not limited to racism, ableism, sexism, heterosexism, and so on. Anarchists, then, argue that we negate all aspects of power over others—the systematization of domination we often refer to as hierarchy.

So anarchists do, in fact, embody a destructive urge—an urge to end domination, to smash power over others, to destroy the means through which working people are robbed and exploited. This communicates the negative aspect of anarchism. Attempts to gloss these over, oftentimes for the purposes of populist messaging, miss out on anarchism's rich history of bravely combating systems of exploitation and relations of domination. But it is true that anarchism is not simply a negative project. In addition to what anarchists oppose, we might also look at what anarchists are for.

"Is Also a Creative Urge."

While it's important to acknowledge that anarchists wish to break with the existing society and contain within them a negative politics, it's also important to recognize that historically anarchists have had a generative politics. That is, within destruction is also creation. So anarchism is also a creative endeavor—this has been demonstrated historically through anarchist attempts to create alternative institutions or, in the words of the IWW, build "the new world in the shell of the old."

In place of a system of private property and systematized robbery, anarchists have proposed the social ownership of society or, alternatively stated, the abolition of property altogether. This might sound absurd in a society that treats property as sacrosanct, but anarchists put forward a specific definition of property: ownership claims on those things that one neither occupies nor uses. Anarchists usually juxtapose this with possessions, or those things that we use or the homes that we live in (i.e. no anarchist wants to take your home or guitar away). This is how bosses and landlords exploit workers, by claiming to own the things they do not use or the places in which they do not live, then extracting rents and value from the people who do actually use them. In place of private ownership, anarchists put forward visions of a social system in which we produce for the needs of the people instead of the profits of capitalists.

Similarly, instead of a state that stands above society, directing it, anarchists typically propose federations of neighborhood assemblies, workplace associations, community councils, and the like as coordinating bodies comprised by the people. We would collectively make decisions that affect our lives rather than having those decisions made for us by politicians or left to the whims of the market. Functions of safety and collective decision-making, then, would be organized through networks "of participatory communities based on self-government through direct, face-to-face democracy in grassroots neighbourhood and community assemblies" instead of representation, police, prisons—in a word, bureaucracy.[5]

And in place of hierarchical social relations, anarchists propose a human community based on autonomy, solidarity, and mutual aid. Thus, the struggle against the state and capitalism must simultaneously be a struggle against white supremacy, heteropatriarchy and all forms of oppression and exploitation. Anarchists propose a society based on a highly egalitarian ethos because no human being should be granted power and control over others. So, anarchists argue, it must be understood that "the war against capitalism must be at the same time a war against all institutions of political power," because "exploitation has always gone hand in hand with political and social oppression."[6] Replacing white supremacy, a world constructed for so-called "able bodies," patriarchy, heteronormativity and all relations of domination would be new sets of social relations that do not arrange groups hierarchically in terms of their access to economic, political, and cultural power.

This very brief introduction is only meant to provide a broad look at anarchism and we'd suggest to anyone who is interested to check out the many anarchist websites, books, magazines, etc. to find out about it themselves. Some anarchists might take issue with our portrayal above—as we said, anarchism is a diverse milieu. We want to be up-front about that, so as not to portray ourselves as speaking for the milieu when we are speaking to our own interpretations of it.

Queer

"Queer" is likewise a contested term. Historically, it was often used to describe something that seemed strange, or not quite right. In more contemporary times, it was/is used as a slur against people who were perceived to be lesbian and/or gay—particularly effeminate men. In contemporary usage, it is often used as a reclaimed sort of shorthand for various identities contained in the LGBT "alphabet soup"—themselves contested groupings of sexual minorities with arguments over who rightfully "belongs" within those identity categories and who might be defined out.

Indeed, part of why "queer" began to be used as shorthand for sexual and gender minorities of all kinds was due to some of these debates over who "belonged," in what contexts, and how we might think about our sexual and gendered selves in ways that weren't based on identities. This explosion in writing about theory, bodies, gender, desire, sexuality, and much more is often referred to as "queer theory" with a simultaneous "queer politics" emerging on the ground, oftentimes in similar historical moments. Groupings such as ACT UP and Queer Nation, events such as the roving "Queeruption" festivals, and so on often reflected radical changes in how participants thought about (the limits of) identity.

These were tailed by the building of queer theory, which put identity categories under a critical lens. Some of the explosion of queer theory is rooted in the work of the French intellectual Michel Foucault. In his famous study of sexuality, Foucault found that "the homosexual," as an identity, could be traced to the rise of sexual science in mid nineteenth century.[7] Thus, the homosexual was an invention. This didn't mean that there wasn't same-sex sexual activity before the mid nineteenth century, but that where before we had an activity, it was transformed through complex historical processes into an identity—complete with borders and, in some cases, rigid in-groups and out-groups. Something a person does (i.e., an act) was transformed into something a person is (an identity). According to Foucault, the homosexual was created as a species of human.

Our available categories of this thing that we came to call "sexual orientation" became based on this historical process of identity-creation, reducing complex desires and relations to the gender of a person and the gender of the people that they desire. This is important because identity is a basic part of how people come to understand themselves and part and parcel of how we become "constituted as socially viable beings."[8] These processes of socially constructing identities led to the complete invisibilization of some people—which was another reason for the development of queer theory and politics.

Think about it: We are told that we are hetero, homo, or bi—perhaps 100% opposite gender attraction, 100% same gender attraction, or a 50/50 split. This is who we are. A good solid majority of our society has internalized this coding and even made oppressive hierarchies out of it. So understanding sexuality and gender in terms of rigid, easily identifiable, and heavily policed identities effectively invisibilizes and robs people who do not fit neatly into our available identity categories of a viable social existence—not just for sexuality, but also (and, of course, relatedly) for gender and sex. This has meant pushing out people whose sexual desires were fluid or whose gender practices or sex didn't make discussions of "sexuality" coherent given our limited ranges of choices and self-understandings. It erased people who did not experience their gender in terms of neatly constructed boxes. We needed a much more fluid, elastic, and broad category that was inclusive and "queer" was, in many cases, an attempt to create that space—an anti-identity, in a sense. Relatedly, "queer" was a word that could be played with.

An Adjective and a Verb

"Queer" served as a space for critiquing identity and playing with theory, bodies, power, and desire that didn't need to be reducible to easy definitions. The implications of thinking about sexuality, sex, gender, and a universe of other ideas in relationship to queer theory and politics are still up for much debate. We hope this collection reflects that. "Queer" has also had a degree of elasticity in use—as a noun, still at times, but also as an adjective and a verb.

Aside from a noun—another marker of identity—"queer" is often used as an adjective. Rather than a description of who a person is, in this way it is typically used as positionality. That is, queer can be seen as a relationship, as a context-defined antagonism to the normal.[9] Halperin, perhaps, describes this best when he writes, "Queer is by definition whatever is at odds with the normal, the legitimate, the dominant. There is nothing in particular to which it necessarily refers. It is an identity without an essence. 'Queer' then, demarcates not a positivity but a positionality vis-à-vis the normative—a positionality that is not restricted to lesbians and gay men, but is in fact available to anyone who is or who feels marginalized because of his or her sexual practices."[10] The normative expectations that exist in society create binary divisions between behaviors deemed "normal" and "abnormal." Whatever behaviors (or desires, thoughts, etc.) fall into the category labeled "normal" are dominant, intelligible, visible, and in many cases, powerful. Other behaviors will fall into the "abnormal" category and become subordinate, unintelligible, invisibilized, and suppressed, reppressed, and oppressed.

What gets labeled "normal" will affect what gets labeled "abnormal." If there are shifts in one sphere, the other sphere will shift with it. Queer, then, is what is at odds with the normal and lines up with the category of "abnormal." Since the normal can change, so can the abnormal, the queer. This is why queer is called a positionality—what is deemed queer is not fixed, it is contextual and related to what is called normal. The reason the term "queer," in this sense, isn't restricted to "gay" or "lesbian" is because many sexual practices are considered abnormal—some that aren't primarily based on gender (for instance, particular ways of having sex—like BDSM—or particular ways of fashioning or arranging sexual relationships—like nonmonogamy or sex work). The normal sexuality, in our own society, isn't just "hetero," it is a particular form of heterosexuality—a heterosexuality that has a goal of a happily married couple in a permanent relationship, abiding by the plethora of norms that make up what is referred to as "heteronormativity"—a very specific type of heterosexuality that reinforces the dominance of the ascribed set of norms: cohabitation, procreation, marriage, monogamous coupling, etc. We might also, then, analyze queer sexual practices and gender embodiment that recognizes that "(h) ierarchies exist within heterosexuality"—allowing us a frame to discuss nonmonogamy, sex work, BDSM, and so on both within same-sex relationship and elsewhere.[11]

This doesn't mean that all of these sexual and gender practices are experienced in the same way or oppressed to the same degree. That too is context-specific and also related to other identities that people might be assigned or the class position that they might inhabit. Rather, it is strategic for all people marginalized and oppressed by heteropatriarchy to organize and struggle together. And that means we need a lens through which to examine a variety of marginalized sexual and gender practices. That does not mean that heteropatriarchy treats all deviants the same. It means that there is no scarcity of liberation and that if liberation, in the final instance, is going to be meaningful, it must include us all.

Further, along with the socially constructed nature of sexuality and gender, as the intersex movement has taught us, we can also put sex under this critical lens. Sex is also put into a binary framework in our society, male and female, which fails to recognize the range of hormonal, sexual, and even chromosomal makeup that people can embody and, importantly, also ignores the coercive nature of the state's attempts to define our sexual selves for us at birth. This allows for a more holistic politics of sex, sexuality, and gender. It also gives us theoretical space to queer our naturalized assumptions about other identities. Consider, for example, people who exist in the margins of available categories for race and how it can make their existence or identity incoherent or, perhaps, changing depending on the context they are in—"white" in some contexts, perhaps Latino in others, and so on. What might politics look like if we began looking at identities in ways that do not treat them as fixed, monolithic, and eternal?

This antagonistic relationship with the normal has also led to an anti-assimilationist ethic that often sets queer politics apart from mainstream "G(lbt)" politics.[12] So the "Holy Trinity" of mainstream gay and lesbian politics—same-sex marriage, Don't Ask Don't Tell, and hate crimes legislation—are often rejected and critiqued within queer politics.[13] Much of this is reflected, as well, in queer tendencies toward a radical politics that is critical of the state. After all, the state forcibly assigns us identity categories and its enforcers mirror the ways that bodies and desires are policed to fit neatly within those categories. The state is also an enforcer of borders in much the same way that our society demands strict and rigid borders around identity. And queer people particularly suffer at the hands of the state in its prisons.[14] Indeed, while part of this ambivalence toward the state is a common trait in queer politics, there is likewise often an ethic of working-class liberation and anticapitalism within queer communities, linking up nicely with anarchist values (another reason that a collection such as this is long overdue!).

This position with regard to the normal is also embedded in how "queer" is used as a verb, particularly in the process of queering. Since queer theory and politics came primarily out of investigations into sex, sexuality, and gender, often times the word is used to connote adding a needed analysis of them to an already existing theory or set of ideas. So we might start the process of queering anarchism in this way, adding a needed critical analysis of sex, sexuality, and gender where it is often either out of date or simply missing. Likewise, it can be used as a verb to describe the process of making a given set of ideas strange, to destabilize dominant understandings and underlying assumptions. So queering anarchism might also refer to making anarchism strange, creating new understandings of anarchism that re(de)fine it using insights from queer theory and politics.

Queering Anarchism

In this collection, one can find all of these uses of "queer"—as a noun, an adjective, and a verb. Rather than trying to fit all of these pieces into a single, coherent definition of the word, we collected chapters knowing that they would at times be contradictory. For us, the purpose of this book was to create a collection that might move conversations forward, and that meant allowing for a huge range of approaches to queer, as well as a diversity of expressing those approaches. So the reader will also find pieces that "queer the script," so to speak, attempting to use creative means to convey ideas outside of the format of theoretical essays. This process of collection and editing took over three years, spanned changes in the editorial collective, and likewise saw some authors stick with us throughout and some lose contact with us in that long process.

When we first put the idea together, we decided that, like most edited collections, we would create discrete sections for the book. We sought out pieces of theory, writings on practice, and reflections on life experiences. In the end, however, we realized that nearly every chapter contained all three of these. So we tried to place them in an order that makes sense, showcases the diversity of thought in the collection, but isn't limited to discrete sections—they'd bleed completely into each other if we tried anyway. We did, however, try to create an order that would draw out familiar theoretical terrain and build on that in a process that, with any luck, will give readers a chance to situate the contents better as they travel through these chapters.

We begin with Ryan Conrad, who has done quite a lot of work critiquing assimilationist strategies and the equality rhetoric of the mainstream gay and lesbian movement. Conrad uses his critique of these assimilationist goals to suggest that we might expect much more than equality under the existing institutions—in fact, we might create a new world. J. Rogue spells out lessons anarchists might learn from the transfeminist movement, suggesting ways that we might update our feminism and build an anarchist gender politics that is nuanced and holistic. Abbey Volcano pens an intervention into radical queer politics arguing to be watchful of inverting hierarchies and basing our politics solely on simplified oppositions. Stacy aka sallydarity reviews existing theories of gender, drawing out a queer anarchist analysis that can serve as a framework for paths out of our current gender practices and understandings. Jamie Heckert explores ways we might queer anarchism and make it strange. In the process, he expresses a need for a creative politics not solely defined by antagonistic oppositions. Farhang Rouhani tells the story of opening a queer social center and the messiness involved in attempting to create and maintain such spaces—where identity categories are simultaneously questioned, created, destabilized, and sometimes celebrated by participants. Jerimarie Liesegang ties the struggle against the state together with the liberation of trans people and shows that the state is intimately involved in coercive gendering and gender assignment suggesting that trans liberation requires the abolition of the state.

Next, Benjamin Shepard argues for queering anarchist organizing that might lead us toward a politics of pleasure. This links up nicely with harm reduction approaches to organizing for better worlds and thinking about queering politics to provide new ways of conceiving of political interventions. Gayge Operaista argues that class struggle must be a central component of queer organizing, asserting in the process that class is not a simple "identity" and that we need to organize as a class against capitalism. The CRAC

Collective queers the script, providing a comic that details conversations among people about how sexual and gender politics relate to their political activity and their lives as radicals and anarchists. Stephanie Grohmann investigates how the economy is involved in our contemporary constructions of sexuality and gender and argues that we might "queer the economy" or shift our understanding of economics to recognize its place in other spheres of life—particularly our gendered and sexual lives. Sandra Jeppesen provides a personal narrative about how queering anarchism might happen in the lives of people who tend to have heterosexual relationships, but do not identify with straightness and heterosexuality.

Finally, Susan Song writes about the intersections between polyamorous sexual practices and relations, and anarchist politics. Diana C. S. Becerra writes a media analysis of *Sex and the City*, paying close attention to how pop cultural forms construct our understanding of gender and sexuality. She compellingly argues that anarchists might use these kinds of analyses to pinpoint the ways that culture influences our understanding of our selves and our relationships with others. C. B. Daring argues that anarchists should have an analysis of sex work that doesn't mirror the moralism that is often connected with "radical" analyses of labor in the sex industry. Jason Lydon ties in anarchist queer politics with a need for resisting the prison-industrial complex. He puts forward an anarchist queer perspective on abolition. Liat Ben-Moshe, Anthony J. Nocella, II, and AJ Withers suggest that we recognize parallels between disability and queerness, making the case that we might not just queer anarchism, but queer-crip anarchism, connecting fights against heteronormativity and other forms of oppression and exclusion with struggles against ableism. Saffo Papantonopoulos contends that straightness is not an identity, but a set of social relations and for liberation to be total and consistent with anarchist principles, those sets of social relations must be uprooted, exposed, and destroyed. Hexe playfully relates BDSM practices to anarchism using this relationship to draw out kinky paths to queering anarchism.

We think the strong connections between anarchist and queer politics are striking. But, as they say, the proof of the pudding is in the eating. We hope this collection serves as a smorgasbord of sorts, providing insights into how we might alter the landscape of this often miserable, violent, and boring world and bring into being different ones. We think the case here is supported quite well that there are many more fruitful engagements to emerge from this meeting of queer and anarchism—and a variety of other partnerships along the way.

1   See e.g. Aragorn!, ed. *Occupy Everything: Anarchists in the Occupy Movement, 2009–2011* (Berkeley, CA: LBC Books 2012).

2   Alexander Berkman, *What is Communist Anarchism?* (New York, NY: Dover Publications 1972, orig. 1929), xxv.

3   Ibid., xxvi.

4   Errico Malatesta, "Anarchist Propaganda," http://recollectionbooks. com/anow/ppl/rev/malatesta/lifeandideas.html (accessed February 4, 2012).

5   Anarchist FAQ, http://infoshop.org/page/AnarchistFAQSectionI5-#seci51 (accessed February 4, 2012).

6   Rudolf Rocker, *Anarcho-Syndicalism: Theory and Practice* (Oakland: AK Press, 2004, orig. 1938), 11.

7   See Michel Foucault, *The History of Sexuality, Volume 1: An Introduction* (New York City, NY: Vintage Books, 1990, orig. 1978).

8   Judith Butler, *Undoing Gender* (New York City, NY: Routledge, 2004), 2.

9   See especially Michael Warner, *The Trouble with Normal: Sex, Politics, and the Ethics of Queer Life* (Cambridge, MA: Harvard University Press, 1999), passim.

10 David Halperin, *Saint Foucault: Towards a Gay Hagiography* (Oxford: Oxford University Press, 1995), 62.

11 Jamie Heckert, "Sexuality/Identity/Politics," in *Changing Anarchism: Anarchist Theory and Practice in a Global Age*, edited by Jonathan Purkis and James Bowen (Manchester, UK: Manchester University Press, 2004), 111.

12 See especially Mattilda Bernstein Sycamore, ed., *That's Revolting!: Queer Strategies for Resisting Assimilation* (Brooklyn, NY: Soft Skull Press, 2004).

13 See especially Ryan Conrad, ed., *Against Equality: Queer Critiques of Gay Marriage* (Lewiston, ME: Against Equality Press, 2010); and Ryan Conrad, ed., *Against Equality: Don't Ask to Fight Their Wars* (Lewiston, ME: Against Equality Press, 2011).

14 See, for example, Eric A. Stanley and Nat Smith, ed., *Captive Genders: Trans Embodiment and the Prison Industrial Complex* (Oakland, CA: AK Press, 2011).

Gay Marriage and Queer Love

RYAN CONRAD

> *Love, the strongest and deepest element in all life, the harbinger of*
> *hope, of joy, of ecstasy; love, the defier of all laws, of all conventions;*
> *love, the freest, the most powerful moulder of human destiny; how can*
> *such an all-compelling force be synonymous with that poor little State*
> *and Church-begotten weed, marriage?*
> —Emma Goldman, "Marriage and Love" (1911)

Mainstream gay and lesbian rights organizations in the United States have mobilized confusing and at times contradictory rhetoric to solidify their moral high ground in the contentious battle over gay marriage. These organizations deploy both the affective rhetoric of an individuals' right to love whomever they choose alongside more analytic rhetoric that demands full and equal access to a myriad of benefits and privileges administered by the state. By pulling on our heartstrings and appealing to the simple logic of equality, many have been duped into entering the shortsighted gay marriage debate when energy would be better focused elsewhere. In 1911 Emma Goldman ripped marriage to shreds in her essay *Marriage and Love* by fiercely critiquing marriage's reinforcement of prescribed gender roles, patriarchy, and the nuclear family. She also wrote critically and extensively on the mobilization of a notion of love to justify the coercive state and church violence we call marriage. Here I will queerly continue where she left off, one hundred years later.

In 2009 I was helplessly kicking and screaming while the national campaigns for gay marriage descended on my mostly poor, mostly rural home state of Maine. Now, in the aftermath of the nauseatingly class-elitist failed campaign,[1] gay and lesbian organizations, and the professional activists that prop them up, remain resiliently resistant to critically questioning what we, as queer and trans subjects, are seeking to be equal to in the first place. Do we really want full inclusion in the institution of marriage, a social contract that explicitly limits the ways in which we can organize our erotic and emotional lives? Furthermore, do we really want to reinforce a social institution where our immediate needs and access to collective benefits are contingent on this singular articulation of partnership? Or have many of us allowed ourselves to be convinced by some vague notion of equality, with all its empty promises,[2] that gay marriage is a battle worth fighting for?

Mainstream gay and lesbian organizations position their campaign strategy and engrossing rhetoric around two competing discourses roughly examined here. By dissecting these competing discourses, one can see that marriage has little to do with love and that the mainstream gay and lesbian organizations' investments in winning the gay marriage battle further erode any possibility for a radically equitable queer future—a future that was once dared to be imagined by radical queer and trans folks organizing with ACT UP, Queer to the Left, and the George Jackson Brigade, and is still imagined today by radical grassroots organizations like Queers for Economic Justice, La Gai-Queer Insurrection, and Gay Shame, to name a few.

The first of these discourses is the highly affective and emotionally charged rhetoric of the individual's right to love whomever one chooses. The messaging that the gay marriage campaigns invoke here actively reinscribes the institution of marriage as one that is defined by and organized around a notion of love. With protest signs displaying slogans like "Who else is fighting for love!?" or "It's my right to love whomever I want!" one is to believe that love is primarily what is at stake in the gay marriage debate. But as many historians have shown,[3] marriage has never been centrally organized around love, but the buying and selling of women as property through a patriarchal dowry system that evolved into the soft coercion of domestic indentured servitude that Goldman so aptly dismantled in her writing. Although many of the more explicitly violent machinations of marriage have abated in the United States, the structural and individual violence continues.

Nearly half of all first marriages end in divorce.[4] If marriage were the loving, providing, social safety net that those invoking family values rhetoric claim it is, then one is left wondering why the divorce rate is so remarkably high. Perhaps it is that nearly 7.8 million women have been raped by an intimate partner at some point in their lives[5] or that domestic violence is the leading cause of injury to women between the ages of fifteen and forty-four in the United States.[6] Or maybe it is that sixty-eight percent of sexually abused children are victims of their own family members.[7] Empiricism aside, the so-called healthy and privatized familial structures through which the institution of marriage seeks to minimize violence cannot be emulated if we, as a radical queer and trans community, are to confront the violence within our own community and families (chosen or otherwise).

In addition to the affective discourse outlined above, a more analytic approach is being deployed in tandem. This rhetoric relies on a certain brand of rugged American individualism that has spawned gay and lesbian organizations that invoke a rights-based discourse in their attempt at achieving what they contend is full equality. It is here we find numerous LGB and sometimes T activists in a rage over their 1,138 rights that federally recognized marriage will bring them, but are denied. These state benefits and privileges, as outlined in the Defense of Marriage Act, are overwhelmingly about the transfer of money and property (including children, as the only way marriage allows us to think about them is like property). The almost exclusive emphasis on property rights highlights that marriage has little to do with love, but with benefits and privileges as doled out by the state to those who adhere to a specific set of moral values determined by the church.

Gay marriage organizations are mobilizing this rights-based discourse focused on "equal" access to state benefits and privileges in tandem with highly effective love rhetoric to win over public opinion by appealing to socialized emotional responses while simultaneously making a more strategic/analytic argument for gay marriage. This two-pronged approach has successfully dragged many LGBT activists into its blinding double discourse by effectively motivating the engagement of many queer and trans folks who would be better off putting their energy elsewhere. What if we, as a queer and trans social justice movement, focused on achieving access to many of marriage's forbidden fruits (i.e., healthcare, freedom of movement across nation-state borders, etc.) for all people, not just citizen couples, gay, straight, or otherwise?

Fortunately this double discourse will fail miserably in the long term because it is impossible to claim marriage is an institution based on love when the only way to do so is to mimic the hyper-conservative family values rhetoric of the Christian right. The normalizing function of this claim, that loving families can only exist within the narrow confines of an immediate nuclear family structure (gay or straight), will continue to mark some families as worthy of survival and others as a deadly threat.[8] As noted by gay historian John D'Emilio in his piece "The Marriage Fight Is Setting Us Back," greater acceptance of gay and lesbian people has largely come from straight people abandoning fantasy familial conservatism opting for queerer more nontraditional ways of organizing both their erotic lives and their families.[9]

The smiling white families posed in picturesque suburban backyards that appeared on pro-gay marriage campaign materials in Maine looked no different than the anti-gay marriage propaganda of smiling white families in picturesque suburban backyards. Not only did the visual narratives mimic one another, save the difference in gendered couples among neo-nuclear gay families, but the accompanying family values rhetoric was nearly identical. The fervent reinvestment in the nuclear family (gay or straight) as a site of financial security, moral aptitude, and physical safety for the child should be horrifying to us all. This kind of logic around familial safety has been challenged by three decades of feminist critique that problematizes the nuclear family as the primary site of sexual violence against children and cannot be erased or obscured through this rhetorical appeal.[10]

This neoliberal fantasy of the nuclear family as the only provider of emotional and economic safety is being recovered and deployed by the contemporary gay rights movement. In a bizarre twist in history, gays and lesbians are turning their backs on the kinds of radical new configurations of "family" that have liberated straight people.

Neoliberalism, which I broadly define here as the concentrated privatization of every facet of our daily lives, depends upon this affective discourse, which asserts that the immediate family constitutes an unproblematized site of safety and security while the rest of the world is rendered a dangerous outside. By insisting that the gay and lesbian nuclear family (a retrograde hetero-mimicry throwback to the 1950s) needs protection, gay marriage activists are further enabling the privatization of social safety nets.

For example, the heightened emphasis on the idea that gay marriage is necessary for same-sex partners to gain health insurance allows the state to further justify not creating a system of universal health care where all people, regardless of marital status receive necessary medical care. In the 1980s, queers agitated for universal health care in the face of a devastating AIDS epidemic that left them caring for those whom the state refused to consider worthy of the most basic care. Today they are calling for the opposite by insisting that only those in state-mandated relationships are worthy of health care.

The campaigns for gay marriage and their accompanying confused rhetoric have been neatly folded into a handful of other issues under the banner of equality across the United States.[11] Equality rhetoric is short-sighted at best and positions our most fantastic queer futures as not only unattainable but also unreasonable. It demands that we put our time and energy into the desperate fight to be equal participants in oppressive and archaic institutions instead of attempting to actualize our dreams of queer utopia.[12] Furthermore, equality rhetoric has created a vacuum of gay pragmatism[13] in which our queer political imagination has withered away, allowing no time or space to even imagine more just, more equitable ways of meeting our material and affective needs as a larger community.

The question remains then: How do we, as radical queer and trans folks, push back against the emerging hegemony of rainbow-flavored neoliberalism and the funneling of our energy into narrow campaigns that only reinforce the hierarchical systems and institutions we fundamentally oppose? How do we reconcile the contradiction of our anger and fervent criticism of so called equality when presently many of our material lives depend on accessing resources through the very subject of our critique? Although I do not have concrete solutions to offer, I believe we must create more space and time to have these vital conversations, be more open and public about our critique of marriage, build coalitions with others who stand little to gain from marriage, imagine other worlds together, and dream up new ways of meeting our material and affective needs.

1   See Ryan Conrad, "Against Equality, in Maine and Everywhere,". *UltraViolet* (December 2009).

2   The promise of health care, freedom of movement across nation state borders, the inheritance of property, etc. These promises only apply if one or both of the people entering into a marriage agreement have a

considerable amount of wealth/property/assets, professional employment, and citizenship status. For many, this is not the case and therefore many will not gain materially from marriage.

3   See Erwin J. Haeberle, *The Sex Atlas* (New York: Continuum Publishing, 1983). See section 3, chapter 11 for an overview of marriage from
ancient history to modernity.

4   According to the US Census Bureau and the National Center for
Health Statistics.

5   Centers for Disease Control and Prevention, National Centers for Injury Prevention and Control, *Costs of Intimate Partner Violence against
Women in the United States* (Atlanta, Georgia, 2003).

6   "Violence against Women, A Majority Staff Report," Committee on
the Judiciary, United States Senate, 102nd Congress, October 1992, 3.

7   Childhelp factsheet, http://www.childhelp.org (accessed July 1, 2010).

8   I would love to see gay marriage propaganda that includes the queer
families I know: two leather daddies and their twink house boy, queer
collective polyamorous households, or the enclaves of queer/trans
street hustlers that still populate some urban centers (like Sylvia Rivera
and Marsha P. Johnson's STAR house).

9   *The Gay and Lesbian Review* (November/December 2006).

10 See Steven Angelides, "Feminism, Child Sexual Abuse and the Erasure of Child Sexuality," *Gay and Lesbian Quarterly* (2004): 141–177.

11 Gay marriage, military inclusion through overturning Don't Ask
Don't Tell, and inclusion in hate crimes legislation make up this holy
trinity of gay neoliberalism. For extended discussion on the intersections of these "equality" issues, see Against Equality's online archive at
www.againstequality.org.

12 I invoke utopia here not as a naively conceived physical time or space,
but rather as a mode of critical inquiry. An understanding that we
should always be attempting to realize our most fantastic and equitable
queer futures in the here and now. Why aim for anything less than the
horizon of becoming?

13 For further clarification on this phenomenon and terminology, see
Jose Esteban Muñoz, *Cruising Utopia: The Then and There of Queer
Futurity* (New York: New York University Press, 2009).

De-essentializing Anarchist Feminism: Lessons from the Transfeminist Movement

J. ROGUE

Transfeminism developed out of a critique of the mainstream and radical feminist movements. The feminist movement has a history of internal hierarchies. There are many examples of women of color, working-class women, lesbians, and others speaking out against the tendency of the white, affluent-dominated women's movement to silence them and overlook their needs. But generally, instead of acknowledging the issues these marginalized voices raised, the mainstream feminist movement has prioritized struggling for rights primarily in the interests of white affluent women. While the feminist milieu as a whole has not resolved these hierarchal tendencies, various groups have continued to speak up regarding their own marginalization—in particular, transgender women. The process of developing a broader understanding of systems of oppression and how they interact has advanced feminism and is key to building on the theory of anarchist feminism. But first, we might take a quick look at the development of feminism—particularly during what is often referred to as its "Second Wave."

Generally, the historical narratives of feminism that suggest that we might look at feminism in "waves" point to the Second Wave as a turbulent period with many competing visions. I'll use that perspective here, though I also realize that the narrative is problematic in a number of ways, particularly its Western and US bias, and I want to acknowledge that.[1] I'm from the United States, which is the context in which I organize and live. This particular narrative is useful here for noting some larger tendencies within feminism—particularly where I'm from, though again I want to acknowledge that this process, while descriptive, engages in some of the kinds of exclusions I am criticizing in this chapter.

I also want to acknowledge that this is a story for drawing out some necessary and important divisions, but any categorization can be problematic (and how could a transfeminism not recognize and acknowledge this problem?). There have been theories of liberal, radical, Marxist, and socialist feminism that do *not* fit this particular narrative. I want to stress, however, that I find it useful in describing theoretical pasts and presents in order to draw out a radically different feminist and anarchist future.

During the late 60s through the early 80s, new forms of feminism began to emerge. Many feminists seemed to gravitate to four competing theories with very different explanations for the oppression of women and their theories had consequences for feminist practices of inclusion and exclusion.

Like their historical predecessors of the "First Wave" who were mainly concerned with voting rights, *liberal feminists* saw no need for a revolutionary break with existing society. Rather, their focus was on breaking the "glass ceiling," getting more women into positions of political and economic power. Liberal feminists assumed that the existing institutional arrangements were fundamentally unproblematic. Their task was to see to women's equality accommodated under capitalism.

Another theory, sometimes referred to as *radical feminism*, argued for abandoning the "male Left," as it was seen as hopelessly reductionist. Indeed, many women coming out of the Civil Rights and antiwar movements complained of pervasive sexism within the movements because they were relegated to secretarial tasks and experienced sexual pressure from male leaders as well as a generalized alienation from Left politics. According to many radical feminists of the time, this was due to the primacy of the system of patriarchy— or men's systematic and institutionalized domination of women. To these feminists, the battle against patriarchy was the primary struggle to create a free society, as gender was our most entrenched and oldest hierarchy.[2] This made a neatly defined "sisterhood" important to their politics.

Marxist feminists, on the other hand, tended to locate women's oppression within the economic sphere. The fight against capitalism was seen as the "primary" battle, as "the history of all hitherto existing societies is the history of class struggles." Further, Marxist feminists tended to believe that the economic "base" of society had a determining effect on its cultural "superstructures." Thus the only way to achieve equality between women and men would be to smash capitalism—as new, egalitarian economic arrangements would give rise to new, egalitarian superstructures. Such was the determining nature of the economic base. This argument was mapped out quite eloquently by Marx's companion, Engels.[3]

Out of the conversations between Marxist feminism and radical feminism another approach emerged called "dual systems theory."[4] A product of what came to be dubbed *socialist feminism*, dual systems theory argued that feminists needed to develop "a theoretical account which gives as much weight to the system of patriarchy as to the system of capitalism."[5] While this approach did much to resolve some of the arguments about which fight should be "primary" (i.e., the struggle against capitalism or the struggle against patriarchy), it still left much to be desired. For example, black feminists argued that this perspective left out a structural analysis of race.[6] Further, where was oppression based on sexuality, ability, age, etc. in this analysis? Were all of these things reducible to capitalist patriarchy? And importantly, for this chapter, where were the experiences of trans folks—particularly trans women? Given this historical lack, feminism required a specifically trans feminism.

Transfeminism builds on the work that came out of the multiracial feminist movement, and in particular, the work of black feminists. Frequently, when confronted with allegations of racism, classism, or homophobia, the women's movement dismisses these issues as divisive or "secondary" (as spelled out in the narrative above). The more prominent voices promoted (and still promote) the idea of a homogenous "universal female experience," which, as it is based on commonality between women, theoretically promotes a sense of sisterhood. In reality, it means pruning the definition of "woman" and trying to fit all women into a mold reflecting the dominant demographic of the women's movement: white, affluent, heterosexual, and non-disabled. This "policing" of identity, whether conscious or not, reinforces systems of oppression and exploitation. When women who do not fit this mold have challenged it, they have frequently been accused of being divisive and disloyal to the sisterhood. The hierarchy of womanhood created by the women's movement reflects, in many ways, the dominant culture of racism, capitalism, and heteronormativity.[7]

Mirroring this history, mainstream feminist organizing frequently tries to find the common ground shared by women, and therefore focuses on what the most vocal members decide are "women's issues"—as if the female experience existed in a vacuum outside of other forms of oppression and exploitation. However, using an intersectional approach to analyzing and organizing around oppression, as advocated by multiracial feminism and transfeminism, we can discuss these differences rather than dismiss them.[8] The multiracial feminist movement developed this approach, which argues that one cannot address the position of women without also addressing their class, race, sexuality, ability, and all other aspects of their identity and experiences. Forces of oppression and exploitation do not exist separately. They are intimately related and reinforce each other, and so trying to address them singly (i.e., "sexism" divorced from racism, capitalism, etc.) does not lead to a clear understanding of the patriarchal system. This is in accordance with the anarchist view that we must fight all forms of hierarchy, oppression, and exploitation simultaneously; abolishing capitalism and the state does not ensure that white supremacy and patriarchy will somehow magically disappear.[9]

Tied to this assumption of a "universal female experience" is the idea that if a woman surrounds herself with those that embody that "universal" woman, then she is safe from patriarchy and oppression. The concept of "women's safe spaces" (being women-only) date back to the early lesbian feminist movement, which was largely comprised of white women who were more affluent, and prioritized addressing sexism over other forms of oppression. This notion that an all-women space is inherently safe not only discounts the intimate violence that can occur between women, but also ignores or de-prioritizes the other types of violence that women can experience—racism, poverty, incarceration, and other forms of state, economic, and social brutality.[10]

Written after the work of, and influenced by, transfeminist pioneers like Sandy Stone, Sylvia Rivera, and Rivera's Street Transvestite Action Revolutionaries (STAR), the Transfeminist Manifesto states: "Transfeminism believes that we construct our own gender identities based on what feels genuine, comfortable and sincere to us as we live and relate to others within given social and cultural constraint."[11] The notion that gender is a social construct is a key concept in transfeminism, and is also essential (no pun intended) to an anarchist approach to feminism. Transfeminism also criticizes the idea of a "universal female experience" and argues against the biologically essentialist view that one's gender is defined by one's genitalia. Other feminisms have embraced the essentialist argument, seeing the idea of "women's unity" as being built off a sameness, some kind of core "woman-ness." This definition of woman is generally reliant on what is between a person's legs. Yet what specifically about the definition of woman is intrinsic to two X chromosomes? If it is defined as being in possession of a womb, does that mean women who have had hysterectomies are somehow less of a woman? Reducing gender to biology relegates the definition of "woman" to the role of child-bearer. That seems rather antithetical to feminism. Gender roles have long been under scrutiny in radical communities. The idea that women are born to be mothers, are more sensitive and peaceful, are predisposed to wearing the color pink, and all the other stereotypes out there are socially constructed, not biological. If the (repressive) gender role does not define what a woman is, and if a doctor marking "F" on a birth certificate do not define gender either,[12] the next logical step is to recognize that gender can only be defined by the individuals for themselves— or perhaps we need as many genders as there are people, or even further, that gender should be abolished. While these ideas may cause some to panic, that does not make them any less legitimate with regard to peoples' identities, or experiences, or the kinds of difficult political projects we might have ahead of us. Trying to simplify complex issues, or fighting to maintain a hold on how gender was taught to us, does not help us understand patriarchy and how it functions. Instead it does revolutionary feminisms a disservice.

Having encountered a lack of understanding of trans issues in radical circles, I feel it important to note that not all transgender people choose to physically transition, and that each person's decision to do so or not is their own. The decision is highly personal and generally irrelevant to theoretical conceptions of gender. There are many reasons to physically change one's body, from getting a haircut to taking hormones. One reason might be to feel more at ease in a world with strict definitions of male and female. Another is to look in the mirror and see on the outside (the popular understanding of) the gender one feels on the inside. Surely, for some, it is the belief that gender is defined by the physical construction of one's genitalia. Too often, however, radicals who are unfamiliar with trans politics and ideas react strongly to individuals' choices with regard to their bodies—rather missing the point altogether. But rather than draw from speculation as to the motivations for the personal decisions of trans people (as if they were not vast and varied), it is more productive to note the challenge to the idea that biology is destiny.[13] Surely everyone would benefit from breaking down the binary gender system and deconstructing gender roles—that is the work of revolutionaries, not fretting over what other people "should" or "shouldn't" do to their bodies.

Thus far, gender and feminist theory that includes trans experiences exists almost solely in academia. There are very few working-class intellectuals in the field, and the academic language used is not particularly accessible to the average person.[14] This is unfortunate, since the issues that transfeminism addresses affect all people. Capitalism, racism, the state, patriarchy, and the medical field mediate the way everyone experiences gender. There is a significant amount of coercion employed by these institutions to police human experiences, which applies to everyone, trans and non-trans (some prefer the term "cis") alike. Capitalism and the state play a very direct role in the experiences of trans people. Access to hormones and surgery, if desired, cost a significant amount of money, and people are often forced to jump through bureaucratic hoops in order to acquire them. Trans people are disproportionately likely to be poor. However, within the radical queer and transfeminist communities, while there may be discussions of class, they are generally framed around identity—arguing for "anti-classist" politics, but not necessarily anticapitalist.[15]

The concepts espoused by transfeminism help us understand gender, but there is a need for the theory to break out of academia and to develop praxis among the working-class and social movements generally. This is not to say that there are no examples of transfeminist organizing, but rather that there needs to be an incorporation of transfeminist principles into broad-based movements. Even gay and lesbian movements have a history of leaving trans people behind—for example, the fight for the Employment Non-Discrimination Act, which does not protect gender identity. Again we saw a hierarchy of importance; the mainstream gay and lesbian movement often compromises (throwing trans folks under the bus), rather than employing an inclusive strategy for liberation. There is frequently a sense of a "scarcity of liberation" within reformist social movements, the feeling that the possibilities for freedom are so limited that we must fight against other marginalized groups for a piece of the pie. This is in direct opposition to the concept of intersectionality, since it often requires people to betray one aspect of their identity in order to politically prioritize another. How can a person be expected to engage in a fight against gender oppression if it ignores or contributes to their racial oppression? Where does one aspect of their identity and experiences end and another begin? Anarchism offers a possible society in which liberation is anything but scarce. It provides a theoretical framework that calls for an end to all hierarchies, and, as Martha Ackelsberg suggests, "It offers a perspective on the nature and process of social revolutionary transformation (e.g. the insistence that means must be consistent with ends, and that economic issues are critical, but not the only source of hierarchal power relations) that can be extremely valuable to/for women's emancipation."[16]

Anarchists need to be developing working-class theory that includes an awareness of the diversity of the working class. The anarchist movement can benefit from the development of a working-class, anarchist approach to gender issues that incorporates the lessons of transfeminism and intersectionality. It is not so much a matter of asking anarchists to become active in the transfeminist movement as it is a need for anarchists to take a page from the Mujeres Libres and integrate the principles of (trans) feminism into our organizing within the working class and social movements. Continuing to develop contemporary anarchist theory of gender rooted in the working-class requires a real and integrated understanding of transfeminism.

1   See e.g., Aili Mari Tripp, "The Evolution of Transnational Feminisms: Consensus, Conflict, and New Dynamics," in *Global Feminism: Transnational Women's Activism, Organizing, and Human Rights*, edited by Myra Marx and Aili Mari Tripp (New York City: New York University Press, 2006), 51–75.

2   See especially Shulamit Firestone, *The Dialectic of Sex: The Case for Feminist Revolution* (New York: Morrow, 1970).

3   Friedrich Engels, *The Origin of the Family Private Property and the State*, http://www.marxists.org/archive/marx/works/1884/origin-family/ (accessed March 20, 2012).

4   See e.g., Heidi Hartmann, "The Unhappy Marriage of Marxism and Feminism: Towards a More Progressive Union," in *Women and Revolution*, edited by Lydia Sargent (Boston: South End Press, 1981); and Iris Young, "Beyond the Unhappy Marriage: A Critique of the Dual Systems Theory," in *Women and Revolution*, edited by Lydia Sargent (Boston: South End Press, 1981).

5   Iris Young, "Beyond the Unhappy Marriage," 44.

6   See Gloria Joseph, "The Incompatible Menage à Trois: Marxism, Feminism, and Racism," in *Women and Revolution*, edited by Lydia Sargent (Boston: South End Press, 1981).

7   Ibid.

8   For an anarchist analysis of intersectionality, see J. Rogue and Deric Shannon, "Refusing to Wait: Anarchism and Intersectionality," http://theanarchistlibrary.org/HTML/Deric_Shannon_and_J._Rogue__Refusing_to_Wait__Anarchism_and_Intersectionality.html (accessed March 23, 2012).

9   Ibid.

10 See especially debates around the Michigan Women's Music Festival on this issue.

11 Emi Koyama, "The Transfeminist Manifesto," http://eminism.org/readings/pdf-rdg/tfmanifesto.pdf (accessed March 24, 2012).

12 In light of the intersex movement, we may need to analyze the social construction of biological sex as well.

13 See Kate Bornstein, *My Gender Workbook* (New York and London: Routledge, 1998).

14 For some notable examples, see the work of Mattilda Bernstein Sycamore, Lesli Feinberg, and Riki Ann Wilchins, among many others.

15 Although this is certainly not a monolithic tendency, as many rowdy queers do indeed want an end to capitalism and call for it explicitly.

16 See "Lessons from the Free Women of Spain"—Geert Dhondt interviews Martha Ackelsberg in *Up the Ante!*

Police at the Borders

ABBEY VOLCANO

Anarchism as a social movement, as an idea, as a practice, is as much about creation as it is about destruction. Mikhail Bakunin wrote "The passion for destruction is a creative passion too."[1] Further, anarchism isn't solely centered on crushing *structures* like capitalism and the state (although we anarchists certainly want that). Rather, we seek to smash *all* institutionalized hierarchies. We reject *all* forms of coerced domination. But imagine if capitalism, the state, white supremacy, patriarchy, etc., were "removed" (if only it were that easy)? What would remain? Unfortunately, not much, one could imagine. Anarchists, then, might also be creative. We might try to create new ways of relating to each other, new ways of relating to the non-human world, new ways of loving, knowing, playing, etc. If we don't create these new social relations, then we will likely fall back on the current ones, at worst, and will not realize our creative potential, at best. Anarchists are often creating new ways of living and relating in the here and now. This chapter gives some thought on how we might do the same with sexuality while not recreating the coercive social relations that confine us now.

An anarchist queer theory might also begin by attempting to tear down the borders between "identities" (as well as unpack their very existence/use) by showing that people are complex (as is the world) and are not easily categorized—at least not honestly. This means tearing down the normative assumptions that are used to uphold a status quo that puts some of us above others in the social order as a result of our sexual and/or gender practices. This is neatly described by the term "heteronormativity," which refers to the culture of understanding, and the institutionalization of heterosexual, cissexual, dyadic, monogamous, and permanent relationships as the only possible and coherent sexuality.[2]

Sometimes (too often), rather than destabilizing the hierarchically organized and institutionalized borders of heteronormativity, folks will construct new "queer" normative assumptions to replace our current organized, normative structures of sexuality. This is a process of inverting hierarchies instead of doing away with them. Instead of recognizing that hierarchically organized sexuality was our problem in the first place, we often flip the current normative expectations on their heads and create a twisted mirror image of the current institutionalized sexuality by hierarchically ordering a new "queer sexuality." This might look like privileging non-monogamy, genderqueerness, and BDSM, for example, over other types of sexuality and gender. Instead of creating a world in which sexuality is somewhat liberated, we instead create new borders and new limitations around sexuality—we have simply inverted the hierarchy and excluded those deemed "not queer enough."

Think of how many times you've sat around with a group of well-meaning folks and the conversation has gone something like this:

"As a working-class person, I have to say…" (a few nods of agreement)

"As a poor woman, it seems to me…" (even more nods)

"As a poor lesbian of color, I think…" (even more furious nodding, making sure everyone registers each other's frenetic agreement)

And so on.

These kinds of displays are often referred to as "the Oppression Olympics." People in these situations seem like they're playing a game together—a grand contest to assert who is more authentic, more oppressed, and thus more correct. It's at this point where identity becomes fetishized; where essentialist understandings of people trump good sense; and where a patronizing belief in the superiority of the wise, noble savage often overrides any sense at all. Often this tactic of agreeing with "the most marginalized in the room" will be used as a substitute for developing critical analyses around race, gender, sexuality, etc. This tactic is intellectually lazy, lacks political depth, and leads toward tokenization.

There is a point to allowing our experiences of various forcefully assigned identities to be at the forefront of conversations. People do have different experiences based on these social constructions and we should take these differences into account. But when they become markers of authenticity and "correctness," it poses a problem for anarchists. After all, we seek to dissolve hierarchical relations, not create new ones formed from the margins.

Queer theory has taken up the disconcerting task of putting identity—and by extension identity politics—under a destabilizing lens. An anarchist queer theory might give us more effective ways of relating than the Oppression Olympics (a set of games no one really wins anyway). And in an anarchist politics of sexuality and gender, this means that care needs to be taken not to invert existing hierarchies, much like the Oppression Olympics do—making more authentic voices out of some over others and creating new hierarchies to replace old ones.

With this piece, then, I want to briefly talk about a few ways that I think radical queer politics and spaces have often come to invert existing hierarchies rather than doing away with them (or perhaps destabilizing them). I want to make it clear that this isn't an argument for a return to heteronormativity, nor is it an argument for an end to celebrating our queerness and the things that we desire. Rather, it is an argument that the ways we fuck, love, and gender ourselves are not inherently revolutionary. But creating a politics that refuses the hierarchical arrangement of people because of their sexual and/or gender practices—and, importantly, one that does not pressure people into certain practices under the auspices of being more authentically "queer"—does, indeed, have radical implications.

Aren't We All Very Public Sluts?

In the next three sections I'm going to outline a few practices within some radical queer circles that I would like to critique and that I think we can learn from. Like I noted before, this is tricky and complicated. While most queer radicals I know (or know of) are working on dismantling structures that (re)produce normative assumptions about sexual identities or expected behaviors, sometimes in our struggles we can inadvertently reinscribe these norms and then organize underneath them (unknowingly). For instance, promiscuity and public sex are for the most part frowned upon in the United States. Sexuality is to be experienced in private monogamous relationships.[3] Public displays of affection are okay in the United States as long as they are heterosexual and PG-13. Throw some similarly-gendered/sexed love in there and bring the rating up to R and you might get the cops called on you (or in the very least receive a lot of scorn and "tsk-tsks," and often a beating to go with it). There are examples of private nightclubs getting raided and folks getting arrested for "risky" sexual activity.[4] We have laws in the United States (they differ throughout the states) against sodomy, BDSM, and other forms of non-normative sexual activity.

Folks who have desires that have been either literally outlawed and/or disapproved of culturally (not always an offense with less "consequences") find themselves in a position of transgressing sexual norms when they practice their sexual desires (whether they "enjoy" challenging those norms or not). Challenging our own desires is an important step in trying to shed the institutionalized, directed, compulsory, organized, and controlled sexualities that have been made available to (and constituted) us. However, one can challenge institutionalized sexual categories and (available) expressions without necessarily having to swing the pendulum to the opposite side with their own sexual practices or with their expectation for others' sexual practices. For instance, just because promiscuity is a non-normative sexual desire/practice doesn't mean that to be in the act of challenging such norms that one must participate in promiscuity, per se. For instance, I can reject and struggle against the sexual/gender status quo without the need to physically embody/practice certain non-normative sexualities. Sexual acts themselves (or lack thereof) are not what we are challenging as queer radicals. We are struggling against sexualities and sexual acts being *categorized and ordered* into hierarchical systems that privilege certain practices/desires over others.

On occasion, I have seen the tendency for radical queers to assume that most (all) radical queers have some particular non-normative sexual desire/practice (for example, assuming that radical queers are generally promiscuous, non-monogamous, enjoy making out with whomever just for the fun of it, are into BDSM or other non-vanilla sex, etc.).[5] Having witnessed this fairly often, I don't believe that folks intend to make these assumptions.

What's peculiar about normative assumptions around sexuality and gender is their ability to be invisible. This is why we also need to struggle at the conceptual level; we need to not only smash the seemingly automatic jump to create and maintain status quos, but we also need to replace the notion of status quo with something else—perhaps an awareness of the very non-necessity of status quos governing cfonsensual sexual practices and a very conscious under-standing of the damage and limitations that these kinds of under-standings can create and maintain. I'm personally a rather shy and private person and at times I have felt pressured to be promiscuous and experiment with non-normative sexual play, often by friends of mine. At times, folks will assume that of course I want to make out with my radical queer friends, of course I want to go to the play party, and of course I wouldn't have an exclusive relationship with only one other person. These assumptions can be cleared up rather easily with an honest conversation. However, the expectation to live up to new queer "norms" is extremely problematic for a struggle that started off as challenging the very existence of those kinds of assumptions and limitations in the first place.[6]

These are oftentimes easy and expected mistakes to make while we struggle. It seems so ingrained in us to conceive of the Correct Line or Correct Path that it's hard to deviate from that if we're not paying very close attention and employing a great deal of self- and collective-reflexivity. The essentialist and egregious dynamic of the Oppression Olympics actually seems to *require* a Correct Line as it attempts to quantify, isolate, and hierarchically order different forms and experiences of multiple and overlapping oppressions. It's important to make sure that while we struggle, we do our best to not re-create what we are struggling against. Inverted hierarchies are no better than the original hierarchies (although perhaps they seem a bit more fun!). It's understandable that a common reaction to expected sexual norms is to find potential value and liberation in doing the opposite—we've all reacted that way, to a degree, to systems of hierarchy at some point in our lives. But understanding that this type of reaction is exactly that—a reaction—is important. Instead of reacting by doing the opposite, we need ways to move forward that don't resemble our original chains, even if they are fastened backwards. A systemic vision of the way sexuality, sex, and gender are hierarchically ordered and organized (and limited) is more fruitful than a reaction that is typified by doing the opposite of whatever feels constraining. For those interested, Nietzsche wrote extensively on this subject, which he termed *ressentiment*.[7] Not only are we still setting limits and creating new hierarchal sexual expec-tations when we define a liberated sexuality as one that is the di-rect opposite of the current socially acceptable and viable sexuality, but we are also continuing to define this liberated sexuality by that which caged us in the first place. If the "opposite" is liberating, then we are still being defined and limited by the original form, since its opposite is defined by itself. A large part of the radical queer project is rooted in the struggle against the creation and maintenance of "the normal" that is used to discipline all of us and our desires.

Will the Real Queer Please Stand Up?

In this section I'd like to develop the case for "queer" as a *position with a context* rather than a stable or fixed identity. One thing this means is defining in queer heterosexualities, to name perhaps one controversial example. A good question to bring this point home might be: Who is more oppressed, erased, and marginalized as a result of their sexuality—an upper-class white gay man living in the Castro or a poor, working-class heterosexual woman of color living in the Bible Belt who has a number of heterosexual relationships, is promiscuous, and is open about it and proud of it? Here we can imagine a heterosexual relationship perhaps being more marginalized in this context as compared to the non-heterosexual relationship that this scenario offers. This question doesn't have an answer—there are a multitude of specific contexts that would affect both of these hypothetical relationships. What this question should do, however, is make obvious that heterosexual relationships aren't always more acceptable or viable than non-heterosexual relationships. It may very well be that a non-heterosexual relationship that mirrors a normative heterosexual relationship may cause less trouble than a heterosexual relationship that involves non-normative sexual acts or manifestations of love that involve more than two people. I am not suggesting that other overlapping positions in society don't affect these scenarios, of course they do. In fact, the intersections of race, class, gender, sexuality, nation of origin, location, culture, etc. will all affect whether someone's style of loving is to be viewed as normative and acceptable or otherwise. This very fact highlights the point that the gender-specificity of a relationship ("straight" or "not") isn't always the axis of acceptance or not. We can see that there are very real ways that heterosexual relationships or styles of loving (or making love) can very much stand in opposition to the "normal," whereas non-heterosexual relationships and ways of loving can very much mirror the "normal" and may not subsequently be scrutinized nor understood as "abnormal" (of course this will be heavily determined by multiple and overlapping positions, oftentimes typified by race, class, gender, and location). It makes sense then to develop "queer" as a relational term vis-à-vis the normal rather than an identity marker that's just short for "LGBT" (or some lengthened version of the alphabet soup).

I have always found it interesting to explore why some practices have historically come to constitute an "identity" while others have not. As Sedgwick writes:

> It is a rather amazing fact that, of the very many dimensions along which the genital activity of one person can be differentiated from that of another (dimensions that include preference for certain acts, certain zones of sensations, certain physical types, a certain frequency, certain symbolic investments, certain relations of age or power, a certain species, a certain number of participants, and so on) precisely one, the gender of the object choice, emerged from the turn of the century, and has remained, as the dimension denoted by the now ubiquitous category of 'sexual orientation'.[8]

In queer theory, the very idea of the *queer* is a shifting terrain that cannot be pinned down to some single definition. Rather, queer can be understood as what is at odds with the "normal" or legitimate. This being the case, there is nothing in particular to which queer necessarily refers, which makes queer an identity without an essence. In this way, as demonstrated above, we can look for hierarchies within heterosexual relationships or ways of loving. A heterosexual relationship of two cisgendered and monogamous people who keep their sexuality indoors is quite different from heterosexual ways of doing relationships that involve non-monogamy, public BDSM, or selling sex for money. I did a small survey at Syracuse University in the fall of 2010 and found that the overwhelming majority of students interviewed believed it was fine that children were raised by two people of the same sex if they were in one monogamous relationship. However, at the same time they also believed that children have no place in the home of someone who is heterosexual but has more than one relationship or is involved in a relationship that consists of more than two people. In this case, the genders within a relationship weren't a factor for judging acceptable environments for children to be raised in, but the *type* of relationship was a factor. Same-sex relationships were fine, as well as heterosexual relationships, but only if they were otherwise normative. Both same-sex or heterosexual relationships that were non-normative, in this case involving either more than one partner or more than one relationship, were not deemed appropriate for raising children. Obviously with this scenario we can see how non-gender-specific ways of loving were the problem for those interviewed, not the gender involved.

Pressured to Poly?

I'd like to focus this section on some personal experiences I've had in which "queer," in part, has become synonymous with "non-monogamous." I've seen people get pressured to be sexually active in queer communities in ways that we'd immediately label as coercive outside of them. Even more absurd, I've seen monogamous same-sex attracted folks defined out of "queer" by poly heterosexuals for being too "normal" or being "homonormative."[9] Again, this understanding forces sexuality into something we *are* instead of something we do—and is a retreat from a radical queer sensibility into policing the borders of identity and practice. After all, we're anarchists because we want to get rid of cops, not be them!

Further, this policing of the borders of identity and practice creates a troubling "outside and against" attitude toward the more "mainstream" LGBT community. Of course not everyone in the more mainstream LGBT community are our comrades, but a lot of them could be (though this might also depend on structural factors too, particularly their relationship to economic and/or political power). This doesn't mean we shouldn't challenge the LGBT community on concepts such as compulsory monogamy, homonormativity, racism in the movement, an uncritical fight for gay marriage, or the problematic struggles for hate crime legislation and for the inclusion of "gays in the military" and what have you. What it does mean is that we shouldn't be positioning the mainstream LGBT community as the "bad guys" and turning our collective nose up at anyone who chooses to use identity labels such as "lesbian." I've witnessed queer people exclaim that anyone using the identity of "lesbian" is oppressive. This is ridiculous and brings us back to my earlier discussion of ressentiment.

Towards a Queerer Conclusion

Queer, by definition, is an ongoing and never-ending process, so this piece certainly isn't intended to be the last word on queer thought or practice. Also, while I'm at it, I should mention that I'm not trying to suggest that we shouldn't be public sluts, polyamorous, etc. (in fact, I enjoy those things at times!). And for all of us, especially those of us who spend a good deal of time in a comfortable circle of queer friends, we need to remember that the dominant society still pressures us to not be publicly queer, and to fit into a heterosexual, monogamous, and cisgender standard that is stultifying, confining, and…well…boring.

As we build movements, an insular, subcultural inwardness is anathema to creating broad based mass movements, which are necessary if we're ever going to topple capitalism, the state, and other related evils. This will require ever queerer conclusions, as it is a process that likely has no definite end.

1   See Mikhail Bakunin, "The reaction in Germany: A Fragment from a Frenchman," 1842, in *Michael Bakunin: Selected Writings*, edited by Arthur Lehning, trans. Mary-Barbara Zeldin (London: Jonathan Cape, 1973), 37–58.

2   Cissexual refers to people who feel that their gender identity matches their body/"sex"—it can also be understood as "non-transgender." "Dyadic" refers to the pairing of two people. Additionally, "homonormativity" is a term describing the same privileging and culture of understanding toward similarly organized sexual relationships between two non-heterosexual people.

3   Please note that I am using a simplistic binary for argument's sake. There are of course many examples of publicly acceptable promiscuous sexual acts, like that of a single, heterosexual, younger male.

4   Chad Garrison, "St. Louis Police Raid Swingers Club 'Red 7'; Consenting Adults Beware!," *River Front Times* http://blogs.riverfront-times.com/dailyrft/2011/05/red_7_st_louis_swingers_police_raid.php

(accessed January 2, 2012).

5   Don't even get me started on glitter.

6   See Gayge Operaista's chapter in this volume for more on new queer norms.

7   See Friedrich Nietzsche, *On the Genealogy of Morals—A Polemical Tract*, 1887, trans. Ian Johnston, (Arlington, VA: Richer Resources Publications, 2009); or see http://www.schoolbytes.com/summary.php?disp=term&id=240 (accessed January 2, 2012).

8   Eve Kosofsky Sedgwick, *The Epistemology of the Closet* (Berkeley, CA: University of California Press, 1990), 8.

9   "Homonormative" refers to same-sex relationships that are dyadic, monogamous, permanent, or otherwise mirroring heteronormative relationships.

Gender Sabotage

STACY AKA SALLYDARITY

Look how your children grow up. Taught from their earliest infancy to curb their love natures—restrained at every turn! …Little girls must not be tomboyish, must not go barefoot, must not climb trees, must not learn to swim… Little boys are laughed at as effeminate, silly girl-boys if they want to make patchwork or play with a doll. Then when they grow up, "Oh! Men don't care for home or children as women do!" Why should they, when the deliberate effort of your life has been to crush that nature out of them. "Women can't rough it like men." Train any animal, or any plant, as you train your girls, and it won't be able to rough it either. Now will somebody tell me why either sex should hold a corner on athletic sports? Why any child should not have free use of its limbs?

These are the effects of your purity standard, your marriage law. This is your work—look at it!

—Voltairine de Cleyre, "Sex Slavery" (1890)

What makes me transgendered is that my birth sex—which is female—appears to be in social contradiction to my gender expression—which is read as masculine. I defend my right to that social contradiction. In fact, I want to live long enough to hear people ask, "What made me think that was a contradiction in the first place?"

—Leslie Feinberg, *Trans Liberation* (1998)

Anarcha-feminists and anarchists in general need to have some new discussions about gender. Feminism has had an ongoing internal argument regarding minimizing or maximizing the meanings of the differences between men and women. Now we are seeing the influence on many anarchists and feminists of newer ideas about gender (e.g. queer theory) that question the idea of a concrete concept of "woman" and "man," even "male" and "female." Yet some radical or anarchist feminists and lesbians remain stubborn about questioning the usefulness of a category called "woman." Meanwhile, identity politics have come under fire in anarchist circles, often characterizing identity-oriented projects as homogenous (represented only by each project's most vocal proponents), and dismissing the importance of focusing on opposition to gender, sexuality, class, or racial oppressions.[1] Yet that which is called identity politics often does involve essentialism, *the idea that there are essential differences between two groups.* In the case of feminism, those who most often get to speak for the "movement" are white with class privilege, and regularly marginalize the experiences of women of color and poor women, and exclude transgender/transsexual people when they organize around a universal concept of *women*. The standard radical feminist characterization of the way gender oppression ("patriarchy") works legitimizes women's exercise of domination (through capitalism or white supremacy, etc.), and makes men's domination seem natural and inevitable. If the criticism of identity politics is that it hardens identities, a queer theory–influenced anarcha-feminism then could be outside of this criticism, and indeed may share it, while still emphasizing the real effects of the group-based oppression.

We've been made to believe that human subordination under the law is natural—that we need to be governed. The legitimacy of imposed government is also emphasized through the seemingly natural differences between people. The differences between people have been made significant so as to promote divisions based on domination and subordination. In doing so, those differences must be(come) clear-cut—a border must be drawn between the two, creating a dichotomy so there is no confusion about who is where in the hierarchy. This takes time, centuries even, to really harden our perception of human nature. It takes laws, but worse it takes discipline, primarily in the form of terror and violence, to pound a sense of hierarchy into us. Despite the possibility that the state and capitalism may be able to function without these imposed borders, the borders must still be destroyed.

To achieve liberation, we must reject the binary gender system, which divides us into two mutually exclusive categories. This gender system not only oppresses in the form of a hierarchy of categories, but also in terms of gender expression—holding up masculinity as superior and policing each person into their gender box. The significance of gender/sex differences must be exposed as a political construct, one which has been used to form a cross-class alliance among men, and to make heterosexuality and women's roles and exploitation in (and outside) the home and family to seem natural.

In effect, we are imprisoned by a gender binary, though a sort of freedom may be accessible to some, and if we don't behave appropriately there are plenty of prison guards to attempt to put us in our place. Clearly those who do not fit into these gender boxes are seen as a threat and are disciplined through threats or acts of discrimination, verbal abuse, harassment, and/or violence. I argue not that gender transgression or deviance is in itself revolutionary, but that we must transcend or destroy the gender-based power relations, as part of a sort of decolonizing. It is crucial that feminists not reinforce these gender boxes, but also that anarchists not minimize our need to pull these issues from the margins. The existence of these identities created by power relations should not be denied, but instead should be examined and opposed in the context of power.

Whereas sex is usually defined by biological differences, gender has been used to describe the prescribed social differences between female and male, defining us as feminine or masculine, traits we can generally agree are not universal throughout time or place. One point of contention among some feminists and gender-transgressors (not that the two are mutually exclusive) is the definition of gender. I agree with others like Kate Bornstein that gender may refer to different concepts: gender roles, gender identity, etc.[2] For lack of a better term, here I will use the term "gender stratum" to refer to the hierarchal binary categories of gender. I argue that what is called "gender identity" is a different aspect of gender, which is separate from, but related to gender stratum. "Gender identity," which I will call "gender inclination" since identity is problematic here, would have different meaning without gender stratum, but should not be confused as meaning the same thing, despite the fact that the two are conflated by many feminists.

We can probably agree that gender stratum is an imposed social construct. We could take it further by questioning whether our concepts of the biological differences between female and male existed before hierarchy, and whether they at least have the same significance before Western culture interpreted the differences we understand today.[3] The possibility that there are really no natural differences between the sexes—that these sexes don't exist other than because of political/social reasons—can be troublesome to nearly anyone. In many ways, these ideas exist almost exclusively in the realm of academia[4] and have little relevance to most people's everyday lives.

On the other hand, throughout the time humans have existed, there have been diverse ideas about the meanings of the physical differences between those with different organs associated with sex/gender. In considering the experiences of intersex people[5] and transgender/transsexual people, it only makes sense that a gender/sex continuum should be the basis for an understanding of human nature. Different ideas about gender and sexuality in various cultures, mostly where untouched by Western civilization[6], show us that not only are Western dualistic ideas about gender/sex, sexuality, and accompanying hierarchy atypical and manipulated to manage the people, but also that the argument that modern capitalism accommodates transgressive gender and expressions of sexuality is beside the point. The transition to capitalism was indeed a main driving force of the conquest over different forms of gender expression and sexuality, enforcing a strict gender/sex binary.

The likelihood is minimal that we could fully understand the origins of the concept of sex or the beginnings of gender hierarchy, even though this may provide answers about the origins of hierarchy itself. [7] Whether biological characteristics once had neutral meaning or not, significance has been increasingly placed on these differences, creating these sex/gender constructs as part of a hierarchy (sex is gendered and therefore I use the two terms somewhat interchangeably), and the construction of the divisions between men and women has been an ongoing process.

Woman as a Different Species

"Certainly we can say that the language of the witch-hunt 'produced' the Woman as a different species."[8]
—Silvia Federici

To understand the construction of a gender binary and hierarchy, we primarily look at Europe because of the ways in which, through colonization/imperialism, Europe violently exported its ideas throughout the world.[9] Before the witch hunts, European peasant women, having a decent amount of social power despite sexual division of labor and Christian-promoted misogyny, were heavily involved in revolts against feudalism and, later, capitalism. It is no coincidence, as Silvia Federici describes in her book, *Caliban and the Witch*, that the witch hunts, which involved the torture and murder of hundreds of thousands of women[10] mostly in the sixteenth and seventeenth centuries, occurred in conjunction with the transition to capitalism and the colonization of the Americas.

Federici also explains how, over the course of a few centuries, women's exploitation, through their unpaid labor in the home, termed "reproduction" (which includes procreation but is not limited to it), as well as slave labor in the Americas, had to be constructed as natural in the setting in which it was in the interest of capitalism to be viewed as voluntary and contractual. By justifying their exploitation, the dehumanization of unpaid laborers (women) allowed capitalists to hide/legitimize the reality that people didn't have a choice in the matter.

The witch hunts were not only counter-insurgency measures. Accusations of witchcraft and prostitution were often made to punish theft and attacks (real or invented) on property, which increased at this time due to land privatization[11] and the exclusion of women from receiving wages. Especially important was capitalism's new demand for workers (partly due to population crisis), leading to the construction of monogamous heterosexual[12] marriage as natural through the forced dependence of women on men, and criminalization of sexual acts that were not for the purpose of reproduction. Peasant women increasingly began to get punished for crimes such as abortion and contraception, and, in the case of witches, also for allegedly causing infertility and impotence in men, in addition to castration and killing children. Queer peasants were disciplined by means of terror in Europe in particular (this is where the term "faggot," meaning kindling, came from[13]), but also during colonization of the Americas as homosexuals and *two-spirit* people were killed, and the continuation of these identities/practices were averted or forced underground.[14]

Federici stresses that while some peasant men participated in and even encouraged these actions against women, and while the church played a strong role, the greater part of the campaign of terror against women would not have been possible without the role and interest of the state.[15] The ruling class's interest in promoting the differences between the sexes is clear, and they accomplished this task by punishing certain behaviors and using terror to discipline women.[16] Early on, European women were defined as unruly, mentally weak, and in need of being controlled. The witch hunts served to reinforce this, but at the same time to discipline women into a new "nature"—that of the docile, moral, and motherly (yet still in need of being controlled).[17] It is worth noting that while capitalism played a strong role in shaping what became understood as the nature of women, there are obvious examples of how those in power in any economic circumstances (not just capitalism) seek to justify their rule by different means, often by controlling sexuality and enforcing gender norms. So while the concept of women and men as two different groups existed prior to the witch hunts, there was now a new significance on the difference between the two, functioning as a clear binary.

The notion of inflexible divisions between humans had to be beaten into all the people as a whole, thus creating profound alienation between men and women, and marginalization, if not extermination, of those who deviate from the norms. In addition, to compel the people to work under the conditions that capitalism requires involved a sort of conquest involving a new perception of the body as a machine or tool, and through the criminalization of various communal activities and non-productive sexuality.[18] Workers' subordination and women's further subordination were made to seem natural. Even though there seems to be no anticapitalist historical study of the shaping of men, this clearly was part of the witch hunts, the transition to capitalism, and colonialism as well.

In discussing human nature, we need to be critical of the ways that certain concepts such as hierarchy, or a need for hierarchy, are made to seem natural.[19] For instance, Andrea Smith wrote, "Heteropatriarchy[20] is essential for the building of US empire. Patriarchy is the logic that naturalizes social hierarchy. Just as men are supposed to naturally dominate women on the basis of biology, so too should the social elites of a society naturally rule everyone else through the nation-state form of governance that is constructed through domination, violence and control."[21] In a speech, she said, "This is why in the history of Indian genocide the first task that colonizers took on was to integrate patriarchy into native communities. The primary tool used by colonists is sexual violence. What sexual violence does for colonialism and white supremacy is render women of color inherently rape-able, our lands inherently invad-able, and our resources inherently extractable."[22]

An example of colonization of the "New World" being ac-complished partly through the promotion of sexual divisions[23] is the French Jesuits' interactions with natives in Canada (called the Montagnais-Naskapi) with no sense of private property, authority, or male superiority, which according to the French had to change if they were to become reliable trade partners. The French taught Naskapi men to discipline their children, and to "bring 'their' women to order."[24] Witch hunts occurred in parts of the Americas (Federici discusses Mexico and Peru) that demonized all natives and Africans, but often focused more on the women.[25] Colonization is an ongoing process which includes patriarchal indoctrination and sexual violence in Indian schools.[26]

Gender Stratum and Race

The sex/gender hierarchy is inseparable from race, colonization, and capitalism. For example, female slaves were treated pretty much the same as male slaves, up until importing slaves was made illegal, at which time female slaves were made more often to breed and were increasingly subject to the sexual violence of white men.[27] As-pects of femininity, defined here as culturally/socially dictated as appropriate for "real" women, were constructed as a distinguishing mark of class (and race), much like landscaped yards that demon-strate that the owners need not use their land to grow food. Women who didn't have to work were to be unnaturally "weaker, delicate, dependent, 'lily-white', housebound" and therefore "the making of the white race involved the politicized unmaking of women to fit into 'white.'"[28]

Race is also a political and social construct. Understanding one politico-social construct can help us better understand another. Bacon's Rebellion, which was a more significant one of many re-bellions in which European indentured servants and African slaves joined together, frightened the state of Virginia into passing a series of laws specifically outlining the freedoms accessible to Europeans/Christians vs. Africans. In doing so, they created race. "Slavery was the most profitable form of labor in colonial Virginia, but racial slavery was the solution to the threat of servile insurrection and the problem of how to efficiently and peacefully get the workers—slave and free—to work... Race emerged from the needs of the Virginia upper class to craft a docile and productive labor force. But as the benefits of whiteness became apparent to English laborers, they came to embrace the system by which privileges were conferred in exchange for policing slaves."[29] While prejudices and ideas about superiority based on differences existed prior, this invention of whiteness created a new significance on physical differences that had a particular function to form a cross-class alliance among white people which still exists today.

The shaping of the categories of race and sex was part of a longer history of hierarchy. Additionally, just as the specific era of the witch hunts lasted a couple centuries, so too was the construction of race an ongoing process, like in the example of the Irish not being included into whiteness until later. Also, after the Civil War, lynching was a prominent way to terrorize—to discipline—Black people into submission. "Before lynching could be consolidated as a popularly accepted institution, however, its savagery and its horrors had to be convincingly justified. These were the circumstances which spawned the myth of the Black rapist—for the rape charge turned out to be the most powerful of several attempts to justify the lynching of Black people," wrote Angela Davis. She explains further in her book *Women, Race, & Class*, "However irrational the myth may be, it was not a spontaneous aberration. On the contrary, the myth of the Black rapist was a distinctly political invention." This also contributed to white women's fear of black men (and to white men's fear of their property, women, becoming tarnished), and was part of the precedent set which began to criminalize people of color, leading to the high rates of people of color in US prisons today.[30]

Despite there being major limitations to drawing parallels between race and gender stratum, the construction of these dichotomies allows us to see partly how hierarchy functions. Those in power divide the people on the basis of a physical difference (ignoring exceptions and gray areas) and amplify the significance of those differences through criminalization[31] and limitations of legal and economic freedoms, as well as through violence (justified by the alleged transgressions), while affording the favored group (men/whites) freedom from most repression. This process functions to make "natural" the divisions and hierarchal positions of those it involves. A cross-class alliance, rewarded with privileges, undermines anti-authoritarian resistance and class solidarity. In the case of women, I should point out that male privilege includes man's ability to dominate the women in his family, which can be seen as more personal while being, in effect, political.

Gender Liberation for Everyone

The naming of political advantages (or "wages") of whiteness or maleness as privileges is a problem, however. If the way I described hierarchy's functioning is accurate, it would not really be in the interest of the favored working-class group to participate in an alliance with the rich rulers since that means they will perpetually be ruled and exploited (this is where the promise of mostly unattainable upward mobility comes in to reinforce the alliance). White people have a responsibility to our/themselves to abolish whiteness for these reasons and to be fully human,[32] in addition, of course, to the responsibility to end racism.

Similar to the case of white people, when men participate in domination, they do themselves harm. While folks assigned male at birth who don't comfortably fit into their assigned gender box are certainly affected by gender oppression, the ones who do conform (willingly or not) would also benefit from undermining the ways gender hierarchy has been naturalized through the socialization of boys and men. They can hardly be free, and the relationships they have with others cannot be fulfilling as long as emotions are suppressed, competitive masculinity has to be established, and inequality (if not abuse) must be maintained with women (and often children as well). Yet why would men choose to change if they are consistently told they are privileged, bell hooks asks.[33] To change means, for one, that men would have to overcome their training to deny their emotions. Implicating women as well as men in perpetuating this damage done to males through parenting, hooks wrote, "Homophobia underlies the fear that allowing boys to feel will turn them gay."[34] Whereas "feminism" tends to imply a fight by and for women, it is, then, also in the interest of men to oppose gender oppression and homophobia/heteronormativity, rather than perpetuate it. It also means that feminism, for lack of a better word, must also address the situation of men.

While it is clear that men largely benefit from this system while women do not, it clearly functions by enforcing this gender border along with the concepts "man" and "woman." We must not, then, continue to reinforce these false concepts as binary, essential, stable, and universal categories. Clearly, even though viewing women as a socially constructed gender/sex within a hierarchy is useful, caution must be taken to avoid a sort of essentialism or sense of universal experience of this oppressed group. Some feminists who see sex/gender as a hierarchical social construct do not accept any other definition of gender, which leads to major disagreements over gender identity.

Some might argue that a realization of gender fluidity rather than a dichotomy would perhaps accomplish the task of undermining the political construction of gender/sex categories for the purpose of domination.[35] This deserves further examination. If we argue, as some have,[36] that hierarchical binaries like man/woman and white/black are created to naturalize hierarchy, this implies that a hierarchy existed prior. Therefore, while it may have been less acceptable to people, this hierarchy existed nonetheless, so the task is surely not simply to abolish the binaries/constructs. Yet again, there is only so much we can know about the origins of the concept of "man" and "woman" aside from the ways in which they have more recently been made more significant.

In this argument for rejecting the binary gender system, it should not be understood to mean that no one should identify as a man or a woman, much less that we should vaguely "smash gender" or implement some utopian androgyny.[37] A truly liberatory position on gender/sex requires self-determination of gender identity/inclination (including bodily alterations) and freedom from coercive gender assignment.[38] Everyone's experiences and sense of identity should be incorporated into an idea of what gender means. One's inclination for femininity (in people assigned male *or* female at birth) for example, should not be dismissed or devalued by others who don't relate to it. Additionally, most trans people face dangers if they diverge much from the standard ideas of femininity (and masculinity), and therefore have to pass by conforming in order to survive (by maintaining safety and employment), despite critical awareness by many about gender hierarchy and heterosexism.

That said, we need to dismantle gender stratum, to separate the power dynamics attached to gender, in that masculinity often means domination, and femininity, subordination. Since men are taught to be dominating—that this is equated with masculinity (being a "real man")—we need to make a particular point to change this. Men are denied their emotions, and as bell hooks writes, "Patriarchy both creates the rage in boys and then contains it for later use, making it a resource to exploit later on as boys become men. As a national product, this rage can be garnered to further imperialism, hatred, and oppression of women and men globally."[39] At the very least it teaches men in general to be apathetic about the plight of others. Because it is instilled in men that their nature requires them to be dominating, we must extract the domination imperative from what it means to be a man. Hooks distinguishes patriarchal masculinity from masculinity, and this deserves further consideration. Without the naturalization of a man/woman dichotomy, masculinity and femininity (gender inclination) and all their various meanings are either exposed as social only, and/or as more about individual tendencies of personality and affinity.

It is this domination that should be opposed, no matter who is doing it or in what form. No one ought to identify domination as part of who they are, nor should women excuse their own (or other women's) participation in domination just because they believe they cannot be oppressors. This applies to male privilege, hetero privilege, class privilege, white privilege, etc., in addition to hierarchies perhaps inadvertently created by those judging others as not revolutionary, queer, or gender nonconforming enough.

In the past there was an expectation that the radical lesbian movement (and before that, women's suffrage) would strongly threaten the dominant order. In fact, it has been viewed as a threat, but as we can see, it has been defeated, recuperated or co-opted under the larger system of domination.[40] If much of radical feminism/lesbianism was really the only real threat to the system,[41] then it served the dominant order to marginalize the particularly militant tendencies and/or those of women of color, or divert the movements to re-embrace essentialism, which reinforced the order of things.

Some radical feminists were certainly on to something. According to Celestine Ware, a black woman activist (1970) who was quoted in bell hooks' *Feminist Theory: From Margin to Center*, "Radical feminism...postulates that the domination of one human being by another is the basic evil in society. Dominance in human relationships is the target of their opposition." Hooks comments, "As feminist move-ment progressed, critiques of the notion of power as domination and control were submerged as bourgeois activists began to focus on women overcoming their fear of power (the implication being that if they wanted social equality with men, they would need to participate equally in exercising domination and control over others)."[42]

Attributing violence and abuse to the nature or necessary politi-cal position of men gives women the opportunity to participate in domination while insisting that they can do so in a more ethical way (or that they are by definition incapable of participating in domina-tion). In addition, this attitude makes male violence seem inevitable and allows us to avoid critical thinking about systemic/institutional oppressions, such as the likelihood that capitalism and the state pro-mote rape.[43] If rape is natural to men, then the survivors (mostly women) can rationalize that their only recourse is through the state. Yet prisons and police are not the solution to this problem. In ad-dition, acknowledging that being a woman, queer, or transgressing gender boxes, and/or having feminist or anarchist politics does not make one necessarily incapable of being a perpetrator of abuse and sexual assault, we must see this as a larger project of addressing is-sues of consent. Additionally, uniting around the freedom to choose what will be done or not done to or with our bodies ties together many people's struggles.

As far as identity politics go, there must be some focus on iden-tity in the sense that there are very real effects of these unreal con-structs. Yet the point is to understand the gender and race divisions not only to end gender and race oppression, but to end domination totally—to undermine these cross-class alliances created in the pro-cess of power seeking to naturalize itself, its law, and its divisions. Certainly capitalism, with the state, made the divisions between genders and races politically significant in a way that they never had been before. This shows that much of the racism and sexism that has existed in the last few centuries is not innate, not organic, not grassroots, but rather manufactured. Part of this struggle will be in exposing the ways in which our beliefs have been shaped in the in-terest of power—that many of the things we consider to be natural are in fact not just man-made, but state-made.

Illuminating the ways that our oppression is not "natural" can be done partly through the actual demonstrations and experiences of gender fluidity and queerness, sometimes referred to with other concepts as "queer." "Queer is…an identity that problematizes the manageable limits of identity. Queer is a territory of tension, defined against the dominant narrative of white-hetero-monogamous-patriarchy, but also by an affinity with all who are marginalized, otherized, and oppressed."[44]

In the sense that *queer* is unstable and destabilizing, it has much potential. Clearly the refusal to participate in privileging political relations would not be co-opted. We know that "LGBTQ" is co-opted just as feminism is, and therefore the potential lies in the ways in which queer is not co-optable. Where identity politics seeks inclusion for its respective group, it chooses participation in domination and reinforces binaries. Would a rejection of inclusion and participation be the antithesis of identity politics, even if it were a politics that focused on a specific group-based oppression?

Gender transgression alone may or may not succeed at destroying the gender hierarchy. If it does, it is because it is able to render the binary meaningless. Yet few are so optimistic about this possibility since it would probably require a lot of participation and clear intent because of this co-optability of transgressions of gender and sexuality by the power structure. However, I argue that binary gender and compulsory heterosexuality have to be destroyed because they regulate us all into our gender and sexuality boxes, limiting our ability to be liberated and to participate in resistance. It is necessary to come up with new ways of resisting gender oppression/patriarchy without reinforcing the idea that woman is a useful category to organize around. Finally, the exposure of gender/sex as a social construct on which a binary hierarchy was naturalized and functions through cross-class/race alliances may activate a clearer general understanding of how this occurs, thereby allowing white women, for example, to better see how whiteness functions similarly, crumbling multiple constructs at once. Imagining new possibilities for gender, race, and power/economic relations is necessary for liberation.

1   See lilith, "Gender Disobedience: Antifeminism and Insurrectionist Non-dialogue," http://theanarchistlibrary.org/HTML/Lilith__Gender_Disobedience__Antifeminism_and_Insurrectionist_Non-dialogue.html (accessed January 28, 2012). In response to Feral Faun/

Wolfi Landstreicher's "The Ideology of Victimization" and other texts on gender.

2   "In hir book, *My Gender Workbook*, Kate Bornstein characterizes gender's components as fourfold: gender assignment, gender role, gender identity, and gender attribution. Gender assignment is what the doctor calls you at birth, so it can be written off as a description of sex (Bornstein reserves the word sex for sex acts so as to circumvent Essentialist argumentation). Gender role is described as what culture thinks your niche should be, while gender identity is totally subjective. Gender attribution refers to how another person might interpret your gender cues." Stephe Feldman, "Components of Gender," http://androgyne.0catch.com/components.htm (accessed January 28, 2012).

3   "Nothing could be less abstract than the idea of a natural social group, or it never occurs except in the context of an existing power relationship, and that is the crux of the matter. An ideology or interpretation of reality which balanced the right of the oppressors against the nature of the oppressed, each conceivable only in terms of the other and both belonging to the actual practice of appropriation, could hardly be described either as reflection (which presupposes the separateness of the practical and symbolic levels) or as rationalization, which presupposes not only the same separateness but also an intellectual ingredient in the exercise of domination which is not always present in hard fact." Colette Guillaumin, *Racism, Sexism, Power and Ideology* (1995), 79.

4   Judith Butler wrote in *Gender Trouble*, "Can we refer to a 'given' sex or a 'given' gender without first inquiring into how sex and/or gender is given, through what means? And what is 'sex' anyway? Is it natural, anatomical, chromosomal, or hormonal and how is a feminist critic to assess scientific discourses which purport to establish such 'facts' for us? Does sex have a history? Does each sex have a different history, or histories? Is there a history of how the duality of sex was established, a genealogy that might expose the binary options as a variable construction? Are the ostensibly natural facts of sex discursively produced by various scientific discourses in the service of other political and social interests? If the immutable character of sex is contested, perhaps this construct called 'sex' is as culturally constructed as gender; indeed perhaps it was always already gender, with the consequence that the distinction between sex and gender turns out to be no distinction at all." Stevi Jackson discusses Christine Delphy's position: "She argues that rather than the difference between men and women being

a self-evident anatomical fact, recognizing that difference is itself a social act... It is not enough, she argues, to treat the content of gender as variable, while assuming that the container (the category woman or 'man') is unchangeable. Rather, we should treat the container itself as a social product." Stevi Jackson, "Theorizing Gender and Sexuality," in *Contemporary Feminist Theories* (1998), 136.

5   "Social construction of biological sex is more than an abstract observation: it is a physical reality that many intersex people go through. Because society makes no provision for the existence of people whose anatomical characteristics do not neatly fit into male or female, they are routinely mutilated by medical professionals and manipulated into living as their assigned sex..." Emi Koyama, "The Transfeminist Manifesto," 2000. The Intersex Society of North America website states that the figures for the total number of people whose bodies differ from standard male or female is one in one hundred births. From www.isna.org/faq/frequency (accessed January 29, 2012).

6   "Patriarchy...rests on a gender-binary system; hence it is not a coincidence that colonizers also targeted indigenous peoples who did not fit within this binary model. Many Native communities had multiple genders—some Native scholars are now even arguing that their communities may not have been gendered at all prior to colonization—although gender systems among Native communities varied." Andrea Smith, "Dismantling Hierarchy, Queering Society," Tiqqun Magazine (July/August 2010). From www.tikkun.org/article.php/july2010smith (accessed February 6, 2012)

7   I am hesitant to argue what John Zerzan does in the following quote because addressing its significance prior to the witch hunt and capitalism is a rather overwhelming task. Yet it is likely significant: "[Gender] is a cultural categorization and ranking grounded in a sexual division of labor that may be the single cultural form of greatest significance. If gender introduces and legitimates inequality and domination, what could be more important to put into question?" John Zerzan, "Patriarchy, Civilization, and the Origins of Gender." From http://theanarchistlibrary.org/HTML/John_Zerzan__Patriarchy__Civilization__And_The_Origins_Of_Gender.html (accessed February 6, 2012). While many feminists see gender hierarchy as the first hierarchy, those materialist feminists who argue that gender/sex categories were created to naturalize an already-existing hierarchy might then argue that gender did not introduce, but did legitimize inequality and

domination. Gender might be the first category-based hierarchy, but may not have been the first hierarchy. The question is whether that hierarchy was in any way gendered prior to the attempts at stabilizing the categories of gender.

8   Silvia Federici, *Caliban and the Witch* (2004), 192.

9   I am not arguing here that gender inequality is only a Western phenomenon. I am arguing that the period of the witch hunt created new meanings for gender, and these meanings were spread throughout many parts of the world. It is worth noting that this has influenced anthropological interpretations of gender as well.

10   The small percentage of those hunted as witches who were men were usually relatives of women charged with being witches. Silvia Federici, *Caliban and the Witch* (2004), 189.

11   Ibid., 200.

12   The terms "heterosexual" and "homosexual" were not used until much later.

13   Ibid., 197.

14   Ibid., see also Walter Williams, *The Spirit and the Flesh* (1986), chapter 7: "The Abominable Sin: The Spanish Campaign against 'Sodomy,' and Its Results in Modern Latin America." Williams describes the motivation resulting partially from the Spanish attempt to regain control of their country from the Moors, who were more relaxed about same-sex relations. Also, the Spanish used the rampant homosexuality in the "New World" to justify their conquest.

15   Federici describes one way women's power in the anti-feudalism movements was broken down involved the state legalizing rape (of proletariat women) and prostitution (during a specific time period, since prostitution was also criminalized for other reasons), making women's bodies the new commons in place of the access to land and other natural resources they were losing. Men were afforded these privileges to damage the more equal relationships they had with women. Interestingly, municipal brothels also served the purpose of addressing the rampant homosexuality of the time. Silvia Federici, *Caliban and the Witch* (2004), 48–49.

16   Ibid., 168. There were plenty of skeptics regarding the reality of witchcraft, but many, like Thomas Hobbes, "approved the persecution as a means of social control."

17   Ibid., 103.

18   Ibid., 136–140.

19 "Like the social Darwinism that preceded it, sociobiology proceeds by first projecting the dominant ideas of current society onto nature (often unconsciously, so that scientists mistakenly consider the ideas in question as both "normal" and "natural"). Bookchin refers to this as "the subtle projection of historically conditioned human values" onto nature rather than "scientific objectivity." Then the theories of nature produced in this manner are transferred back onto society and history, being used to "prove" that the principles of capitalism (hierarchy, authority, competition, etc.) are eternal laws, which are then appealed to as a justification for the status quo! What this procedure does accomplish," notes Bookchin, "is reinforce human social hierarchies by justifying the command of men and women as innate features of the 'natural order.' Human domination is thereby transcribed into the genetic code as biologically immutable." Murray Bookchin, *The Ecology of Freedom: The Emergence and Dissolution of Hierarchy* (2005), 92, 95. Quoted in "What Does Anarchism Stand For?," An Anarchist FAQ Section A.2, http://infoshop.org/page/AnarchistFAQSectionA2 (accessed January 28, 2012).

20 "By heteropatriarchy, I mean the way our society is fundamentally based on male dominance—dominance inherently built on a gender binary system that presumes heterosexuality as a social norm." Andrea Smith, "Dismantling Hierarchy, Queering Society," *Tikkun Magazine* (July/August 2010). From www.tikkun.org/article.php/july2010smith (accessed February 6, 2012)

21 Andrea Smith, "Indigenous Feminism without Apology." (2006) http://www.awid.org/eng/Issues-and-Analysis/Library/Indigenous-feminism-without-apology-Decentering-white-feminism.

22 US Social Forum 2007, Liberating Gender and Sexuality Plenary, http://www.youtube.com/watch?v=x5crWlrksZs (accessed January 28, 2012).

23 Overall, though, and especially after the first phase of colonization, men and women were equally accused as devil worshippers and treated as such. This was done to justify to Europe and to the church specifically that the conquest was a mission of conversion, not a conquest for riches. Federici, *Caliban and the Witch*, 220–21.

24 Ibid., 111.

25 The witch hunts in the Americas were "a deliberate strategy used by authorities to instill terror, destroy collective resistance, silence entire communities, and turn members against each other. It was also

a strategy of enclosure, which depending on the context, could be an enclosure of land, bodies or social relations. Above all, as in Europe, witch hunting was a means of dehumanization and as such the paradigmatic form of repression, serving to justify enslavement and genocide." Ibid., 220.

26 "Strengthening of this male power [in tribal councils] is inextricably linked to a long history of colonialism, as well as to federal government policy and law, such as Indian boarding schools... The boarding schools' purpose, for example, was to insert patriarchy into tribal communities and to socialize children to believe in patriarchal gender norms." Renya Ramirez, "Race, Tribal Nation, and Gender: A Native Feminist Approach to Belonging," *Meridians* Vol. 7, No. 2 (2007), 22–40

27 Angela Davis, *Women, Race and Class*, (1981) 5–7.

28 Butch Lee and Red Rover, *Night Vision*, (2000) 29.

29 Joel Olson, *Abolition of White Democracy*, (2004) 37. I would say that "peacefully" is not a good word here, as Olson elaborates on some of W. E. B. DuBois's analysis of this cross-class alliance as ensuring the stability needed to maintain capitalism "largely through the terrorization and subordination of the rest of the working class."

30 See Angela Davis, *Women, Race and Class*, (1981).

31 In the case of race, criminalization is now used in such a way as to not seem related to race, even though it clearly targets people of color at a disproportionate rate. Race-based identity politics, focusing on inclusion and exceptionalism, tend to overlook the criminalization of people of color.

32 "So-called whites must cease to exist as whites in order to realize themselves as something else...in order to come alive as workers, or youth, or women, or whatever other identity can induce them to change from the miserable, petulant, subordinated creatures they now are into freely associated, fully developed human subjects." Noel Ignatiev, "The Point Is Not to Interpret Whiteness but to Abolish It," paper presented at the University of California-Berkeley conference, "The Making and Unmaking of Whiteness," April 1997. From race-traitor.org/abolishthepoint.pdf (accessed February 6, 2012).

33 bell hooks, *Feminist Theory: From Margin to Center*. (1984): 73–75.

34 bell hooks, *The Will to Change* (2004): 45.

35 "Like the apartheid of race, blurring of class boundaries is the gravest offense because it challenges the reality of the division of reality...sexual continuity is threatening—it destroys the male-dominated power

structure completely. If there are no hard and fast sex types, then there can be no apartheid of sex." Martine Rothblatt, *The Apartheid of Sex*, (1995): 19. "The continued oppression of women proves only that in any binary there's going to be one up and one down. The struggle for equal rights must include the struggle to dismantle the binary." Kate Bornstein, *Gender Outlaw*, (1994): 106.

36 See Collette Guillaumin. *Racism, Sexism, Power, and Ideology.* (1995).

37 "Many in the movement who yearned not only for women's liberation, but also for human liberation, embarked on a bold social experiment. They hoped that freeing individuals from femininity and masculinity would help people be viewed on a more equal basis that highlighted each person's qualities and strengths. They hoped that androgyny would replace masculinity and femininity and help do away with gendered expression altogether. Twenty years after that social experiment, we have the luxury of hindsight. The way in which individuals express themselves is a very important part of who they are. It is not possible to force all people to live outside of femininity and masculinity. Only androgynous people live comfortably in that gender space. There's no social compulsion powerful enough to force anyone else to dwell there. Trans people are an example of the futility of this strategy... People don't have to give up their individuality or their particular manner of gender expression in order to fight sex and gender oppression. It's just the opposite." Leslie Feinberg, *Trans Liberation* (1998), 53.

38 See Emi Koyama, "Transfeminist Manifesto." (2000) From eminism. org/readings/pdf-rdg/tfmanifesto.pdf (accessed February 6, 2012); Michelle O'Brien, "Trans Liberation and Feminism: Self-Determination, Healthcare, and Revolutionary Struggle." (2003) From anarchalibrary.blogspot.com/2010/09/trans-liberation-and-feminism-self. html (accessed February 6, 2012); and Carolyn, "Politicizing Gender: Moving toward Revolutionary Gender Politics." From www.spunk. org/texts/pubs/lr/sp001714/gender.html (accessed February 6, 2012).

39 bell hooks, *The Will to Change*, (2004): 51.

40 I would note that "bisexual" denotes a binary, and thus does not necessarily upset gender, but pointing to the recuperative nature of the power structure, Paula Rust wrote, "Thus lesbianism was initially constructed as a challenge to gender. But once 'woman' was reconstructed to include 'lesbian', lesbians became part of the prevailing gender structure. In effect, lesbianism was co-opted into gender and ceased to be a challenge to it. Furthermore, the rise of cultural feminism reified

rather than challenged gender, maximized rather than minimized the differences between women and men, and created a concept of lesbianism that was dependent on the preservation of gender. Given lesbians' initial challenge to gender, one might expect bisexuals' efforts to break down gender to be well received among lesbians. But because of the change in the relationship of lesbianism to gender…, bisexuals' contemporary challenge to gender is also a threat to lesbianism." Paula Rust, "Bisexual Politics," reprinted in Judith Lorber, *Gender Inequality, Feminist Theories and Politics* (Roxbury Publishing Co., 1998), 93–94.

41 "The development of sisterhood is a unique threat, for it is directed against the basic social and psychic model of hierarchy and domination…" Mary Daly quoted in Peggy Kornegger, "Anarchism and the Feminist Connection." (1975) From anarchalibrary.blogspot.com/2010/09/anarchism-feminist-connection-1975.html (accessed February 6, 2012).

42 bell hooks, *Feminist Theory from Margin to Center.* (1984): 83.

43 Angela Davis, "Rape, Racism, and the Capitalist Setting," in *Angela Y. Davis Reader* (1998), 129.

44 Mary Nardini Gang, "Toward the Queerest Insurrection," From zinelibrary.info/toward-queerest-insurrection-0 (accessed January 28, 2012).

Anarchy without Opposition

JAMIE HECKERT

> *To oppose something is to maintain it.*
> —Ursula K. Le Guin, *The Left Hand of Darkness*

I have a memory. It was 1984: a presidential election year in the United States. We had a mock election in school. To learn about the process? To start practicing early? I was eight years old. Only one person in our class voted for Walter Mondale against Ronald Reagan. When these results were read aloud, the girl in front of me turned around and pointedly asked, "It was you, wasn't it?" It wasn't.

After school (that day? another?) a boy from my class asked me if I was a Democrat or a Republican. When I said, "Neither," he was perplexed. "You have to be one or the other," he responded, with all the assurance of one stating an obvious and unquestionable truth. "Well, I'm not," I insisted. I knew you didn't have to be; my parents voted, but they didn't identify themselves with either party. In my mind's eye, this boy's face screws up with outraged and frustrated disbelief. "You have to be one or the other!"

Democrat or Republican? Gay or straight? Man or woman? Capitalist or anticapitalist? Anarchist or archist?

Us or them?

I have a memory from a very different time and place: London, 2002. I traveled down from Edinburgh with a woman from ACE, the social centre we were involved in, to attend Queeruption. It was my first queer anarchist event. On the way, I learned loads about menstruation. Once there, I remember chatting to another guy. He found out I identified as an anarchist and started asking me, were you at such and such summit protest? Nope. How about this one or that one? No. No. He looked really puzzled and maybe even asked how I could be an anarchist without converging outside the G8, WTO, IMF, or other gatherings of elites. Isn't that what anarchists do?

~·※·~

Anarchist politics are usually defined by their opposition to state, capitalism, patriarchy, and other hierarchies. My aim in this essay is to queer that notion of anarchism in a number of ways. To queer is to make strange, unfamiliar, weird; it comes from an old German word meaning to cross. What new possibilities arise when we learn to cross, to blur, to undermine, or overflow the hierarchical and binary oppositions we have been taught to believe in?

Hierarchy relies on separation. Or rather, the belief in hierarchy relies on the belief in separation. Neither is fundamentally true. Human beings are extrusions of the ecosystem—we are not separate, independent beings. We are interdependent bodies, embedded in a natural world itself embedded in a vast universe. Likewise, all the various social patterns we create and come to believe in are imaginary (albeit with real effects on our bodyminds). Their existence depends entirely on our belief, our obedience, our behavior. These in turn are shaped by imagined divisions. To realize that the intertwined hierarchical oppositions of hetero/homo, man/woman, whiteness/color, mind/body, rational/emotional, civilized/savage, social/natural, and more are all imaginary is perhaps a crucial step in letting go of them. How might we learn to cross the divide that does not really exist except in our embodied minds?

This, for me, is the point of queer: to learn to see the world through new eyes, to see not only what might be possible but also what already exists (despite the illusions of hierarchy). I write this essay as an invitation to perceive anarchism, to perceive life, differently. I'm neither interested in recruiting you, nor turning you queer. My anarchism is not better than your anarchism. Who am I to judge? Nor is my anarchism already queer. It is always becoming queer. How? By learning to keep queering, again and again, so that my perspective, my politics, and my presence can be fresh, alive.

Queering might allow recognition that life is never contained by the boxes and borders the mind invents. Taxonomies of species or sexualities, categories of race or citizenship, borders between nations or classes or types of politics—these are fictions. They are never necessary. To be sure, fictions have their uses. Perhaps in using them, we may learn to hold them lightly so that we, in turn, are not held by them.

Of Opposites and Oppositions

How to be one's self and yet in oneness with others, to feel deeply with
all human beings and still retain one's own characteristic qualities.
This seems to me to be the basis upon which the mass and the indi-
vidual, the true democrat and the true individuality, man and woman,
can meet without antagonism and opposition.
—Emma Goldman, "The Tragedy of Women's Emancipation"

If everyone inspired by anarchism agreed exactly on what it was,
how it worked and how it felt, would it still be anarchism?

> *Everybody on earth knowing*
> *that beauty is beautiful*
> *makes ugliness.*
>
> *Everybody knowing*
> *their goodness is good*
> *makes wickedness.*
> —Lao Tzu[1]

I notice how often anarchism, and anarchy, is defined in opposition to the state, capitalism, and all other forms of hierarchical structure. Not domination, but liberation. Not capitalist, but
(libertarian) communist. Why?

Oh, I'm not opposed to opposition! I just have some questions.
One is about borders—drawing lines on a map and then claiming that
they are real. Isn't this the operation at the heart of the state? And
isn't this what happens when you or I want to draw a clear line between us, good anarchists, and them, evil archists? We this, they that.

The questioning of borders is at the heart of queer theory.

Conventional lesbian, gay, bisexual, and transgender politics is
based on opposites: we an oppressed minority and they the privileged majority. In this version, the problem is inequality and the
answer is legal protection. Queer theory troubles this, suggesting
instead, in my mind, that the problem comes from belief in the
identities. The thing about opposites is that they depend on each
other to exist: straight is not gay, gay is not straight and bisexual-
ity still confuses people. This leads to all sorts of possibilities for
control—we learn to ask ourselves and each other, is he really...? Is
she really...? Am I really...? We're encouraged to believe that our

sense of gender and who we fancy tell us who we are and where we fit in a sexual hierarchy imagined to already exist. Whereas a state-oriented LGBT politics tries to challenge the hierarchies of heter/homo, cis/trans, while keeping the identities, queer politics might ask how the identities themselves might already be state-like with their borders and policing.

I have similar questions about anarchist and other identities. How much energy that could go into creating other-than-state-like ways of living gets lost to efforts to appear anarchist enough? I know I'm not the only one who suffers from anarcho-perfectionism! Likewise, I've seen loads of energy go into arguments about whether so and so is really anarchist or not, or such and such is really anarchism.

On the flip side, I once had a very interesting conversation with a man who owned a furniture-making company. We had a lot of areas of agreement and he seemed very interested in anarchism. I suggested that when he retired he could leave his factory to all of the workers to be run as a cooperative. He responded, plaintively, "but I'm a capitalist."

What kinds of politics might become possible if we all learn to be less concerned with conforming to certain labels and more capable of listening to the complexity of our desires? My concern, here, is that opposition—a politics of opposites that push against each other, lean on each other—might get in the way of the listening.

A memory-story[2]: a few years ago, I lived in a former mining village outside of Edinburgh. I was greatly distressed at hearing the single working-class woman next door shouting horrific things at her children nearly every morning. She would curse at them, sometimes shouting how she hated them. It was nearly unbearable. How could I talk to her about it? Then, I took a course on non-violent communication—a strategy without opposition (more on this below). It taught me to communicate in a way that made it easier for her to hear my feelings and desires. The opportunity came when I found a ball in "my" garden (we don't own land, we are part of land) and she was in "hers." I threw the ball over the privet hedge and asked her how she was finding single parenting. "It must be hard," I said. I then told her that when I heard her shouting in the mornings I felt frightened because it reminded me of things from my own childhood.[3] She didn't say anything to me then, but the shouting stopped and her daughter started talking to me.

More recently, this skill again served me well. On my way to London, where I was going to speak about academia and activism, I got into a conversation about politics with a man who identified as conservative. Terrorism came up and I asked if we were any better than them; quoting a Chumbawamba T-shirt, I said, "War is terrorism on a bigger budget." He looked thoughtful and a hippie-looking French guy behind him laughed and wrote it down. Then a very big and very angry looking man stood up and asked if I had just said that war is terrorism. I nodded, and he said, "I'm in the Army." He looked furious and I thought there was a good chance he might punch me. I suddenly found myself in his shoes, sensing what he might be feeling, wanting. I looked him in the eye and asked gently, "Are you angry because you want respect for yourself and your fellow soldiers?" He looked away, his face and shoulders softening, and muttered, "I guess everyone is entitled to their opinion."

What might have happened if I had opposed him?

What might an anarchy refusing to be contained by the borders of its opposites look like? How might anarchism be continually queered, listening across lines of identity and ideology? Now, I'm not saying that anarchism should include everything. I am saying that interesting things are likely to happen if folk inspired by anarchism make connections with folk who see things differently, who do things differently. To do so is not simply to try to convince others that anarchism is right, but perhaps even to let go of such judgments.

> *Beyond right and wrong, there is a field.*
> *I will meet you there.*
> —Rumi

I yearn for honesty, complexity, and compassion. I don't want to be asked, or told, to choose from a list of options already defined, already decided, already judged. I want to have a discussion. Connection. Intercourse. A chance to listen and to be listened to: giving and receiving, receiving and giving. Let's experience different possibilities for identities, for relationships, for politics. Let's meet.

It is this which draws me again and again to anarchism. And not just to anarchism; I am too promiscuous for that.[4] My anarchism has no straight lines, no borders, no purity, no opposites. No living things do. And I like my anarchy alive.

Okay, I'll be honest. My anarchism can grow rigid, bordered, oppositional. I know the satisfaction of imagining myself more radical than others. The thing is, this comes with the risk of being not-radical-enough, or even not really an anarchist. It also gets in the way of getting along with people, of working together, of even meeting. So, when my anarchism is rigid, what are the chances of experiencing anarchy?

Reading Stories Differently

But these stories weren't gospel. They weren't Truth. They were essays at the truth. Glances, glimpses of sacredness. One was not asked to believe, only to listen.
—Ursula K. Le Guin, *The Telling*

A friend of mine, who does both activisty and scholarly things, recently made disparaging comments about the queer theory that is only about "learning a different way to read a novel." And indeed, one of the first books to be labeled queer theory was Eve Sedgwick's *Between Men*, a book about nineteenth-century English literature. It was, at the same time, an exploration of patterns of oppression in particular cultural norms of love, sex, friendship, gender, and intimacy. Recognizing these patterns came from learning to read novels differently. In drawing attention to love and desire between men in apparently heterosexual novels, the point is perhaps not to say that this is really what the story is about. Rather, it unsettles our notion of how things really are and, therefore, what is possible.

Is this so different from the storytelling of Peter Kropotkin? *Mutual Aid: A Factor in Evolution* invited a different reading of Darwin's theory, different from those who saw evolution as justification for empire, those who imagined that survival of the fittest meant the most fit, the most dominant, the most masculine, the most "advanced." For Kropotkin, and I think for Darwin, too, fittest meant best able to fit in with other beings in an ecosystem. In other words, to cooperate.

~❀~

So, is cooperation better than competition? Is queer better than straight? Are those the right answers? Is that how I should live my life?

The way I see it, at the moment anyway, neither queer nor anarchy is about finding the right answers or working out the right way to live. Both are about the experience of connecting with others, with self. I almost always find it harder to connect with someone who is insisting that their story is *the* story, their truth *the* truth. Where's the space left for my story, my truth? Your story, your truth? How can different people, different creatures, different stories and voices learn to fit together if any one story tries to take up all of the space? Like the Zapatistas, I want to live in "a world where many worlds fit."

One of the principles of permaculture, an ethical design system or perhaps a revolution disguised as gardening, is that edges are the most productive areas in a system. Where the river meets the bank, the forest the meadow, or the sea the shore, there will be an abundance of life. The more that anarchism, a many branched river in our social ecosystem, mixes and mingles with swamp and stone, soil and soul, the more diverse forms of life will benefit.

Conversely, moral high ground is a cold, barren, and lonely land. I know—I've been there and I return from time to time. Highly rational and fiercely intellectual, it leaves no space for doubt, for complexity of feeling. Warmth toward self and other dwindles, for the cold numbs the heart. Shelter from pain, numbness, may be a form of protection from the horrors of witnessing violence and violation. Ah, but the numbed heart is also impervious to joy. And how queer can life be without joy? Seeking further distance and separation from the pain by climbing that moral high ground, I risk forgetting that my heart yearns for community, vitality, and play. Perhaps it is less of a forgetting and more of a learning not to listen. For pain is a signal, an awareness of being alive, a reminder of what is desired. Learning not to listen. Isn't that, too, the nature of the state?

Care of the Self

The interplay of the care of the self…blends into pre-existing relations, giving them a new coloration and greater warmth. The care of the self—or the attention that one devotes to the care that others should take of themselves—appears then as an intensification of social relations.
—Michel Foucault, *The History of Sexuality, vol. 3: The Care of the Self*

In a queerly anarchist paper, Sian Sullivan asks, is an *other* world possible?[5] When state/empire/capital depends on carefully and continuously producing clear and hierarchical divisions between and within people, how can we make space for that which has been designated *other*? Declaring a politics to be nonhierarchical, anarchist, feminist, safe, or queer does not magically make this happen. It takes a different kind of magic—practice.

These hierarchies aren't just "out there." They are also in here: in the way we hold our bodies, in our thoughts, in our emotional reactions, in the ways we learn to see the world and to imagine what is real and what is possible. These hierarchies arise in the ways we relate to ourselves, to other humans, and to the rest of the natural world. And that's okay.

(Bear with me, here!)

There's this social psychologist called Thomas Scheff who was trying to understand why people conform (or, perhaps, why it's hard to be queer).[6] Drawing on a rather Kropotkinesque view of evolution, he reckoned that humans are basically cooperative and that maintaining this cooperation is a basic function of our emotions. We feel good ("pride") when our social bonds are strong and we feel bad ("shame") when relationships are at risk, because we depend on these relationships to live. Now, this is all well and good for getting along with each other. The trouble starts when we feel ashamed of our shame and get into this nasty spiral of beating ourselves up. He calls this pathological shame and offers it as a suggestion for understanding all the ways in which people conform to things that we know aren't good for us, for other people, or for the rest of the planet. This is why I say it's okay that hierarchies arise. If trying to be a good anarchist means always being anti-hierarchical, then anarchist relationships are always at risk of not being anarchist enough, thus feeding the spiral of pathological shame, of rigidity, of the state. Modesty may offer the middle ground, the convivial edge, between excessive pride and pathological shame.[7]

Since then, another radical social psychologist has developed a more complex emotional model of domination. Marshall Rosenberg, the founding practitioner of nonviolent communication (NVC), also reckons that conformity and domination start in our everyday relationships.[8] He talks about the concept of emotional slavery—feeling responsible for other people's emotions. What happens when the beautiful anarchist desire for freedom and equality is held in this cage? I see in myself and in others an overwhelming compulsion to try to make everything equal, to make myself and others free. To make everything okay.

What if everything is already okay, even pain and shame?

Rosenberg offers the radically compassionate perspective that absolutely everyone is doing the best thing they can imagine to meet life-serving desires/needs (e.g., order, community, play, food, shelter, etc.). There is no such thing as evil; there is nothing to oppose. Instead, we might learn to both empathize with the desires of others and to express our own. Sure, we might disagree about strategies for meeting those needs. I still get angry, sometimes, when seeing strategies that meet some people's needs while ignoring others (like war, private property, or bullying). And blaming someone for that can be temporarily satisfying. The thing is, if I blame other people for not being perfectly anarchist already, then I end up blaming myself too. I'm no perfect anarchist either. How could I be? Where would I have learned these skills? Like everyone, I'm still practicing.

This is why I invite you to consider the very queer notion of an anarchism not based on opposition, but a politics that starts off accepting everything just as it is. From the basis of acceptance, we might then ask, what service can be offered? How can anarchy be nurtured, rather than demanded, forced? What ways of living and relating can we practice that are even more effective at meeting the needs of everyone for life, love, and freedom? And in what ways might we learn to accept the pain we feel when that doesn't happen, instead of distracting ourselves with resentment or chocolate? And in what ways might we learn to be gentle with ourselves when we realize we've been drawn to strategies of distraction or even domination?

Stillness in Motion

Prefer what is positive and multiple, difference over uniformity, flows over unities, mobile arrangements over systems. Believe that what is productive is not sedentary but nomadic.
—Michel Foucault, Preface to *Anti-Oedipus: Capitalism and Schizophrenia*

Bodies need to move, to play, to be well. Sedentary culture leads to great suffering. Bodies kept in line, in chairs at work stations or school desks. Bodies kept in order. The same goes for thoughts, for feelings.

To hold tightly—to shame, resentment, or any emotion or any story of how the world really is—is to be held tightly. This is not freedom. To hold gently is to be held gently. This, to me, is freedom. No opposition, no tension, between intimacy and spaciousness. Instead, there is a gentle dance that comes from a deep stillness.

To become anarchist, to become queer, is not easy. To learn to cross lines, to see that the lines are not even real, is a radical transformation for those of us who were raised to believe in them. But it need not be a struggle. Struggling against the world as it is, struggling against my experience, gets in my way. Sure, the world is not the world of my dreams. Why should it be? To stop my pain, or yours? Running from pain is a noisy affair. It distracts.

To learn to listen to yourself, to "let your life speak,"[9] requires silence, peace. Otherwise, I know I get caught up in a rush of stories and feelings about what I should be doing, how I've not done enough. I forget to rest, to play. Is that radical?

Hold on, you might say. Of course we all need to rest and play. But how can we not oppose, for example, the Wall in Palestine/Israel? How can you say it's a fiction? It's concrete. Material. So too are the bullets and the tanks that maim and kill.

Bodies and the bullets are real. Painfully real. The concrete does not self-organize into the Wall. No border, invented by human minds, asserts its own existence. No gun shoots itself. There is human action behind every border, every wall. And behind these actions: emotions, beliefs. Why do some Israeli people support the Wall? Because, as I understand it, they are afraid. They are taught to believe that at least some Palestinians are dangerous enemies. They desire security, life. When people act as soldiers, they believe, perhaps, that the border is real and must be defended. They may believe that those on one side are inherently different from those on the other. Or perhaps they believe, with their hearts and minds, that they have no choice other than to follow orders. To do otherwise, to relate otherwise, might simply be unimaginable.

A State of Mind

The challenge we face is made up of specific patterns of behaviour among Settlers and our own people: choices made to support mentalities

that developed in serving the colonization of our lands as well as the unrestrained greed and selfishness of mainstream society. We must add to this the superficial...justifications for the unnatural and misunderstood place and purpose of human beings in the world, an emphatic refusal to look inward, and an aggressive denial of the value of nature.
—Taiaiake Alfred, *Wasáse: Indigenous Pathways of Action and Freedom*

Queer ecology is both about seeing beauty in the wounds of the world and taking responsibility to care for the world as it is.
—Catriona Mortimer-Sandilands, "Unnatural Passions?: Notes Toward a Queer Ecology"

I find myself coming again and again to what seems to me as a very queer conclusion. The most radical thing I do is meditate daily.

Raised in Settler society, I've learned to resist looking inward, to be frightened of what I might find there. But it's the best way I've found "to be one's self and yet in oneness with others, to feel deeply with all human beings and still retain one's own characteristic qualities," as Emma has called us to be, to feel. And so I invite you to consider, just to consider, meditation as an anarchist practice of freedom.

Here's a queer proposal: the state is always a state of mind. It's putting life in boxes and then judging it in terms of those boxes, those borders, as if they were what really mattered. It's trying to get other people to do what you want them to do without so much regard for their needs, their desires. It's self-consciousness, self-policing, self-promotion, self-obsession. It's anxiety and depression. It's hyperactivity stemming from the fantasy that being seen to be doing something is better than doing nothing, even if what you're doing might cause more harm than good. It's resentment at self and others for not doing it right, for not being good enough. It's the belief that security comes from control. And it's a source of tremendous suffering in the world.

It's also something I do. When I look inward, when I meditate, I can see how much the mind is attached to individualistic stories of myself: as important, as weak, as wonderful, as useless, as victim, hero, or villain. The stories fluctuate and change form. And when I believe them, they affect all of my relationships. I, too, can perform the state.

Judith Butler may have taught me that the performance of a role is merely a copy without original, but it is meditation that lets me see it with clear vision. Sitting down each morning, focusing my mind, observing the thoughts and emotions that pass through, I learn to not identify with them, to not get caught up in them, to not reject them. I'm learning the "art of allowing everything to be as it is,"[10] which in turn helps with the many challenges of caring "for the world as it is," of seeing beauty in wounds. I'm learning to be playful with my sense of who I am, to let go the borders, the policing. It's so much easier for me to connect with others when the walls of the heart, of the individualized self, come down. And it's easier to let go of the walls if I don't judge them. Of course we learn to protect ourselves.

I practice meditation, not just for myself, but so that I can go out into the world unarmed. Unarmored. Enamored. When I feel a love for life itself, I see anarchy everywhere. I notice all the little ways, and not-so-little ways, that people already support each other, already speak for themselves, already listen to each other, already make decisions, and act together. These aren't just "seeds beneath the snow," as Colin Ward put it. They are blossoming flowers. An *other* world is not only possible, it already exists. I've felt it.

And when I again get caught up in my own thoughts, my own desires, my own stories about who I am, and who you are, what should have happened, how the world should be…then I see so little outside the dramas of my own mind. Everything I see, everyone I meet, I reinterpret through the lens of those fictions. I take myself and my beliefs very, very seriously. Just like the State.

Is it radical to hate myself for that? Is it radical to hate "cops," "capitalists," "politicians," "racists," or "homophobes" for that? In my own experience, the two are intimately intertwined. Inseparable.

And so I go inward before going out into the world. Letting my mind grow still, I am not ruled by my thoughts. Letting my heart open, I am able to love myself and others. And if I am called to fight, to protect those under threat, let me do it with love. Because if I'm not loving, it's not my revolution.

1   Lao Tzu (trans. Ursula K. Le Guin), *Tao Te Ching: A Book about the Way and the Power of the Way* (Boston, MA: Shambhala, 1997), 4.

2   I borrow this term from Kristina Nell Weaver whose anarcho-buddhist geography writing reminds me that memories are not the truth of what has happened in the past, but the stories that our minds create in the present.

3   I've written about this in an essay. See "Fantasies of an Anarchist Sex Educator," in *Anarchism and Sexuality: Ethics, Relationships and Power*, edited by J. Heckert and R. Cleminson (London: Routledge, 2010).

4   See D. Shannon and A. Willis, "Theoretical Polyamory: Some Thoughts on Loving, Thinking, and Queering Anarchism," *Sexualities*, 13 No. 4 (2010): 433–443.

5   See S. Sullivan, "An *Other* World is Possible? On Representation, Rationalism and Romanticism in Social Forums," *Ephemera*, 5 No. 2 (2005): 370-392. Online at http://www.ephemeraweb.org/journal/5-2/5-2ssullivan.pdf (accessed January 25, 2012).

6   See T. J. Scheff, *Microsociology: Discourse, Emotion, and Social Structure* (Chicago: University of Chicago Press, 1990).

7   See Ursula K Le Guin, "The Conversation of the Modest" in *Wild Girls* (Oakland, Ca: PM Press, 2011).

8   See Marshall Rosenberg, *Nonviolent Communication: A Language of Life* (Encinitas, Ca: PuddleDancer Press, 2003).

9   See Parker J. Palmer, *Let Your Life Speak: Listening for the Voice of Vocation* (San Francisco: Jossey-Bass, 1999).

10 See Adyashanti, *True Meditation: Discover the Freedom of Pure Awareness* (Louisville, CO: Sounds True, 2006).

Lessons from Queertopia

FARHANG ROUHANI

Paths to Queer Anarchism

I discovered anarchism later in life than most people. By this, I don't mean to suggest that there is a maximum age requirement for entry to become an anarchist or that there is any kind of linear way through which we develop our ways of thinking and acting, but I would like to begin this essay by saying a little bit about how I got here. In my undergraduate and graduate educations in literature, political geography, and cultural studies, I came across few, if any, opportunities to study anarchist thought closely, nor was I involved in any kinds of movements or communities organized around anarchist ethics. My thinking about the world, as it developed in graduate school in particular, was shaped largely by Foucault, Gramsci, and Lefebvre and their descendants, specifically focused around Marxist political economy, queer theory, and the everyday practices of state formation and globalization. My doctoral thesis centered on how middle-class young residents of Tehran, Iran, experience themselves as citizens and consumers in relation to theocracy, democracy, and neoliberalism within their practices of using satellite television and the internet. It is very curious to me now that I was influenced by so many theories that were themselves influenced by anarchist ways of thinking without the word "anarchism" every really being uttered. This reveals a lot, I think, about our education and wider social systems in the United States and their ignorance and anxieties about approaching anarchism. There is so much work clearly derived from and aligned with anarchist approaches that does not call itself that.

In any case, my first introduction to anarchism came in the Commonwealth of Virginia of all places, when shortly after I started my teaching job at Mary Washington College (now called the University of Mary Washington) in 2001, I was approached by a group of radical students to be the advisor of a newly formed student group, the Anarchist Social Theory Club (ASTC). I, of course, said yes, knowing very little but also being very interested. Over the next few years, we collaborated on yearly reading groups and seminars ranging in topic from anarchist social-philosophical history to anarcha-feminism and the intersections of queer theory and anarchism to a much more practice-oriented project called Rights to the City, which focused on a squatting experiment in downtown Fredericksburg, Virginia. From the beginning, I approached anarchism with a good deal of skepticism, especially in the ways that anarchist scholars until recently unproblematically talked about (human) nature in essential terms. But at the same time, I felt more and more drawn in to more recent anarchist critiques of domination, coercion, and identity politics, and the emphasis on ethics-based, rather than rights-based, practical models of creating new worlds in the shell of the old.

One of the projects organized by ASTC was a yearly workshop series on different radical activist and community projects in the region, ranging from Richmond Indymedia to Helping Individual Prostitutes Survive (HIPS). In 2004, two members of the Richmond Queer Space Project (RQSP hereafter) came to Mary Washington for a workshop, and I immediately connected to their theoretical and practical engagement with creating a queer space around a set of anarchist ethics. RQSP was a micro-scale activist and community building project based in Richmond, Virginia, which lasted from 2001 to 2006, which had a very dynamic presence in the city. While active in organizing rallies and workshops and holding weekly consensus-driven meetings, RQSP was made particularly vibrant by its creation of a material space, Queer Paradise, which at different times operated as political, social, and living spaces for different members of the group.

It was largely through the combination of my involvement with ASTC and my exposure to RQSP that I, in my mid thirties, came to identify myself as an anarchist. I wanted to start my essay with this personal story partly to provide full disclosure of how I became interested in anarchism and how my interest in anarchism was initially of an academic nature, but also to emphasize the widely different paths and trajectories that bring people to particular ideas, movements, and practices.

What I would like to argue in this essay is that while queer and anarchist theories offer inspiring, creative, utopic alternatives, they often do not get into the complex, contradictory, messy processes through which ideals are enacted. We tend, for example, to valorize consensus-driven practices without paying critical attention to the critical gap between our idealized consensus models and the complex ways in which they are practiced. My goal is to describe the rise and demise of RQSP as a way of taking these complexities seriously and as a way toward understanding how such movements can be better sustained. I will begin by examining three analyses of queer anarchism in practice, and then observe the complex processes through which RQSP created a queer material space, with an emphasis on the sometimes contradictory politics of affinity and identity that emerged. What I present here is the product of a year-long research project interviewing ten members of RQSP and is a shorter, hopefully more accessible version of a forthcoming article in the free online academic journal, *ACME: An International E-Journal for Critical Geographies*.

Affinity, Prefiguration, and Queer Anarchisms

Within the academic world, anarchist perspectives have recently inspired and been inspired by a variety of radical theoretical frameworks, including queer theory, feminism, critical race theory, and radical environmentalism.[1] Two important recently developed aspects that have a direct bearing on the formation of queer anarchist politics and projects such as RQSP are affinity and prefigurative politics. Scholars conceptualize affinity as a group of people coming together, sharing a common ground, and developing spaces of support and communication. Affinity politics, then, involves perceiving the hopes and fears of seemingly culturally and regionally different people as interlinked, forming coalitions that can negotiate a temporary common ground, and moving beyond divisive identity politics.[2]

Prefigurative politics demands that activists adhere as much as possible to the world they would like to see in how they live and act in the world today. As such, it presupposes equality and imagines a collective subject of resistance, rather than arguing for individual rights that can be added into the existing statist status quo. The processes of politics are as important as the result, involving the employment of non-hierarchical, participatory, and consensus-based models of action. The result is a dynamic vision of utopia as an ongoing process, rather than as a goal that can be achieved through granting individual rights.[3]

Affinity and prefigurative politics, as such, share a radical confluence with queer politics in their critique of identity politics, concern for ethics in relationships, and advocacy of practicing utopia through experimentation. For a deeper look into these elements, I will now discuss the works of three scholars on queer anarchist practices.

Jamie Heckert conceives of anarchism as an ethics of relationships.[4] He critiques the extent to which sexual orientation is a state form, one of the many everyday processes of state formation through which people's opportunities and actions are rigidified and controlled. Ultimately, people's desires and identities cannot be contained in state-sanctioned state forms, and those people produce alternative realities in relation to their partners that sometimes evade control of the state. Heckert's take on resistance to sexual orientation continues a central tradition of anarchism, but expands it to a realm, sexuality, not extensively dealt with by anarchists. In addition to serving as a critique of the state, he presents ways in which people are actively engaged in a prefigurative project in their everyday life. In a similar vein, Gavin Brown synthesizes anarchist perspectives on affinity, autonomy, and play with a geographic perspective on queer space in his research on Queeruption gatherings.[5] The temporary spaces of the gatherings provide opportunities for the creation of a "queertopia," through the ways in which they construct a non-hierarchical, ethically aware, sexually positive community and space. Furthermore, the gatherings provide opportunities to challenge the social divisions that result from identity politics through providing temporary spaces for the creation of autonomous, affinity-based relationships centered on ethics and mutual respect. Lastly, Eleanor Wilkinson examines the role and politics of emotions in the work and daily lives of queer activists.[6] She argues that emotions are often undervalued in how we think about activism, and that a queering of thought on activism involves, among other things, challenging the notion that only certain kinds of emotions are appropriate in certain kinds of spaces. For example, she suggests that the seeming openness and consensuality of autonomous activist organizing often depends on silencing certain kinds of emotions, such as anger and frustration, and bracketing sexuality as a private or a secondary matter. Instead, she argues for a reflexive openness to discussions of emotions that potentially lead to greater emotional sustainability for individuals and groups.

These research pieces converge around their desire to expand the field of anarchism to revalue sexuality, emotions, and relationships to people, groups, and movements, and to present a full range of spaces of activism beyond our fixation on street politics, to include the range of everyday spaces and practices through which people engage with constructing new worlds. Wilkinson, in particular, goes far in considering the complexities and contradictions of such a project. While anarchist perspectives on affinity and prefigurative politics are inspiring in their explorations of opportunities for solidarity and creating new possible worlds, they often do not present the complications and complicities that can be involved in building a new world in the shell of the old. For a closer look, I now turn to some observations on the Richmond Queer Space Project.

RQSP and the Messy Politics of Space-Making

The Richmond Queer Space Project was founded in 2001 by four self-described Richmond queers who had previously established chapters of the Lesbian Avengers and the Queer Liberation Front and were seeking to create a material and symbolic space that would support queer political actions and community formations. The original space that the group occupied as Queer Paradise was a cheaply rented, dilapidated loft in downtown Richmond. The group members I interviewed reflected proudly on their accomplishments with creating this first space. As a large warehouse, it held endless possibilities in how space could be allocated, and from the beginning they could make conscious collective decisions on how a queer space should look. For example, one of the members of the collective used a wheelchair, and the group made a conscious effort to build a space for her that would suit her needs, such as a low door, and that would make others conscious of disability issues. The experience was empowering on both an abstract level and on a practical level of gaining building and construction experience. Also, the space served simultaneously as a living space for some members and as a meeting space for RQSP and other activist Richmond groups, adding to its general character of having endless possibilities.

The use of this space ended in April 2002 when police and city inspectors condemned the building and gave the residents two hours to leave. The group floundered after that, meeting periodically in people's houses, in university campus buildings, and on a farm. Queer Paradise reemerged in November 2002 as a leased office space in a location just a few blocks away from the first space. From the beginning, there were conflicts and concerns about the extent to which this space had the effect of de-radicalizing the group. Some members considered this new kind of space to be very conventional and un-queer, but it was ultimately consensually agreed to largely because it would be a more publicly visible space that might be more accessible and safe for new potential members.

There were other ways in which a de-radicalization of the project was happening in this moment, for example in the change of RQSP from an underground to a nonprofit organization. While group members actively tried to maintain the nature of the organization, any official state-sanctioned organization must adhere to certain rules, including having a hierarchical power structure.[7] This de-radicalization is also evident in changes in the mission and goals of the collective. The first mission statement identified the goals of the RQSP as:

- To provide a space to promote community among queer-identified people and encourage queer activity in Richmond.
- To provide free meeting space for queer-positive groups who work to challenge heterosexism, sexism, ableism, racism, and classism.
- To educate on queer and related issues through pamphlets, speakers, conferences, queer cultural activities, and a lending library.[8]

The new, more generalized mission statement associated with the second space was: "The Richmond Queer Space Project maintains a queer-friendly space and resource center, promotes queer culture in Richmond, and links queer experience to the wide spectrum of social justice work."[9] This reflects a significant change, from the more radical tone of the first statement to the more generic, inclusive, social justice tone of the second. These changes were not uniformly accepted within the group, and came to a dramatic head in the context of one event in particular.

This happened in June 2004, in the context of a rally in opposition to House Bill 751, the so-called Marriage Affirmation Act. The state's largest mainstream LGBT rights organization, Equality Virginia, had organized a rally and was set to have its members and allies speak on behalf of gay marriage rights, and the members of RQSP spent a considerable amount of time and energy debating whether and how to be involved. Ten members were set to deliver a strong anti-marriage statement, but other members of the collective did not want to antagonize the mainstream LGBT movement in the presence of the larger threat of the bill. They rewrote the speech in a way that could establish a temporary ground of affinity with the LGBT marriage movement, while at the same time including the collective's own beliefs of marriage as a normalizing institution. The speech that was ultimately given clearly identifies RQSP as "queer," makes linkages between queers and other marginalized groups, and argues for solidarity based around the fact of the bill being as much about further controlling the lives of individuals as about marriage specifically. It concludes as follows: "As HB 751 came straight into our lives, it created activists. And in that respect there is an opportunity on our horizon. Let us figure out how to struggle not just for our own group rights, but against our common enemy. And let us not grow comfortable when it is not our group that is under attack."[10]

Participation in this event provided opportunities for building connections, by establishing temporary ground while broadcasting a critique of marriage and state control, but it also led to the most severe conflict, ultimately leading to the demise of the group. Some members ended up feeling betrayed about the conciliatory tone of the speech, criticizing it as a form of assimilation politics, and ended up forming a separatist "queer posse" within RQSP. The members who had supported rewriting of the speech were also left with ill feelings about the queer separatists, expressing that their actions were divisive, lacked an ethics of care, and were overly dismissive of the concerns of the LGBT activists. Basically, what ensued was a divisive form of identity politics, of who was queerer than whom, within a project that was consciously attempting to be opposed to identity-based political divisiveness. The split also represented a breakdown in processes of consensus building. The processes of consensus building around participation in this event were time-and-energy-draining, and ultimately unsuccessful. I think this brings up an important question of whether consensus-modeled groups should always have agreement as their goal. Perhaps the irreparable fracture that developed during this moment could have been avoided if members could have agreed to a temporary ideological separation, with the idea that RQSP did not need to have a singular ideological vision.

There were other significant sources of conflict that were voiced in my interviews with members of the collective. Age appeared as a divisive issue. One of my interviewees, an older male member of the collective at thirtysomething, argued that the younger members tended to be more narrowly focused on using RQSP as a platform for carrying out queer activist projects, that the older members were more focused on creating a space and a community, and that those in between often felt stretched in both directions. I think that age is an important, underrepresented source of conflict in anarchist politics, and particularly so in the United States where the scale of the movement is so small and discontinuous through time that there aren't the same kinds of cross-generational ties there can be in other radical activist cultures. Race and racism, also, were important issues, as RQSP consisted primarily of white radicals and Queer Paradise was situated within a Richmond neighborhood that was the product of long-term segregation. The neighborhood consisted mostly of a combination of long-term poor African-American and affluent gentrifying white and African-American residents. The tensions from these changes made RQSP members feel at times like white colonists and at other times totally excluded from the narrative of urban decline and renewal in the neighborhood. Lastly, there were important issues having to do with scale and the limits of radical activism in a small, relatively conservative southern city like Richmond. During its existence, RQSP had as few as ten and as many as about thirty members. For those in the collective who were seeking to make the space more accessible, it was shocking that the group didn't grow beyond that. A trans-identified member of the collective told me that he had recently wanted to start a chapter of Gay Shame in Richmond, but given the small size of the mainstream visible gay community in Richmond, it seemed wrong to start an organization that would serve to critique it. Such a statement, I think, has important implications on the nature and extent of radical queer politics possible in certain kinds of places.

What We Get When We Admit Our Limitations

I do not mean to diminish the significance and vitality of autonomous queer collectives like the Richmond Queer Space Project. The members I interviewed informed me of all the ways in which their association empowered them, sexually, politically, and culturally, and ended up impacting their professional futures as well. My concern has much more to do with how to cultivate longer-term impact and sustainability. I realize that much of the vitality of projects such as RQSP is related to their temporariness and the looseness of affinity associations. But among other things, it concerns me that very little queer activism has taken up the role of RQSP in Richmond since its demise four years ago.

I would like to end by suggesting that we need to develop a much more extensive knowledge base and practical toolkit for being able to deal with problems when they appear. For one thing, it is tremendously important to appreciate the challenges of trying to build a new world in the shell of the old, the need for all the forms of emotional support and reflexivity that activists and academics alike tend to ignore, and the specific kinds of opportunities and constraints provided by different kinds of spatial contexts. More specifically in the context of queer anarchist politics, we need to pay more attention to ways in which identity politics is bound to impact us, as a part of the sexual world that we currently inhabit, so that we can engage and deal with its divisiveness when it appears. And we need to approach the notion of queertopia as an ongoing, constantly reimagined process, within which contradictions and capitulations need not be equated with the end or failure of the project. The long-term sustainability and dynamism of our movements and spaces depend on admitting our limitations and learning from the critical gap between the ideals and enactment of our projects.

1   See Randall Amster, Abraham DeLeon, Luis Fernandez, Anthony J. Nocella, II, and Deric Shannon, ed., *Contemporary Anarchist Studies* (New York: Routledge, 2009).

2   ibid., 82–92, 213–223.

3   See Ibid., 11–17; J. Shantz, "Anarchist Futures in the Present," *Resistance Studies* No. 1 (2008): 24–34; and J. Rancière, *Disagreement* (Minneapolis: University of Minnesota Press, 1999).

4   See J. Heckert, *Resisting Orientation: On the Complexities of Desire and the Limits of Identity Politics*, PhD dissertation (Edinburgh: University of Edinburgh, 2005).

5   See G. Brown, "Autonomy, Affinity and Play in the Spaces of Radical Queer Activism," in *Geographies of Sexualities* edited by K. Browne, J. Lim, and G. Brown, (Burlington, VT: Ashgate Publishing Company, 2007), 195–206.

6   See E. Wilkinson, "The Emotions Least Relevant to Politics?: Queering Autonomous Activism," *Emotion, Space and Society* No. 2 (2009): 36–43.

7   For other examples, see M. Andrucki and G. Elder, "Locating the State in Queer Space: GLBT Non-Profit Organizations in Vermont, USA," *Social and Cultural Geography* (8)(1) (2007): 89–104.

8   RQSP literature, January 10, 2002.

9   2004, queerspace.org (now defunct).

10 June 30, 2004.

Tyranny of the State and Trans Liberation

JERIMARIE LIESEGANG

"STAR is a Revolutionary Group. We believe in picking up the gun and starting a revolution if necessary. Our main goal is to see 'gay' people liberated and free"
—Marsha P. Johnson, "Rapping with a Street Transvestite Revolutionary"[1]

"Trans Liberation is the phrase that has come to refer to all those who blur or bridge the boundary of the sex or gender expression they were assigned at birth: cross-dressers, transsexuals, intersex people, Two Spirits, bearded females, masculine females and feminine males, drag kings and drag queens. Trans Liberation is a call to action for all those who care about civil rights and creating a just and equitable society"
—Leslie Feinberg, *Trans Liberation: Beyond Pink or Blue*[2]

Anarchists (should) understand the importance in opposing the regulation of sexual and gender behavior by governments and other allied forces such as the church and capitalism. In fact there has been a long history of anarchism as a movement and a philosophy recognizing and embracing the pivotal importance of sexual and gender liberation. Within this history there has been a prominent role of queer anarchist sex radicals who kept this significant engagement at the forefront of the anarchist movement and philosophy. Yet despite the pioneering anarchist sex radicals at the turn of the century and those during the heyday of the (gay, feminist, black) liberation movements of the sixties and seventies, there has been an increasing trend by the Lesbian, Gay, Bisexual, and Transgender (LGBT) liberation movement toward embracing the government and its role in regulating sexual and gender behavior. And this current "liberation" movement has worked in complicity with the state simply to broaden and *reform* the definitions and social norms of sex and gender, as well as focus on the assimilation of LGBT within the State through marriage reform, Don't Ask Don't Tell, and by enacting laws that seek to entrench and empower the police and incarceration system through increased funding and engagement through hate crime legislation. And so we see a liberation movement that moved from a focus on fighting the state and its associated systems of corrupt police, politics, and social norms to a liberation model complicit with a state and its allied power structures that makes no excuse regarding its control, regulation, definition of, and legal boundaries regarding, sexual behavior and gender identity and expression.

This chapter details the historical roots of sex and gender radicals within the anarchist movement as well as within other allied liberation movements. From this historical perspective, we can reexamine the state of the LGBT liberation movement, and attempt to solidify and redefine a trans liberation movement outside the current so-called LGBT liberation movement. The aim of this chapter is to reconsider Trans liberation within the contexts of the current social, economic, and political environments within primarily the United States, though given the penetration of a global LGBT movement led by marriage advocates, it can also be viewed from a global lens. In this process, it is hoped to reveal that the core of the trans existence and persona is radical and anarchistic, if not insurrectionary, in its embodiment—such that pure liberation of sex and gender will not come through complicit reform within the state but rather through rejecting the state and its many social constructs.

Queer Anarchists/Sexual Radicals 1850–1930 (aka First-Wave Sexual Liberation)

During the late nineteenth and early twentieth century there emerged an articulation of a politics of homosexuality. In 1897 Berlin, the German sexologist and sex radical Magnus Hirschfeld and several colleagues formed the Scientific Humanitarian Committee (SHC)—the world's first homosexual rights organization. The members of the SHC were radical intellectuals who helped create new understandings of homosexuality and championed new political goals and ideas as well as strong critiques of oppressive social norms and values.[3] During this first wave of sexual liberation many of these radical intellectuals shaped new understandings and forms of same-sex political and social consciousness that had immediate and long-term impacts on the lives of European people. Within the United States, unlike Europe, the politics of sex radicals did not arise from a blossoming homosexual rights movement. Instead, it arose from the anarchist movement of the time. Anarchist sex radicals like Emma Goldman, Alexander Berkman, Leonard Abbott, John William Lloyd, and Benjamin R. Tucker wrote books, articles, and lectured across the United States regarding same-sex love. Emma Goldman [1869–1940] is without question the first person to openly lecture on homosexual liberation (emancipation) and openly supported Oscar Wilde against his persecutors. Though not an anarchist himself, Magnus Hirschfeld praised Emma Goldman as the "first and only woman, indeed, one could say the first and only human being, of importance in America to carry the issue of homosexual love to the broadest layers of the public."[4] The US anarchists of this time were unique in articulating a political critique of American social and legal rules as well as the societal norms that regulated relationships. In this effort, and through leveraging the anarchist movement of the time, they were able to center homosexuality within the political debate. By doing so, they created a fundamental shift in the sexual, cultural, and political landscape of the United States, not only during their time but also for decades to follow. As Terence Kissack notes: "The anarchist sex radicals were interested in the ethical, social and cultural place of homosexuality within society, because that question lies at the nexus of individual freedom and state power…The anarchist sex radicals examined the question of same sex love because policeman, moral arbiters, doctors, clergymen and other authorities sought to regulate homosexual behavior."[5]

So we see that during this first wave period within Europe much of the dialogue by sex radicals was around a civil rights and educational venue with a focus on acceptance within the constructs of the state. However, the anarchist US sex radicals did not come to the issue of sexual liberation through a lens of homosexual identity and reform, but rather from a more fundamental and radial anarchist alternative denouncing the principles of the state and its allied power structures within the church and its mandate of adherence to social norms. Following World War I and the passing of the 1918 Sedition Act, sex radicals and the anarchist movement began a sharp decline as many of the activists were imprisoned or deported and their vital propaganda vehicles were shut down. And not much later, on

May 6, 1933, the Nazis took power within Germany and attacked Hirschfeld's Institute and burned many of its books. So there came about a closing to this first-wave sexual liberation as the state (in both the United States and Germany) commenced its crackdown on the sex radicals and the revolutionary dialogue around sexual liberation that they had created.

Homophile Movement 1930-1969 (aka Second-Wave Sexual Liberation)

By the late 1930s the anarchist movement and sex radicals were a shell of their original heyday of the late nineteenth and early twentieth century. Coincidental with this decline in the anarchist movement we saw the rise of the Communist Party (CP) as the primary vehicle of the left. Sex radicals of this period began to work under a left that was dominated by the CP, which marginalized the ideas and ideologies of their anarchist predecessors.[6] The CP was an organization that, contrary to the anarchists, enforced uniformity of belief and action. And in regards to homosexuality, the CP had a policy of discouraging membership of gays and lesbians who refused to be silent about their private lives (clearly a 180 degree reversal from the beliefs and actions of anarchist sex radicals like Emma Goldman and Alexander Berkman). In theory the CP enacted the first "Don't Ask Don't Tell policy" against homosexuals, even though many prominent sex radicals and homosexuals of the left were members of CP.

Whether it was state actions against sex radicals and anarchists following World War I, or the rise of the sex radical oppressive CP, the second stirrings of a sexual liberation movement did not begin to arise until after World War II. And sadly, many contemporary histories of the gay movement in the United States have focused not on the sex radicals and anarchists of the first wave of sexual liberation, but rather on this second-wave postwar era with a focus on the organizations and individuals who shared the primarily reformist view of gay liberation.

Following WWI there were no sustained homosexual or sex radical movements until 1948 with the publication of the Kinsey report titled *Sexual Behavior in the Human Male* and in 1953 with the publication of the study titled *Sexual Behavior in the Human Female*. Both of these reports astounded the general public and were instantly controversial and sensational. "The findings caused shock and outrage, both because they challenged conventional beliefs about sexuality and because they discussed subjects that had previously been taboo."[7] Yet as we learned from the first-wave sex radicals, this was far from the first open discussion about sex, sexuality, and gender. Rather than this dialogue arising from radical intellectuals and anarchists, it instead arose from the mainstream scientific community and sexologists. These reports, as did the writings and lectures of the first wave sex radicals, permanently altered "the nature of the public discourse of sexuality as well as society's perception of its own behavior."[8] These publications were widely read and revealed to the general public that a large number of men and women engaged in same-sex love. Also during this period Harry Hay (1912–2002), a prominent gay man within the second-wave sexual liberation movement, founded in 1950 the *Mattachine Society*, the first enduring LGBT rights organization within the United States. Harry Hay was a prolific and vocal advocate for the gay liberation movement (or as Hay framed in it those days "the homophile movement"). Hay learned about activism and organizing during his early days within the CP, however in order for him to pursue his sexual politics he needed to leave the CP since the CP did not allow gays to be members.[9] During this onset of the Mattachine Society and the homophile movement, we saw the rise of the lesbian counterpart to Mattachine—Daughters of Bilitis, as well as One, Inc., the publishers of *ONE Magazine*, the first US pro-gay publication. However, the dialogue was far different from that of the first-wave sex radicals who challenged and critiqued the constraints and oppressions of the state. The second-wave dialogue was centered on identity, whether homosexuality was a mental illness, and improving homosexuals' standing within a capitalistic and hierarchical state, as well as seeking to exercise the rights to congregate in bars without fear of arrest and to distribute their magazines through the state-controlled postal system.

In many respects, this movement represented an organizational movement like Hirschfeld's SHC, as opposed to the individual discourses and writings of the anarchist sex radicals. In 1948 Harry Hay understood that "[a]ctivating the political potential of homosexuals in the United States depends, in Marxist terms, on their becoming a class for itself, aware of their common interests, rather than merely a class within itself…Without consciousness of themselves as a class mobilization of Gays and Lesbians for gay issues is chimerical. Without a broad base of people representing themselves in politics, the project of liberation devolves to political action committees and single-issue lobbying."[10] We see the roots in the United States of a strong sense of identity and its relationship to effecting social change and movement building. This is a very different liberation tactic from that of the anarchist sex radicals who did not seek to reform legal codes or lobby politicians in order to stop bar raids. Instead, the vision for change of anarchist sex radicals was more fundamental—a radical alternative to the existing state system, which cannot be reformed but must be totally dismantled for true liberation of all.

Gay Liberation 1969–1980 (aka Third-Wave Sexual Liberation)

It may be apropos to start this section with a quote from an article by Dennis Altman, whose book *Homosexual: Oppression and Liberation* (1972) was viewed as the definitive writing on the subject of ideas that shaped gay liberation of this time: "A relatively small group of white middle-aged males are in a position to make the major decisions to define the boundaries within which all of us must function. It is by and large this group who benefit from the existing distribution of resources; the productivity of American Capitalism and the success of the ideological persuasion are such that the great majority of persons rally to defend the system that enables this minority to maintain their dominance."[11] Altman warned that commercialization and capitalism threatened the sexual revolution. The capitalist class promulgates successfully their dominant ideology and it is reflected in institutions in this society. It is, amongst other things, anti-sex/gender liberatory.

The start of this phase of the liberation movement dates from the Stonewall riots of 1969 when a police raid on a Greenwich Village bar called the Stonewall Inn provoked a series of riots that mobilized drag queens, street hustlers, lesbians, and gay men, many of whom had been politicized by the ongoing police brutalization of queer street youth as well as the civil rights and antiwar movements.

The second wave of sexual liberation viewed the struggle for sexual liberation through a "politically conservative" homophile civil rights movement, although their calls for social acceptance of same-sex love and transgender people were seen as radical views by the dominant culture of the time. However, at the onset of the third wave, the Stonewall riots crystallized a broad grassroots mobilization across the country. Many early participants in the movement for lesbian, gay, bisexual, and transgender people's rights were also involved in various leftist causes of the 1960s, including the civil rights movement, the antiwar movement, the student movement, and the feminist movement. However, this early gay liberation movement took a radical departure from their second-wave counterparts. The first political organization formed in wake of the Stonewall riots was the Gay Liberation Front (GLF). The organization was named in honor of the National Liberation Front, the Vietnamese resistance movement, and as a gesture toward the unity of the struggles of blacks, the poor, women, and the colonized in the "Third World." One early flyer, distributed in the Bay Area in January 1970, proclaimed, "The Gay Liberation Front is a nation-wide coalition of revolutionary homosexual organizations creating a radical Counter Culture within the homosexual lifestyles. Politically it's part of the radical 'Movement' working to suppress and eliminate discrimination and oppression against homosexuals in industry, the mass media, government, schools and churches."

At this point in the evolution of the liberation movement, we begin to see a transition from a focus on identity-based politics and working within the state and its arms of oppressions (prisons, legal, police, etc) to a consciousness similar to that of the early sex radicals where total radical change of the system was mandated—albeit this consciousness was short-lived during this wave. Still, the importance of the early stages of the gay liberation movement is critical to our eventual understanding of trans liberation. During the 1960s, we saw the rise of an anti-authoritarian movement where full liberation was intricately tied to the liberation of *all* oppressed communities, be it the gay and lesbian brothers and sisters, street youth, trans folks, people of color, or feminists. In these early days, following the rebellions at Compton (1966) and Stonewall, many gay, lesbian and trans activists aligned with organizations like the Gay Liberation Front, the Young Lords, the Black Panthers, etc. The liberation politics of that time aimed at abolishing the oppressive institutions that reinforced traditional sex roles and at freeing individuals from the constraints of a sex/gender system that locked them into mutually exclusive roles of homosexual/heterosexual and feminine/masculine. Gay and, implicitly, trans liberation advocated a radical transformation only after sex and gender categories had been eradicated.

During this period there were two prominent revolutionary organizations that were formed. The Gay Liberation Front (GLF) formed a month after the Stonewall rebellion and the Street Transvestite Action Revolutionaries (STAR) formed following the occupation of Weinstein Hall at NYU in September of 1970. The GLF's statement of purpose explained: "We are a revolutionary group of men and women formed with the realization that complete sexual liberation for all people cannot come about unless existing social institutions are abolished. We reject society's attempt to impose sexual roles and definitions of our nature."

STAR advocated for an inclusive gay liberation that strongly embraced trans rights, nurtured homeless street youth, and worked to create a communal trans family unit. They worked to dismantle the very state institutions of a capitalistic society that they deemed responsible for their oppressions. In a publication by STAR, they noted in closing: "We want a revolutionary peoples' government, where transvestites, street people, women, homosexuals, Puerto Ricans, Indians, and all oppressed people are free, and not fucked over by this government who treat us like the scum of the earth and kills us off like flies, one by one, and throw us into jail to rot. This government who spends millions of dollars to go to the moon, and lets the poor Americans starve to death."[12]

Both the GLF and STAR formed during the early stages of this third wave of sexual liberation but were undone by ideological factions within the gay liberation movement. In the case of STAR and the budding trans liberation portion of the movement the severe fractionation of the movement unveiled itself at the 1973 Christopher Street Liberation Day rally. The bitterly public feud—Sylvia Rivera storming the stage to speak out for imprisoned Trans folks and street youth, Jean O'Leary of the Lesbian Feminist Liberation condemning men who impersonated women for entertainment and profit, and Lee Brewster of the Queens Liberation Front castigating lesbians for their refusal to let drag queens be themselves—thereby exposed the dramatically contrasting views on the meaning of gay liberation.[13] In the case of GLF, it was a move from multi-issue movement building to a single-issue, white-dominated, legislative-focused vision dominated by GLF's successor, the Gay Activist Alliance (GAA).

At the beginnings of the third wave we saw an anarchist style tendency similar to the first-wave sex radicals of the United States; who realized that their true liberation was intricately and necessarily tied to the liberation of their gay and lesbian brothers and sisters, people of color, and feminists, while maintaining a common fundamental rejection of the state, its capitalistic institutions, and the church. However, from the mid seventies onward the anarchist-style liberationist framework became less important to the dominant gay and lesbian organizations, who increasingly favored an ethnic model that emphasized community identity and cultural difference (as originally championed by the homophile movement). Today we can see that marriage equality is a core example of identity-based politics and operates to the exclusion of others desiring nontraditional families and relationships not requiring state sanction or regulation. In essence, sexual liberation evolved from the precept of the anarchist liberationists into an assimilationist and identity-based liberation of "different but equal under the law of the State." During the middle part of this period as the mainstream LGBT organizations, media, and communities embraced assimilation within a capitalistic society, there was the ever-present undercurrent of radical social change organizations such as ACT UP, OutRage, and others that embraced "queer," not LGBT, as an identity label that pointed to separatist and non-assimilationist politics. And the evolving area of queer theory, which was originally associated with the radical gay politics of these queer organizations, developed out of an examination of perceived limitations in the traditional identity politics of recognition and self-identity.

Trans Liberation (aka Fourth-Wave Sexual and Gender Liberation)

Any semblance of a trans liberation movement of today is rooted within the predominant gay liberation movement from the eighties to present: a hierarchical, identity-based, single issue, gender-conforming, free market, and state/electoral-based movement. Yet, as noted in the introduction, the trans community defies the "accepted" social constructs of sex and gender, of free market capitalism, and the state with its need for society's adherence to strict social norms/constructs in order to maintain its operating systems of power, keeping its focus on assimilation within a system that by definition constrains the core concept of trans. As we learned from the revolutionary history of gay liberation within the context of GLF and STAR, we understand that their vision for emancipation was dependent upon radical social change. STAR in its call for a "full voice in the struggle for liberation of all peoples" and a demand for "identification of the opposite gender" for transvestites foreshadowed the queer theoretical contention that "biological sex" is not equal to gender, as well as its affirmation of gay liberation's refusal to assimilate.[14]

With the evolution of queer theory in the early 1990s, more than two decades after Stonewall, we see the promotion of radical social change both similar and yet different to that of the first-wave anarchist sex radicals and the gay and trans liberationists of the early phases of the third wave. queer theory has expounded upon and extended the challenges set forth by our anarchist sex and gender radicals by challenging not just categories of sexual orientation/identity but also of categories *per se*. The subjective interpretations of sexuality within Queer theory subvert any monolithic traditional notion of sex, sex roles, gender, and even sexual orientation. (Some) queer theorists, as with anarchist sexual liberationists, rather than demanding inclusion, equal rights, and end of discrimination dominated by the current LGBT mainstream, challenge the core assumptions of society and the normative construction of sexuality. Whereas anarchists and anarchist theory need to look at struggle on the conceptual level that queer theory provides, queer theory needs to be coupled with anarchism's critique of structural domination, such as the state and capitalism.

Trans people, as laid out by anarchist sex radicals, gay liberationists, and queer theorists, defy society's precepts of gender identity and expression and challenge, at its core, societal, religious, and state demands and constructs. Sadly I fear that we, as truly inherently revolutionary peoples, will instead seek the "safe" route of assimilation, as some of our gay and lesbian brothers and sisters have done before us. Yet through serious self-reflection, political analysis, and dialogue, particularly through an anarchist lens, I postulate that we can avoid the same reformist road that the majority of the homosexual movement has been trapped in. To this point, I have remarked over many years how ironic it is that the transsexual person defies society's construct of man and woman while at the same time many in our community work so very hard to subscribe to a binary system that our bodies defy. Granted this is a complicated analysis and there are many reasons for so strongly subscribing back to the binaries (major drivers being safety and survival); at the same time it is something that we as a community and as individuals must seriously challenge.

For me, it is clear that any so-called liberation movement for the trans community today is, like its gay and lesbian counterparts, entrenched within an assimilated and capitalistic framework. And in this liberation framework the trans community is still securing its liberation to the same wagon of its gay and lesbian counterparts. If we are to liberate society and ourselves from the tyranny against those who traverse gender and sex, we liberate ourselves from the mental and physical constructs that manipulate us into subordination for the benefit of the "greater good of society, religion, and state." It is now time for the trans community to embrace and continue the militant and revolutionary paths our trans elders laid down for us if we are seeking revolutionary (rather than reformist) changes. So a key tenet of trans liberation lies within the liberation of one's self (and others) from the tyranny of the state, religion, and society; and equally important—from our own self-imposed tyranny.

And with that said, viewing trans liberation with an anarchist lens has proven an invaluable vehicle for such an analysis. As Emma Goldman so eloquently stated in her 1911 essay "Anarchism: What It Really Stands For": "Anarchism is the only philosophy that brings to man [*sic*] the consciousness of himself; which maintains that God, the State, and society are non-existent, that their promises are null and void, since they can be fulfilled only through man's subordination. Anarchism is therefore the teacher of the unity of life; not merely in nature, but in man."

Challenging the state is a daunting and challenging task for all oppressed peoples (and for me personally—I am a strong believer in civil disobedience and direct action—when the cause and reasons are just). However, the fear of challenging the state as a non-operative trans person is a significant challenge and barrier to putting my beliefs into actions. My heart and soul told me that by not acting upon my beliefs I was allowing the state to control my individual expression—preventing my rebellion of a system that works to subjugate my individual identity. I actually needed to go through a two-year process of dealing with a conscious and subconscious fear of being controlled by the system. It turned out that through a long and convoluted process I was able to put my individual beliefs ahead of those of submission to, and fear of, the state's total control of my gender identity. Oddly, one night before an affinity group and I were to risk arrest shutting down a government building in New York, a dear friend and I saw the opening of *V for Vendetta*. For me the transformation of Evey Hammond was pivotal to my personal transformation. For those not familiar with Evey's transformation, I paste the following from a wiki on *V*:

> In her cell between multiple bouts of interrogation and torture, Evey finds a letter from an inmate named Valerie, an actress who was imprisoned for being a lesbian. Evey's interrogator finally gives her a choice of collaboration or death; inspired by Valerie's courage and quiet defiance, she refuses to give in and is told that she is free. To her shock, Evey learns that her imprisonment was a hoax constructed by V, designed to put her through an ordeal similar to the one that shaped him. He reveals that Valerie was another Larkhill prisoner who died in the cell next to his; the letter that Evey read is the same one that Valerie had passed on to V. Evey's anger finally gives way to acceptance of her identity and freedom.

The heart of this point was reinforced at a recent demo protesting the hypocrisy of Human Rights Campaign, where one of the chants included the words "*Fuck you* HRC." Several people asked with all seriousness, "Are we *allowed* to say that?" Then when the first police car came, they were convinced that the police were called because of our using the words "*Fuck You*." In reality the cops didn't really give a damn what we were chanting about. Clearly on the surface this is all kind of silly and a nit, except for the fact that the reaction and fear of this trans person typifies the implicit warnings of Emma Goldman—that the tyranny, or fear of such tyranny, by the state has a profound impact on our actions and our behaviors. This clearly ties in very closely with our goal of achieving trans liberation.

1   Karla Jay and Allen Young, ed., *Out of the Closets: Voices of Gay Liberation* (New York: Jove Publications, 1977), 113.

2   Leslie Feinberg, *Trans Liberation: Beyond Pink or Blue*, (Boston: Beacon Press, 1999).

3   Terence Kissack, *Free Comrades: Anarchism and Homosexuality in the United States, 1895–1917* (Oakland: AK Press, 2008), 1.

4   Ibid., 4.

5   Ibid., 5.

6   See ibid.

7   Ibid., 171.

8   "Kinsey Reports," Wikipedia, http://en.wikipedia.org/wiki/Kinsey_Reports (accessed July 14, 2010).

9   See Harry Hay, *Radically Gay*, edited by Will Roscoe (Boston: Beacon Press, 1996).

10   Ibid., 339.

11   Jeff Hayler, "Homosexual Oppression: Does Capitalism Really Affect It," Australian National University, http://www.anu.edu.au/polsci/marx/gayleft/oppression_cap.rtf (accessed January 27, 2012).

12   Stephan L. Cohen, *The Gay Liberation Youth Movement in New York: An Army of Lovers Cannot Fail* (New York: Routledge, 2008), 37.

13   Ibid., 9.

14   Ibid., 23.

Harm Reduction as Pleasure Activism

BENJAMIN SHEPARD

In 2004, organizer Adrienne Maree Brown described the links between pleasure activism and harm reduction: "Some people think
I've spent the last several years of my life working with raising
awareness about HIV/AIDS, destigmatizing drug use, and ending
overdose, but really it's about breaking down barriers to pleasure.
So I'm a pleasure activist."[1] Certainly Brown is not alone in this
sentiment. "I don't think we do acknowledge the pleasure though,"
explains Allan Clear, "not as much as we should."[2] The following
takes up where Brown and Clear leave off, considering the anarchism of harm reduction and the pleasure of sexual civil liberties
activism, and their cross currents. Both anarchism and queer activism have long challenged anti-pleasure ideology.[3] Through decades
of social struggle, the two overlapping movements have come to
share an embrace of the insurrectionary possibilities of pleasure, a
rejection of social controls and formal hierarchies in favor of mutual
aid networks and DIY community building, the use of direct action,
and a culture of resistance.[4] Pleasure activism manifests itself in any
number of these cross currents.

Yet the relationship between harm reduction and pleasure is
anything but simple. "Take yir best orgasm, multiply it by twenty
and you're still fucking miles off the pace," writes Irving Welsh
in his novel *Trainspotting*, musing on his romance with heroin.[5]
"The passion for destruction is a creative passion," Bakunin famously asserted.[6] Thus the paradox of pleasure is often pain as
the characters in Welsh's novel soon find out. Still, this right to
pleasure finds its roots in any number of expressions of sexual and
social freedom, as well as the intersections between drug use, and
anarchist and queer movements.[7] Often obscured, the need for
pleasure fuels the imperative to reduce harm. After all, what inspired the movement's formation but a struggle over expression
and desire. While drug use is often about numbing pain, it is also

fundamentally about pleasure seeking and sensuality.[8] As such it is useful to contend with their multiple meanings, viewing such experience as a vehicle for "symbolic and creative play," as Kane Race writes, a space where new ideas and identities are formed.[9] "[G] reater attentiveness to pleasure and its qualities and social dynamics may also provide crucial resources for devising more effective strategies of care."[10] Finding the pleasure in harm reduction is akin to queering anarchism at its foundation.

Harm reduction has long been recognized as a movement with roots in anarchist direct action.[11] And there are good reasons for this. In the same way Gandhi challenged social mores to make salt, even when the practice was outlawed in colonial India, harm reduction activists have challenged penal codes to create needle exchange programs in the spirit of direct action.[12] Such gestures of freedom are a fundamental part of anarchist practice. "You may already be an anarchist," Crimethinc suggests. "Whenever you act without waiting for instructions or official permission, you are an anarchist. Any time you bypass a ridiculous regulation when no one's looking, you are an anarchist. If you don't trust the government, the school system, Hollywood, or the management to know better than you when it comes to things that affect your life, that's anarchism, too. And you are especially an anarchist when you come with your own ideas and solutions."[13]

Part of this impulse involves breaking down socially imposed barriers to pleasure. Such thinking helped queers invent safer sex when the AIDS epidemic began.[14] Direct action was also the inspiration for the proliferation of harm reduction programs around the world; here sexual risk reduction and drug use practices shared common cause.[15] "I have often pointed out the importance of considering the essential role played by pleasure in drug use—even in the most chaotic use—and its life-endorsing 'usefulness,'" explains Walter Cavalieri, BSc, MSc, MSW, Director of the Canadian Harm Reduction Network, "as well as the need to draw on the parallels between the gay liberation and the drug users' rights movements."[16]

At their core, harm reduction and anarchist-queer movements embrace pleasure, autonomy, and self determination. In doing so, they challenge core elements of a social structure bent on social controls. Anti-pleasure ideology, after all, has deep roots. From the Temperance Movement to prohibition, over and over, authorities have sought to curb the expression of pleasure or consumption of intoxicants. Yet few movements have built on the lessons of the failure of prohibition. The following pages consider some of the history of anti-pleasure ideology as well as forms of pleasure activism, which have challenged this thinking in a safe thoughtful way. Case examples from drug user, HIV prevention, and social organizing are explored. Through them, I consider core questions: How can we create an agenda to support both the affirmation of pleasure and the rejection of prohibitive politics? What would such an agenda look like? What are obstacles and best practices? How can harm reduction take up the issue of pleasure, linking understandings of multiple forms of pleasure, with a progressive agenda aimed at rejecting prohibitions that support war and violence, rather than affect and care, pleasure and abundance?

Anti-pleasure Ideology

The history of struggles over pleasure involves an ongoing dialectic between expression and repression. While the Dionysus cults embraced intoxicants, drink, and collective expression of ecstasy, the Romans recognized these pursuits represented a fundamental challenge to power relations and the Roman authorities sought to crush the cults.[17] Yet those who embraced pleasure continued to find their way into trouble. Adam ate the apple and anti-pleasure religious doctrine took a foundation that we are still grappling with today.

Deep within his dissent to the *Lawrence v. Texas* Supreme Court ruling repealing US sodomy laws, Justice Antonin Scalia offered a telling clue about the continuing phobia conservatives experience concerning the practices in pleasure. "If sodomy laws are unconstitutional," Scalia wrote, then so are "laws against bigamy, same sex marriage, adult incest, prostitution, masturbation, adultery, fornication, bestiality, and obscenity." Few assumed that any laws against masturbation were still on the books anyway.[18] Well, not technically. But for those with a keen eye on hierarchies of transgression, the seemingly trivial topic takes on inordinate meaning. To make sense of Scalia's dissent, it is useful to look back to thirteenth-century Christian theology, specifically St. Thomas Aquinas's categorization of "luxuria," signifying crimes against nature in which masturbation signaled the beginning of a slippery slope leading to sodomy, adultery, and bestiality. For Aquinas and the rest of the "every sperm is sacred" crowd, masturbation is a sort of gateway pleasure, like marijuana is to heroin. It is not very dangerous in and of itself. Yet left to the active imagination, it is capable of opening doors to a vast arena of possibilities.[19] Hence Scalia's reference to the subject in a Supreme Court decision about sodomy. While one would assume Aquinas's *Summa Theologica* is not applicable to American law, given the quaint notions of the separation of church and state, its cultural influence cannot be underemphasized. However deeply flawed they remain, teachings on crimes against nature have established the basis for laws that continue to criminalize countless sexual practices, including homosexuality. Concurrently, they propel abstinence-only sex education, which fails to acknowledge either evidence-based practice or the complexity of sexual expression.[20]

The roots of anti-pleasure ideology stretch far and wide. From Aquinas to Calvin, Cotton Mather to Comstock, a puritanical streak permeates US politics. When Republican Senate candidate Christine O'Donnell recently spoke out against masturbation, she was participating in a storied tradition. The Puritans famously condemned those who deviated from their religious doctrine and emphasis on work rather than play, torturing religious non-conformists. Yet there were those who fought back. While we hear a great deal about the Tea Party these days, in the 1794 Whisky Rebellion Pennsylvania whisky makers tarred and feathered tax collectors who sought to tax whisky sales.[21]

The founders had many reservations about the threat of the widespread expression of sexual desire and drunkenness seen in the colonies. Thomas Jefferson famously warned those in the new nation not to visit Europe, where one: "is led by the strongest of all human passions into a spirit of female intrigue…for whores…and in both cases learns to consider fidelity to the marriage bed as an ungentlemanly practice, and inconsistent with happiness."[22] When founder of US psychiatry Benjamin Rush was not busy experimenting with torture devices designed to treat mental illness, he railed against bodily pleasure as "a disease of the body and the mind."[23]

Over the years, this prohibitive logic only gained steam. The nineteenth-century Temperance Movement sought moral reform and the prohibition of the consumption of alcohol.[24] The Eighteenth Amendment of the US Constitution was ratified in January of 1919. The era set in motion a cavalcade of unintended consequences as markets for alcohol consumption moved from legal, regulated commerce into the providence of an unregulated black market, which involved illegal approaches catering to market demand. Violence and crime followed. What did not occur, however, was the reduction of the consumption of alcohol. By 1933, the Eighteenth Amendment was repealed. Throughout the period, a queer public commons took shape in places, such as San Francisco, where prohibition was not enforced.[25]

Over the next three decades the welfare state expanded simultaneously with social movements involving labor, civil rights, women, and people on welfare. By the mid-1960s, these movements started to encounter a backlash over the expanded welfare rolls. With his unsuccessful presidential campaign of 1964, Goldwater introduced crime as a panic issue. While it failed in 1964, crime succeeded as an election issue in 1968, and Nixon was elected, with the help of his "Southern Strategy," which racialized crime, welfare, and poverty. Policy emphasis shifted to crime control, rather than welfare provision or prevention. Nixon's election marked a striking policy shift, with a new emphasis on a prohibitive approach to crime under a new "War on Drugs." Rather than provide services to alleviate poverty, the new emphasis was on criminalizing it. The Rockefeller drug laws of the early 1970s are a prime example.

Faced with increased attacks on social movements under the new administration, a number of groups fought back. The Black Panthers organized a food program to support their community in Oakland. The Young Lords, a Bronx-based direct action group of the same vein, organized a number of forward-thinking, audacious acts of direct action aimed at cultivating a more responsive system of public health for social outsiders. In 1970, the group took over Lincoln Hospital. The group's list of demands included calls for Spanish-language translation for services, acupuncture to aid detox services, and a consumer bill of rights. Most would later become common practices and policy.[26]

One of the early members of the Young Lords was Sylvia "Ray" Rivera, a leader in the transgender movement. Rivera was also a veteran of Gay Activist Alliance and the Street Trans Action Revolutionaries (STAR). Much of the gay liberation impulse shared common cause with the anarchism of the era.[27] Pleasure activist

Charles Shively described "indiscriminate promiscuity as an act of revolution."[28] Through this organizing, gay liberationists challenged the social system, rather than embrace marriage, militarism, and law and order social policies. Instead, the movement fought homophobia, sexphobia, and anti-pleasure ideology. It borrowed from Wilhelm Reich's argument that anti-sex politics support the docile bodies linked to fascism as well as anti-sex ideology;[29] such thinking only fuels abstinence-oriented policies, sexualized and racial fear, prohibitive politics and disconnection from the body.

Throughout the early years of the AIDS epidemic, activists grappled with core questions about the appropriate approach to HIV prevention. While some suggested HIV prevention should include a Temperance-era abstinence approach that called for strict prohibitions of sexual contact,[30] others called for a more humanistic, sex-positive approach. Dr. Joseph Sonnabend, Richard Berkowitz, and Michael Callen worked on an HIV prevention pamphlet in New York in the early 1980s. They recognized that if one asks gay men, much less anyone else, to give up sex, the result is usually anger. All or nothing propositions result in variations between hysteria, repression, and inevitable lapses. For many, a world without sex is not worth living in. Prohibition is often more dangerous than acknowledgement, careful expression, and prevention. In response, the three recognized that latex was the life-saving compromise needed. From here Berkowitz and Callen built on the lessons of gay liberation to draft, "How to Have Sex in an Epidemic." The result was a revolution allowing for personal and political protection and cover for both sex and the liberation movement that dismantled the shackles around it.[31] The lessons of the tract became core principles of HIV prevention activism of the next two decades:

- Get informed about high- and low-risk activities.
- Be honest about needs, desires, and risks.
- Meet a person where they are.
- Practices, not places spread HIV.
- Provide safer sex information, condoms, lube, and clean syringes.

Reflecting on the invention of safer sex, pleasure activist and ACT UP veteran Douglas Crimp argued, "We were able to invent safe sex because we have always known that sex is not, in an epidemic or not, limited to penetrative sex. Our promiscuity taught us many things, not only about the pleasures of sex, but about the great multiplicity of those pleasures. It is that psychic preparation, that experimentation, that conscious work on our own sexualities that has allowed many of us to change our sexual behaviors...it is our promiscuity that will save us."[32]

Yet, over the years, the use-a-condom every time condom code started to wane. In a 2007 podcast, Donald Grove, a veteran of ACT UP's needle exchange committee reflects on this moment and its lessons for the harm reduction movement:

> The mere fact that society disapproves of something does not mean it isn't going to happen. For me harm reduction is about working with drug users where they're at. Which means recognizing that lots of them are very interested in stopping, but until you can provide them with the kind [of help or alternative] they need they aren't going to stop, or can't stop. Therefore, you need to address the fact that drug use is an ordinary part of their daily lives. And not only that, but I think where it becomes really particular and really special is it's an ordinary part of their daily lives. [I]t is highly stigmatized, something they have to do in secret, something they have to do with a lot of other dangers and harms piled on top of it by the legal system and that this is going to impact everything else about their lives which isn't stigmatized. We as a culture, approach the impact that the drug use, we take the impact that those things have on the rest of their life and say, 'well that wouldn't be happening if you weren't using drugs.' What I keep coming back to is, but they are using drugs.
>
> When I was still in my early thirties, thirteen years ago, I realized that we have a lot, including in the gay community, a big dialogue around how you ought to be doing things rather than how you are doing things. And what happened to me in the back room of the Wonder Bar, after a decade of impeccably safe sex, I was sucking off a guy in the back room and he came in my mouth. And I swallowed it, and it was as though I had been struck like a gong. And I vibrated

for days after that, because I realized how much I had missed for so long, and how important that is to me, and how utterly erotic that is to me. And I realized that this was something I did not want to stop. And you know it was a struggle. I talked to some of my harm reductionist friends about it. But the way I learned to put it at that time is everyone wants to talk to me about what I ought to be doing, and no one talks to me about what I am doing. And I see that as the essence of the harm reduction approach when interacting with drug users who for instance need sterile syringes. So that's the essence of harm reduction for me, is to say, accept that people, or work with people based on what they are doing rather than what you believe they ought to be doing.[33]

Through Grove's narrative, one can see the lessons of Crimps's[34] thinking intersecting with a burgeoning harm reduction movement pioneered through needle exchange programs, such as ACT UP's illegal exchange in New York.[35]

Throughout the period, activists came to build a movement around the recognition that abstinence is unsafe, repression unhealthy. As queer theorist Eve Sedgwick explained, "There is an ethical urgency about queer theory that is directed at the damage that sexual prohibitions and discriminations do to people."[36] Building on these practical understandings, the US harm reduction movement organized to support the needs of drug users in the United States. A group of activists moved to change the way cities around the United States cope with policies such as syringe exchange. Like using a condom, harm reductionists recognized syringe exchange as life-saving intervention. Activists in New York's ACT UP committed civil disobedience to make sure clean needles were accessible to those who needed them. After arrest, they made the legal argument that faced with an AIDS crisis, syringe exchange was a "medical necessity." Activists started a public health pilot program, with the support of the city of New York. Over the years, the syringe exchange would be recognized as a successful intervention.[37] According to the New York department of health, HIV affected sixty percent of injection drug users in 1990. As of 2001, that rate was down to ten percent. The Harm Reduction Coalition defines the practice as a set of interventions that seek to "reduce the negative consequences of drug use, incorporating a spectrum of strategies from safer use, to managed use, to abstinence."

One of the primary activists involved with the early syringe exchange programs in New York was Greg Bordowitz, who worked with ACT UP's syringe exchange committee. Bordowitz reveled in ACT UP's ethos of pleasure.[38] "Looking back on it now, it was a place you could have romance. Well, everybody was in love with everybody. There was this intense sense of comradeship and closeness. We were all brought together and felt close because of the meaningfulness of the work, and the fact that people were dying, and people in the group were getting sick. It created this feeling, a heightened intensity. Emotions were very powerful within the group, and they were on the surface of the group. Often people would cry in meetings, or people would get enraged in meetings. It was intense that way. And also, that fuels Eros. That fueled attraction that—people clung to each other, not necessarily in a desperate way, but people found comfort in each other. They enjoyed each other." For members of ACT UP, pleasure was a resource.[39]

Yet over the years, syringe exchange programs would increasingly become entwined with departments of health, funding, and the pitfalls of the nonprofit industrial complex. Today much of harm reduction is about evidence:

- Science
- Linear thinking
- Positivism
- Collaboration with health departments
- Service provision and struggles—against co-optation
- Funding

But where did the pleasure go? The plenary of the ninth Social Research Conference on HIV, Hepatitis C and Related Diseases, Australia, 2006, was titled: *StigmaPleasurePractice*. Here participants asked, "Why is it difficult to consider pleasure in drug policy and practice? What are the consequences for practice? How might a greater focus on the pleasures of drugs invigorate harm reduction?"[40]

To start the process, it is useful to reconsider the ways direct action practices inform movements for social and sexual freedom, including anarchism, sexual civil liberties activism, and by extension harm reduction.[41] "I joined Sex Panic! because there's no group making the same connections between the renewed sexual repression of the past several decades," explained Chris Farrell in 1998. "The failure of the left to identify pleasure as a political principle worth fighting for does a lot to explain the moribund state of progressive politics." Here Farrell calls for the activists to "return sexual pleasure to the progressive agenda....Until the left learns the function of the orgasm, our fight against repression is doomed."[42]

From sex worker organizing to parties celebrating public sexual culture, examples of such practices are many. Groups such as AIDS Prevention Action League and Jacks of Color have helped support a broader push for safer promiscuity with large scale parties, which in turn support and facilitate pleasure. The late sexual civil liberties activist Eric Rofes rejected paternalism, while writing that gay men are far more comfortable and capable of embracing complicated choices. CHAMP's Julie Davids has used data to challenge public health panics, rejecting stigma. Through events, such as the Artgasm Big Bang Party,[43] pleasure activists have supported both harm reduction and public sexual culture: "We are a group of radical queers who are creating a space that is sex-positive, gender-inclusive, anticapitalist, affordable, size-positive and feminist where we can fuck, make art, engage in kink, dance and play." To do so, this sex party depends on "a radical definition of consent." Here, consent is recognized as "the presence of 'yes' and not just the absence of no,' with the understanding that everyone can change their mind, stop, or back up at any time. Consent must be established each and every time sexual activity happens." Through such endeavors, pleasure activists have taught us that without pleasure there can be no justice.

Throughout the movement, leaders such as housing works co-founder Keith Cylar, helped keep the expression of pleasure as an integral component of harm reduction. Squatter Louis Jones started Stand Up Harlem within the same spirit of anarchism. "That to me felt so incredible. You talk about emotions. I just felt such pleasure. Everyone thinks about pleasure in terms of decadence, but there was more to it than that. I was moved...It brought fulfillment. I felt animated. We were living together, sleeping together, and working for change." Yet, more to it, "[u]sing was dying with dignity—with dignity because it was my choice. No one was making it for me. I took a stand for those I knew who chose drugs when they were facing death." Jones recognized that when facing death, there were those who "would want to cop in the midst of all that pain." He explained: "For some it was just to get that old familiar, this old feeling, relationship, lover, what have you. This pain relief that the doctor might not give or it might not be enough. It was on your own terms. The liberty was what I was elated about—the choice without shame. That was what I was doing."

At CitiWide Harm Reduction, where I worked for four years, we grappled with pleasure as part of a tragicomic continuum of human experience. When a member died, we said goodbye in a circle. Here, grief was transformed into a space for care, song, drumming, and happiness born of authentic lived experience. And members knew they had faced the negative, moved through it, and come out the other side. The tenacity of those in the circle made the scene one of the most pulsing spaces I have seen. In their daily transforming of the negative into a new way of living, those in the program achieved a kind of magical power.[44] In this way, harm reduction is understood as a place where members build healing communities, spaces for care, and solidarity. Through such connections, they challenge the insurmountable. And they share lives and authentic experience together outside of the prohibitive logic of criminal justice and coercion.

Building on these lessons, one can come to see components of an agenda for pleasure, care, and just human relations. In *Three Essays on the Theory of Sexuality*, Freud rejected Puritan mores by suggesting that everyone has some form of perversion in them.[45] There is no shame in it. This is part of being human. Yet shame exists and causes harm. To do away with shame and the repression it fuels,[46] pleasure activists push to transform the social order.[47] Yet, to be effective, the process must include a respect for self-determination, choice, and pleasure. If we do not acknowledge the importance of pleasure, we risk mirroring the prohibitive politics we reject.[48] Without justice, there can be no pleasure. After all, what we are protecting is a right to social imagination that rejects both paternalism and positivism, while opening spaces for alternative social relations and ways of embracing experience outside the realm of the rational experience. The failure of the political left to articulate a pro-pleasure argument is nothing short of a failure of the political imagination. It leaves a huge void to be occupied by moralists. There is another route—one built through practices in pleasure, justice, and freedom.

1   Adrienne Maree Brown Brown, "I Hate Politics: Confessions of a Pleasure Activist," in ed. A. M. Brown and W. U. Wimsatt, *How to Get Stupid White Men out of Office: The Anti-Politics, Unboring Guide to Power* (Brooklyn, NY: Soft Skull Press, 2004), 20.

2   Quoted in B. Shepard, *Queer Political Performance and Protest* (New York: Routledge, 2009).

3   See Terence Kissack, *Free Comrades: Anarchism and Homosexuality in the United States, 1895–1917* (Oakland, CA: AK Press, 2008).

4   See B. Shepard, "Bridging the Divide between Queer Theory and Anarchism," *Sexualities* No. 13 (August 2010), 511–527.

5   Irving Welsh, *Trainspotting* (New York: W.W. Norton, 1996), 11.

6   Mikhail Bakunin, "The Reaction in Germany," (1842) in *Bakunin on Anarchism*, edited by Sam Dolgoff (Montreal: Black Rose Books, 2002), 57.

7   See Shepard, *Queer Political Performance and Protest*.

8   See Kristine E. P. Kennedy, Christian Grov, and Jeffrey T. Parsons, "Ecstasy and Sex among Young Heterosexual Women: A Qualitative Analysis of Sensuality, Sexual Effects, and Sexual Risk Taking," *International Journal of Sexual Health* (22)(3) (2010): 155–66.

9   Kane Race, *Pleasure Consuming Medicine: The Queer Politics of Drugs* (Durham, NC: Duke University Press, 2009), xii–iii.

10 See ibid.

11 See Christopher Smith, Luke Dunn, Kathy Rigby, and Jon Paul Hammond, "Harm Reduction as Anarchist Practice," 8th Annual Harm Reduction Conference, Austin, 2010.

12 E. Springer, "Effective AIDS Prevention with Active Drug Users: The Harm Reduction Model," in, *Counseling Chemically Dependent People with HIV/AIDS* edited by M. Shernoff (Binghamton, NY: Haworth Press, 1991), 141–158.

13 Quoted in Smith, "Harm Reduction."

14 Douglas Crimp, "How to Have Promiscuity in an Epidemic," in *AIDS: Cultural Analysis/Cultural Activism*, edited by Douglas Crimp (Boston: MIT Press, 1988), 237–271.

15 See Springer, "Effective AIDS Prevention."

16 Walter Cavalieri, e-mail correspondence with the author, December 2010.

17   See Barbara Ehrenreich, *Dancing in the Streets* (New York: Metropolitan Books, 2007).

18   Hendrick Hertzberg, "Northern Light," *The New Yorker* (July 7, 2003), 24.

19   Thomas Laqueur, *Solitary Sex* (Brooklyn, NY: MIT Press/Zone Books, 2003), 142–43.

20   Chris Collins, Priya Alagiri, and Todd Summers, "Abstinence-only vs. Comprehensive Sex Education: What Are the Arguments? What is the Evidence?" Progressive Health Partners, AIDS Policy Research Center & Center for AIDS Prevention Studies AIDS Research Institute, University of California, San Francisco, Policy Monograph Series, March 2002, http://ari.ucsf.edu/pdf/abstinence.pdf.

21   See Thaddeus Russell, *A Renegade History of the United States* (New York: Free Press, 2010).

22   Quoted in ibid.

23   Quoted in ibid.

24   See J. R. Gusfield, *The Symbolic Crusade* (Champaign: University of Illinois Press, 1986).

25   See Shepard, *Queer Political Performance and Protest.*

26   See ibid. and B. Shepard, *Play, Creativity, and Social Movements* (New York: Routledge, 2011).

27   See Kissack, *Free Comrades*; and Shepard, "Bridging the Divide."

28   See Charley Shively, "Indiscriminate Promiscuity as an Act of Revolution," in *Come Out Fighting*, edited by C. Bull (New York: Nation Books: 2001).

29   See Wilhelm Reich, *The Mass Psychology of Fascism* (New York: Farrar Straus and Giroux, 1980).

30   See Gusfield, *The Symbolic Crusade.*

31   See Richard Berkowitz, *Staying Alive: The Invention of Safer Sex* (New York: Basic Books, 2003).

32   Crimp, "How to Have Promiscuity in an Epidemic," 253.

33   Ibid., 253.

34   See ibid.

35   See Springer, "Effective AIDS Prevention."

36   Dinita Smith, "'Queer Theory' is Entering the Mainstream," *New York Times* (January 17), B9.

37   See Springer, "Effective AIDS Prevention."

38   Greg Bordowitz, Oral History with the ACT UP Oral History Project, 2002, http://www.actuporalhistory.org/interviews/interviews_01.

html#bordowitz (accessed December 26, 2010).

39   See Shepard, *Queer Political Performance and Protest.*

40   Martin Holt and Carla Treloar, "Pleasure and Drugs," *International Journal of Drug Policy* No. 19 (2008), 349–352.

41   See Shepard, "Bridging the Divide."

42   Quoted in Shepard, *Queer Political Performance and Protest.*

43   Big Bang Party, Artgasm for Radical Queers, 2007, http://www.bigbangparty.org/party.html (accessed December 24, 2010).

44   See Shepard, *Play, Creativity, and Social Movements.*

45   Peter Tatchell, *Freud and the Liberation of Sexual Desire,* June 12, 1989, http://www.petertatchell.net/psychiatry/freud.htm (accessed December 24, 2010).

46   See Reich, *The Mass Psychology of Fascism.*

47   Tatchell, *Freud and the Liberation of Sexual Desire.*

48   See Holt and Treloar, "Pleasure and Drugs."

Radical Queers and Class Struggle: A Match to Be Made

GAYGE OPERAISTA

While radical queers identifying with anarchism, anti-authoritarianism, and/or anticapitalism seem to be on the up-swing, there exists a profound misunderstanding of class struggle within radical queer circles and a lack of class analysis that hurts both specifically queer analyses and anticapitalism as a whole. Let's face it, the task is not to "queer" anarchism, which has become a signifier for every countercultural, edgy activist project out there, to the point where it now has as little shared meaning among radicals as queer does in the radical milieu. *The task is for radical queers to become class struggle militants.* We need to be constantly conscious of moving toward a holistic queer praxis, one that examines the conditions of the lives of all queers, and also that locates those lives in the larger context of the struggles of all workers and all the oppressed. This is not only a position of solidarity and a refusal to leave other queers behind, but it is also the realization that queer liberation is inextricably tied with the self-emancipation of the working class.

Queers, like other oppressed groups, are hit particularly hard by capitalism, and this is especially true of the queers most often erased, ignored, or left behind by queer and feminist movements: queers of color, trans and gender-nonconforming people, queers with disabilities; and queer sex workers are some examples. Many queer anarchists and other anticapitalists come from anti-oppression backgrounds, and, while analysis in anti-oppression circles continues to improve and greater understandings and explications of intersectionality continue to be the case in those circles, a good, critical anti-oppression analysis is not enough. We need to be both anticapitalists and to understand how capitalism functions to truly understand the conditions of the lives of the working class, from those struggling against multiple systems of oppression to the "middle class" existing in a position of (far too often temporary) comfort in the suburbs. Through this understanding of class struggle, we can contribute to mass movements for collective liberation.

Without this understanding of class struggle, our critique of the state can only be both flawed and limited; we must have an understanding of class struggle to see the state as an instrument of the domination of one class over all other classes and our anti-state project as the need to destroy the bourgeois state as inseparable from the project of abolishing all classes. It is a social and not an antisocial project. To paraphrase Kropotkin, we want no rulers, not no rules, and failing to acknowledge class struggle leads to a view of the state as an independent institution, not as an instrument of class rule. Also can lead to a glorification of antisocial acts as some sort of resistance to the state, when in reality they are juvenile, futile, and reactionary. Unlike Leninists, we neither want to seize the state nor even to replace it with a "proletarian" state. We know that if classes remain after the revolution, and there is the need for a hegemonic governing body separate from the people to maintain social relations, then the revolution has failed.

However, many queers come to anticapitalist movements retaining liberal ideas about class and how capitalism functions, treating class as just another way someone can be oppressed or privileged, rather than a relationship to the means of production that is continually re-created. Applying an anti-oppression analysis to class becomes problematic in many ways. It causes us to continue to use the definitions of class that the bourgeoisie (capitalist class) use for us, that serves to split the working class and convince members of it to act against their own class interests. It prevents us from articulating how and why some queers are hit so hard by capitalism, and results in us far too often ignoring the struggles of trans people, for instance, and rephrasing them in terms of people being voluntary "drop outs," as if the state of being "middle class" was an immutable, inherited thing rather than a term created to get portions of the working class to side with capital against other workers.

The solution to these issues, of course, is educating ourselves about class struggle, and capitalism, and to see the movement for queer liberation as both indispensably a part of the struggle of the working class and indispensable to that struggle.

On "Classism"

A standard practice from anti-oppression circles is writing a list of oppressions that we oppose, and oftentimes "classism" is included in that list. Leaving aside the fact that the lists are, by necessity, incomplete, capitalism is a structure of a different sort from white supremacy or heteropatriarchy, for instance. We do not seek to cease to engage in practices we currently call queer in undoing heteropatriarchy; however, the goal of anticapitalist struggle must be the negation of first the capitalist class (through seizing the means of production), and the subsequent negation of the working class, as the exploitation of labor ends with control over both one's labor and the necessities of life, the abolition of property, and the socialization of the means of production. To struggle for any less than this is to struggle only against class elitism, to merely want the rich to treat us better, for the lives of the poor to not be so hard. This is not the sum of our desires. We want a world without rich and poor, and it's time our analysis, our organizing, and our actions reflected that!

Furthermore, due to the analysis of class carried over from liberal or reformist analyses, there is the tendency to use accusations of classism to maintain divisions within the working class, to silence, erase, or render the marginalized powerless, and to invisibilize a wide variety of the experiences of queer people. And these all draw upon flawed analyses of class. The post–World War II restructuring of the working class, particularly in the post-industrial world, has lead to ever greater levels of education in the working class, and greater employment in the service sector and technical jobs. Meanwhile, many stereotypical assembly-line jobs have moved to the developing world or been replaced by machines. Not only do sociological definitions of class that are based on old stereotypes about education and work performed conceal social relations, they obscure the reality of the proletariat in the post-industrial world. Furthermore, presumptions about who is a "true prole" and what "true proles" are intellectually capable of both insult those who do blue-collar work, and serve to either implant anti-intellectualism into mass movements or to maintain intellectual labor as the specialized domain of academics. Also, with the increasing privatization of education and the rapidly rising costs of both public and private higher education, student debt is becoming an increasingly large factor in proletarian struggle, and pretending that a mythical "middle class" exists, composed of everyone outside the increasingly scarce assembly-line worker, cuts us off from a variety of important terrains of struggle. Too often, our discussions of class turn into a competition over whose childhood was harder rather than figuring out how we're going to liberate ourselves. And while there are real socioeconomic differences between various groups within the working class, we cannot let that obscure our analysis of the class as a whole.

To overcome this infighting, flawed analysis, and erasure, we need a truly anticapitalist analysis of class. We need to understand capitalism as creating a class system based on relationship to the means of production, and understand that an essential component of working-class struggle on the way to destroying capitalism is to win day-to-day struggles, such as less hours, greater pay, safer and more comfortable work environments, in so much as those things reduce the amount of value the capitalist class extracts from us and can be won directly, without mediation. Another goal of day-to-day struggle is to create and maintain effective self-organization. Winning these intermediate struggles does not take workers out of the working class, and can (and must, if we, the working class, are to liberate ourselves) serve both to improve the conditions we are struggling from and also build our capacity and ability to struggle by encouraging our self-organization as a class. It is foolish to buy into the same logic that the capitalist class uses to divide us against ourselves.

Another flaw of this sociological/liberal analysis of class as just another oppression is that it is the first step in breaking our solidarity with the entire proletariat. When we view class as a way that the poor are oppressed and that the so-called middle class and the capitalists are privileged (with the capitalists merely more privileged than the middle class), we inevitably fall into arguments of who is "working class enough"; did the queer who grew up in a single-parent home in poverty cease to be working class when she worked her way through school and became a teacher? Is the struggle of a trans person who is unable to get steady work under capitalism illegitimate due to the fact that they grew up in a two-parent household in the suburbs? Do we write off cis straight white workers due to their being "too privileged" to be in the same struggle as us? Do white queers continue to fetishize people of color, conflating race with class, without an analysis of how capitalism constructed and maintains racism? We cannot resolve these questions within queer anarchist circles while retaining an analysis of class drawn from an anti-oppression politics grounded in sociology or liberalism.

The most serious flaw, however, by putting class merely on the level of an oppression, is failing to have the realization, to paraphrase Marx, that the workers are the ones with radical chains; the exploitation of the working class is the entire basis of the system we want to destroy, and it is only by identifying, struggling against, and destroying those chains that any of us can be liberated. Once we realize that we can begin to understand how stratification based on race, gender, and sexuality were built into the working class as a means of control and hyperexploitation and as the midwife to capitalism's birth.

Beyond the Limits of Identity Politics

"Queer" arose as a critique of the assumptions that underlie identity politics. These assumptions were that oppressed groups were well-defined, had clear borders, that all members of the oppressed group have common desires and needs, and that a small portion of that group could thus speak for the entirety of the group. "Queer" was purposefully reclaimed to be a term of solidarity and struggle, and to include gay, lesbian, bi/pansexual people, and trans and other gender-nonconforming people. Initially, there was the acknowledgment that these groups had different desires and needs, but formed a coalition uniting around oppression based on gender and sexuality. However, queer liberation movements remaining rooted in identity politics have led us down the road of debating the precise boundaries of queer and arguing over whose concerns are legitimate, all the while pretending that we were not participating in identity politics, and thus can ignore the very real power differentials that occur within the queer community. To break away from the negative aspects of identity politics, we must look at material conditions and specific effects on particular subgroups, and struggle from those material conditions.

Furthermore, by defining a common struggle only along the lines of queerness, we are faced with the question of whether we want to organize for the same struggles as bourgeois queers. While queer anarchist/anti-authoritarian/anticapitalist circles make a big point of espousing "anti-assimilationism" and anticapitalism, often the analysis deteriorates into "being like the straights is bad" and "capitalism is bad." By generalizing "the straights" as a coherent group that hegemonically oppresses "the queers," and that the reason we don't want to assimilate is because we don't want to be like them, it becomes both too easy for us to ignore struggles that do not directly touch the entire queer community and to reduce anti-assimilation into nothing but a way to police the desires and identities of other queers.

We need to oppose the institution of state-sanctioned marriage because it strengthens the nuclear family as the consumptive and reproductive unit of capitalism, not because many straight people get married. Trying to invert the relationship hierarchy to shame people who are happy with a long-term relationship and shared household with a partner does not bring us a step closer to ending capitalism and ending oppression. It merely is one method by which queers police the identities, expressions, and ways of life of people in our community. If anti-assimilation is to be of any value, it needs to be founded on the idea that we want to destroy the current order and help build a better world, not keep ourselves separate from "the straights" because queers are somehow a well-defined group that do not find themselves as part of any other groups and can be kept apart from the rest of the world.

It is also necessary to keep in mind our class interests; no matter how well bourgeois queers play the part of a "radical" queerness, we can find nothing in common with their class interests, and are in struggle with them, and not the straight members of the working class. If we assume that our commonality lies in our queerness, not only can we be forced to ignore the other ways we are oppressed, we also assume that bourgeois queers are our allies and straight working-class people are our enemies, when we want only one thing from bourgeois queers—to take back that which is rightfully ours, and share it in common amongst ourselves according to our needs. This is the same thing we want from bourgeois straights and a desire we have in common with more and more straight members of the working class every time class recomposition occurs.

Without incorporating an analysis beyond identity, we are unable to go beyond the limitations of identity politics. While an understanding of intersectionality helps us to understand that some queers face issues that other queers do not, intersectionality is not enough, as it does not address the fact that the interests of bourgeois queers are in direct contradiction to the interests of the majority of queers, and this conflict can only be resolved through furthering class struggle, and ultimately by social revolution. We need to be wary of critiquing identity only to create a singular in-group and a singular out-group, and having the composition of that in-group have more to do with hipness and popularity rather than sexuality or gender. We also need to be wary of a politics that has us make alliances with the people in power rather than with members of other marginalized and exploited groups.

Struggling Autonomously, or, "Who is Queer, Anyway?"

It is often necessary for oppressed groups to engage in class struggle autonomously—i.e., to self-organize against their specific material conditions, fight against them, and bring their struggle back to the working class as a whole. While I am about as interested in arguing the precise definition of queer as I am about arguing about how many angels can have a circle jerk on the head of a pin, it's pretty clear what queer in general is—the state of being not-heterosexual, and/or the state of being trans, genderqueer, or gender-nonconforming. This, in the main, is the definition that has been used for "queer," as a reclaimed term of solidarity, by queer communities in struggle for decades. While "queer" is a purposefully imprecise term, we should avoid it becoming either a hip label or something that only belongs to those we agree with politically.

Working-class queer communities have often been targeted from both sides, first by bourgeois LGBT organizations looking for numbers and legitimacy, and by radical organizations that seek to co-opt queers and queerness that they feel comfortable with. Both sides erase and silence the queers they are not comfortable with. Ultimately, working-class queers need the ability to self-organize, and to do that they need to not be controlled by either bourgeois LGBT organizations or radical organizations coming in from the outside to lead them. While of course there are radical working-class queers in radical organizations, working-class queer community organizations need to arise out of the self-organization of all working-class queers, and not exclude non-radicalized queers from membership, as people are radicalized through struggle, and excluding them from the organs of struggle is saying that we both know best and that they are beyond change.

While queer communities have often defined "queer" too narrowly—examples of excluded groups from dyke communities being bisexuals, femmes, butch/butch and femme/femme couples, butches and femmes at some points in time, and trans women—we need to not be so broad as to be meaningless; we need to retain a notion of queer that highlights the separation from traditional notions of the family, and the additional reproductive labor (in the sense of being able to reproduce one's labor power for the next day) that comes from being a member of an oppressed group that is in constant danger from a hostile world and lacks traditional means of support.

If we want queers to be able to join in the broader class struggle (not like we haven't been there all along), we need spaces and organizations where we can approach the class struggle from working-class queer standpoints. We need spaces where we can formulate the questions about what being a working-class queer means to our material conditions, to our exploitation under capitalism. To truly be able to do that we need spaces where we can form organizations that don't need to make every hetero radical comfortable, and spaces that aren't controlled by bourgeois queers. If we, ourselves, bring those spaces into being, we will be able to organize our own struggles, link them up to the larger struggles of the class, and bring queer fierceness back to the class struggle. We do not need anyone from the outside to lead us; we will do things for ourselves by focusing not on academic definitions of what it is to be queer but rather the material conditions of queer lives.

The Dead End of Anti-Assimilation

Anti-assimilation, in-so-much as it has been a critique of the bourgeois cooptation of movements for queer liberation, has been valuable. Anti-assimilation, in-so-much as it has been hostile to seeing queer struggles as part of the larger class struggle and as it has policed the identities of queers, by casting out queers who can pass, trans people who access medical transition, monogamous queers, queers who must be closeted in their working lives to retain employment, has been a hindrance. The assimilationist/anti-assimilationist dialectic is unhelpful. The proper questions we should ask ourselves about queer organizations, movements, and struggles are: What is the class composition? Are the forms of organization a benefit or a hindrance to working-class struggle? Are the goals ones that would strengthen the working class or the bourgeoisie? In which struggles will our efforts as revolutionaries be most valuable toward our ultimate goal of communism? We must also ask how we can broaden the struggle—what opportunities does each queer struggle bring to spread to the rest of the working class?

These are far more important questions to me than whether the queers participating in the struggle reach an appropriate level of anti-assimilationist purity, which often at its core is just a reflection of the stratification built into the working class, twisted on the surface, but true to that stratification at its core. Another problem with anti-assimilationist purity is, as mentioned earlier, the idea that there is a need for queers to discipline themselves to adhere to a hegemonic idea of queerness that stands in opposition to a hegemonic idea of straightness. We run into the danger of cutting out far more queers that we should desire to struggle alongside than those whom we do not wish to struggle alongside, our comrades being working-class queers who may be monogamous, vanilla, or gender-conforming, for instance.

Ultimately, we must remember that any movement that sees itself as divorced from class struggle, that does not incorporate an understanding of the logic of capital into its organization and goals, will go on to serve bourgeois ends as it will be easily cooptable, or be able to expand to other sectors of the working class, and allow itself to be resolved into demands that capital can easily meet without being weakened. The task of queer communists in relation to queer movements is to place themselves into mass organizations, arguing for working-class queer issues in straight-dominated organizations, and arguing for true anti-capitalist class analysis, direct action, and unmediated struggle in queer organizations. We cannot afford to seclude ourselves in a radical queer bubble, divorced from both radicalized straights and non-radicalized queers; nor can we afford to dilute our politics in united front–type politics. Instead, we see the need to form both specific political organizations with a great deal of unity, and to advocate for our revolutionary ideas in mass organizations.

Questions to Be Asked

Of course, we are long from the days when any serious communist considers queerness to be a "bourgeois deviation." However, while we have anarchist and Marxist feminisms to draw from, we are left with a queer theory that is totally divorced from class and transfeminisms without a solid class foundation, and a queer movement that has left behind its roots in the struggles of working-class queers. This leaves us with many questions that have yet to even be solidly asked.

On the theoretical level, we have questions regarding how queerness affects the conditions of productive and reproductive labor of working-class queers. Such questions as "what is it like to choose to not form the same sort of long-term romantic relationships in terms of how it impacts how one's labor is exploited (harsher exploitation, less assistance in dealing with work, and loss of family support)? Or, when we do, when both partners are perceived as/are women, the assumption that neither is the primary breadwinner and thus how those lower wages and being thrown into a mothering role in the workplace brings that alienation to our social relationships? Or the extra unpaid reproductive labor (in the sense of reproducing one's labor power for the next day) that is required for one to do when one lives in a world that is hostile to one's very existence?" must be posed, analyzed, and hopefully provide guidance in our participation in struggles.

On a somewhat more practical level, we have such questions as "where are the potentials for broadened struggles that originate among working-class queers? How did the process of the queer movement losing its revolutionary character and acquiring a reactionary character occur? What forms of self-organization would serve us, as working-class queers?" While these questions may seem more pressing than the theoretical ones suggested previously, just as theory without practice is useless, practice without theory will forever leave us running every which way, and unable to identify the best places and moments for our energies. If we are to truly build a queer movement with a proletarian character, and return queer struggles to the proletarian struggle, we need both.

Conclusion

Queer anarchists are faced with a choice: do we stay with an analysis based on identity, and see our liberation as an independent entity? Or do we directly engage in class struggle with the rest of the working class, and see our liberation as inextricably linked with the liberation of all? One choice politically isolates us and can lead us to make alliances with the capital that exploits us and harms the self-organization of mass movements; the other has the potential to lead to true liberation, as divided we are weak, but, united, nothing in this world happens without the sweat on our brows.

This is to not say that queers can only take from class struggle, and give nothing in return. Many of us have been cast out of our families of origin, and can provide a lot of practical experience in creating new communities of mutual aid and solidarity. We provide our own unique viewpoints on the operation of oppression, and, by observing how it has created divisions in our own communities and disrupted our struggles for liberation, we can provide a lot of first-hand knowledge of how intersecting oppression and power imbalances can harm and derail the struggle of the proletariat. We have, in the past, mobilized large numbers of us when our community was threatened, acknowledging the power imbalances in our community, how portions of our community were disproportionately affected, and how the crisis went beyond our community. We came together to respond to the initial phases of the AIDS crisis and to directly struggle against the neglect of the state and the profiteering of corporations, but have subsequently, with the power and influence gained by bourgeois queers and their organizations, been told to turn our attention to inclusion in marriage and the military, against our own interests and abandoning those of us who are multiply marginalized. We can retake that power by identifying the ways queer members of the working class are affected by struggles around unions (and struggles toward workers' organizations that are not merely the negotiating agent between labor and capital), housing, access to health care, the disproportionate effects of environmental destruction on the working class and oppressed groups, and against controls on immigration and toward a world without borders, in the form of nation-states *and* in the form of constraining, bordered, and policed identities. By identifying how queers are affected by these struggles, we can form bonds of true solidarity with other communities in these struggles, communities that many of us are already a part of. By building mass movements truly self-organized by the people in struggle themselves, and seeing how our issues are interconnected, we can bring about a serious challenge to capitalism and the state.

To me, someone who is committed to the end of all oppression, and the end of capitalism and the destruction of the bourgeois state, and the achievement of communism, a classless, stateless society, where production is according to our abilities and strictly for human needs, the choice is clear; as a queer communist, I must engage in class struggle and participate in the self-organization of the working class, as it is not enough for me, as a queer person to be in the same circumstances as a straight person in the same social position—nothing but social revolution will suffice. And the only way for that social revolution to occur and succeed is by struggling from our own material conditions, and broadening that struggle across sectors of the working class. The class struggle is the broadest and deepest struggle, reaching everywhere and getting to the root of things, and only through our self-organization can we truly be in solidarity with workers everywhere.

Recommended Readings and Resources

• "Queers Read This," ACT UP NY, http://www.actupny.org/documents/QueersReadThis.pdf (accessed January 26, 2012).
• Deric Shannon and J. Rogue, "Refusing to Wait: Anarchism and Intersectionality," http://theanarchistlibrary.org/HTML/Deric_Shannon_and_J._Rogue__Refusing_to_Wait__Anarchism_and_Intersectionality.html (accessed January 26, 2012).
• Queers Without Borders, http://www.queerswithoutborders.com (accessed January 26, 2012).
• Pink Is a Shade of Red, http://queeranarchism.blogspot.com/ (accessed January 26, 2012).
• The author blogs at Autonomous Struggle of the Glittertariat: http://glittertariat.blogspot.com

• One cannot hope to understand the capitalist mode of production without some familiarity with Marx; while there are several good books, lecture series, and/or blogs on reading Marx's *Capital*, one should start with just reading, and, indeed, struggling through the first volume of *Capital*, without it being interpreted by someone else. Of these guides to Marx's *Capital*, Harry Cleaver's *Reading Capital Politically* is probably the best.

• *Caliban and the Witch: Women, the Body, and Primitive Accumulation* by Sylvia Federici, detailing the bloody birth of capitalism from feudalism, the beginning of a new patriarchal era, and how the process of primitive accumulation incorporated hierarchies of race and gender into the proletariat cannot be recommended enough.

• Libcom (http://www.libcom.org) has an extensive library of what we might term libertarian communist writings—the work of anarcho-syndicalists, anarchist communists, left communists, autonomists, council communists, the ultra-left Marxist humanists, etc. that I highly recommend browsing, and in which one can find interesting and enlightening threads.

toé, le besoin de sexualité, on le questionne pas souvent... J'ai l'impression que ça peut devenir presque une contrainte, la sexualité....

ben oui, combien de fois que tu baises par semaine ... ok une fois.. ou bien deux fois par mois pis tout le monde te regarde comme si tu étais un extra-terrestre. Mais ça, on en parle pas dans le milieu anarchiste vraiment ... y'a pas ce genre de chose

Pas vraiment. Like i don't think we've created some kind of perfect <u>bubble</u> where relationships can be whatever but i think there's a lot less judgement in terms of the kinds of relationships we can have with people

So there's a lot less pressure with anarchist to fit norms of relationships and therefore like sex and what sex has to be for you. We don't even have the same definition of sex. Cause i think most anarchist, or at least Feminist Anarchist, don't think that sex has to be vaginal penetration, there's just a more open scope of what sex can mean.

The idea of coupling, i find there's a lot of focus on that and to me that's really fucked cause that's so straight world to me. Like "who are you dating" and "how come you're not dating anyone?" and that not even has to be serious or super intimate or anything, whatever the fuck that means, but it's like "why are you not with someone in some way?"

It's still the idea if you are alone you are a looser.

In '95 no one was talking about queer any thing or any kind of polyamory necessarily or explicitely but there was way more men qui cruisaient les filles de manière explicite pis harassing a bit...

then, once the antiauthoritarian sort of thing started being talked about, then it sort of calm down and feminist also talking about this sort of thing and there was a shift!

Ça me fait penser à un autre aspect... Je m'affirme en tant que féministe et je cherche à le vivre dans mes rélations... J'ai été avec un latino et la sexualisation des femmes versus la sexualisation des personnes migrantes c'est devenu un enjeu. Pour moi, c'est majeur dans mon expérience de vie, le fait de parler de sujets aussi sensibles, en étant dans des réalités différentes... Les féministes dénnoncent le fait que les femmes sont sexualisées, mais d'autres aussi le vivent, dans ce cas-là, les hommes migrants.

Ils se font cruiser de façon intense mais il n'y a pas d'espace pour le dénoncer... et c'est très difficile à aborder...

i almost think that in the anarchist scene that i know about like, now i'm not talking about the queer scene, but i always find it really asexual

that's so true yeah yeah!

C'est ça qui est weird. En fait c'est super valorisé quand même la bisexualité chez les femmes anarchistes. C'est comme "wow c'est super hot"

mais du coup moi maintenant je suis comme mal à l'aise par rapport à ça parce que je suis "ben, c'est pas parce que tu es une fille que t'as le droit de me toucher"

c'est rushant, c'est difficile, c'est aussi des fois avec une amie, pis de dire "tu m'envahis, c'est plus cool"

pis en même temps les gars sont là, pis les gars ne peuvent pas toujours se toucher. Tsé, la bisexualité c'est quand même bien pour les filles...

mais surtout pas pour les gars. Les gars ils veulent beaucoup en théorie.

Like many anarchist straight men they're all like "oh i should have a relationship with a man.... next subject!"

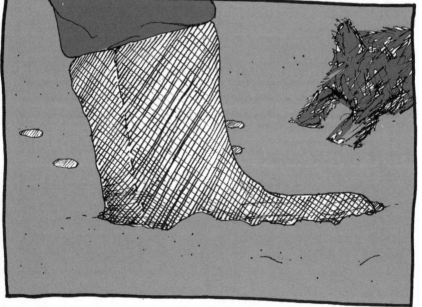

so, do people think that we have better relationships and better sex because of anarchist values or principles or ideologies or politics or all of that?

C'est pas parce qu'on est anarchistes que nos relations sont meilleures. Je pense qu'elle correspondent plus à nos valeurs.

Capitalist ideals aren't actually geared towards happiness. Just the fact that anarchist are more self reflexive and knowing that they don't have to accept that and knowing that it's something [we] can create and with somebody else so that it's this interactive thing that's about us and our needs and it's not like everything is better but i feel like there's more of a chance for things to be better and actually more organic and based in your own desires.

to be continued

Queering the Economy

STEPHANIE GROHMANN

Queer theory and practice challenge some of the basic assumptions around gender and sexuality that form the basis of modern society. They question the idea that human beings throughout history have fit neatly into the categories of "male" and "female," both physically and in their social selves, and that heterosexuality is the normal and natural way of sexual expression. Queer theory shows that gendered identities as well as sexualities are not fixed and "natural" but rather that they are socially constructed, fluid, and changeable—both socially and with regard to physical bodies. Gender and sexuality, in this view, are not something we are born with but something we do—or "perform"—on a daily basis. Queer politics therefore calls for a subversion of fixed identities such as "man," "woman," "straight," "homosexual," and so on by exploring individual performances that break out of these categories altogether. As a result, queer practice can mean a lot of different things—from cross dressing to S&M, from making visible intersexual or transsexual identities to DIY pornography. The goal is not to create new categories to label people, but to show that the categorization of individuals is repressive and violent as such—most of all the dominant heterosexual binary of "male" and "female."

Critiques of queer politics typically point out that this focus on the individual deconstruction of identity categories neglects the material conditions that the dominant gender binary is based on. In this article, I would like to explore some of the ways these material conditions—what is commonly referred to as "the economy"—relate to gender and sexuality and what queer politics can mean on the level of concrete economic practice. My basic argument here is that the connection between economic practice and gender goes much deeper than issues like sexism or homophobia in the workplace or the persisting pay gap between men and women. While these forms of oppression doubtlessly exist, they are not random aberrations of an otherwise egalitarian economic system, as market liberals claim, or a historical residue of hundreds of years of patriarchy. On the contrary—the heteronormative, hierarchical two-gender system in its current form is a result, rather than a predecessor, of modern capitalism.

One of the basic assumptions of queer theory is that categories like "male" and "female" are not the same for all societies at all times. In fact, as theorists like Thomas Laqueur have pointed out, the heterosexual gender binary as we know it has only been around for a few hundred years. Its emergence in "Western society" coincides with that of another category that in this form did not exist before—that of "the economy" as a specific sphere that is separate from all other aspects of society, such as politics or the family.

Only a few centuries ago, when most people lived subsistent lives in larger social units such as extended families and village communities, it would hardly have occurred to anyone to refer to some of the things that needed doing as "economical" as opposed to "non-economical." At the same time, while no doubt the domination of men over women has a history of at least a few thousand years, until the advent of what we now call capitalism, people did not consider men and women to be fundamentally different creatures. Women were considered somewhat lesser men, similar to slaves, and in a thoroughly hierarchical society like the feudal system of the middle ages, had their place below their fathers and husbands. It was not, however, assumed that by virtue of their sex they had particular characteristics that men had not and vice versa.

The advent of capitalism fundamentally changed these circumstances by creating "the economy" as a separate sphere, disconnected from other aspects of life. In a massive wave of expropriation, millions of peasants were forced off their land and made to work in factories that were located somewhere other than where they lived, thereby creating the now common distinction between the workplace and the home. The traditional social structures thus destroyed, the new system created a new form of gender relations—while it was the men who went to earn a wage, women were supposed to stay in the home, look after the kids and provide the necessary regeneration for the working male so he could turn up for work the next day.

Of course, this gendered allocation of roles was always a more ideological than actually existing one—just as today, women from poorer backgrounds or without a male breadwinner in the house still have to flock into the factories by the thousands. As an ideology, however, it was powerful enough to create the binary, heterosexual gender system as we know it today. The new world order began to sweep up larger portions of the population; from an ever earlier age men and women were trained into their respective roles. The world of wage labor, based on the market ideology of individual interest and cut-throat competition of all against all, required individuals who were rational, calculating, aggressive, and competitive. The world of the home, on the other hand, needed to be populated by people who would be gentle, manageable, emotionally supportive, and nurturing.

This resulted in the "gendered division of labor," which excluded women from wage labor, put almost all economic resources into the hands of men, and confined women to the home, thus making them entirely dependent on marriage as a means of economic survival. This dependency—and women's resulting vulnerability to male violence—has been among the main issues for feminist movements over the last centuries. Their struggles resulted in at least a partial inclusion of women in the labor market and thus relative economic independence. This inclusion, of course, was not achieved for all women in the same degree, as divisions by race and class became more obvious within the feminist movements. While it was acknowledged, however, that black and working-class women, as well as lesbians and transgender persons were excluded from full economic participation in multiple ways, the market liberal point of view regarded these forms of oppression as just another obstacle on the way to full inclusion. That this inclusion (in market liberal terminology: "equal chances") was the goal largely appeared to be self evident.

However, despite at least two centuries of feminist struggles, the gendered hierarchy within the capitalist economy seems strangely resilient to attempts at "equality" that want to include women in the male sphere of wage labor. Not only are women under-represented in certain areas, particularly higher-waged jobs, while at the same time still bearing the bulk of responsibility for reproductive work, also any sector of wage labor women enter into automatically becomes de-qualified and devalued. It is my point here that the reason for this is not so much sexist resistance to women's emancipation and independence—although that surely plays a major role—but the very nature of capitalism itself.

Let us take a closer look at what we mean by capitalism. Traditional Marxists as well as some Anarchists tend to focus their critique of capitalism on the exploitation of the working class by capitalist elites. This form of oppression is regarded as the "main contradiction" within capitalism, while all others (sexism or racism for example) are "side contradictions" that will eventually resolve themselves if the worker's struggle is successful in ending capitalist exploitation.

This point of view has unsurprisingly been met with harsh criticisms from people who regarded the forms of oppression they had to deal with by no means a "side contradiction" to the problems of white working-class men. But apart from nonchalantly declaring sexism, racism, and homophobia secondary problems, the "class struggle" perspective posed yet another problem: since it focuses on struggles and contradictions *within* capitalism (and takes a particular side in these), it fails to address the fundamental principles of the system that pitches different groups against each other in the first place. These fundamental principles are the very core categories that make the capitalist economy tick—Marx therefore started his analysis of capitalism in *Capital* not with class struggle, but with the unassuming categories of commodities, labor, and value.

According to Marx, capitalism functions like a great social machine. The worker's energy (labor power) is put in at one end and "infused" into the products of their labor—figuratively, of course, but in a sense that also marks a social "reality." In order for two things to be exchangeable at a certain rate, they must have something in common—otherwise, how could one say a car "has the same value as" for example two motorbikes? What they have in common is that both are the products of human labor—and the amount of labor that "goes into" a product determines its exchange value. While the workers thus spend their energy to produce value, they on the other hand have to buy back the very products of their labor from those they sold their time and energy to. During this cycle, a certain amount of (imagined) energy is siphoned off and creates "surplus value"—which is the whole point of capitalist production. The meeting of human needs is, if anything, a by-product but certainly not the purpose of this machinery.

Traditional Marxism, as well as socialist feminism, has mainly focused on the appropriation of surplus value by the capitalists as the core problem, while anarchism has emphasized the hierarchical and violent nature of this process. Much less attention has been paid to the process of turning human energy into an object as such—what Marx calls commodity fetishism. "Fetishism" in this context means the belief that material objects in some way "carry" certain amounts of energy that constitute their value. This belief does not have to be consciously held—it is enough if people act *as if* it were true. This way, all products of human labor can be related to each other as quantities of value, while their producers at the same time are separated from each other and do not organize production according to any kind of conscious agreement, but instead according to the "invisible laws" of the market.

This way, the circuit of labor and exchange comes to seemingly exist as an independent system from the social relations existing "outside" of it. At the same time, this system requires subjects that will readily conform to the behavior required by the market—competition, a commitment to growth at all costs, and the domination of "nature." Not coincidentally, this subjectivity is more or less congruent with the modern notion of masculinity. The "white, Western white-collar worker" is the full embodiment of this generic masculinity that at the same time has come to be the blueprint for "generic humanity" as such.

At the same time, not all human behavior can be organized in terms of market relations, least of all the kind of "nurturing" that is necessary to continually reproduce labor power. Consequently, all that cannot be expressed in terms of "value" becomes literally "devalued" and feminized (while at the same time it is a necessary precondition for the value circuit to exist). Despite its best efforts, the value circuit has never been completely able to incorporate each and every aspect of human life into the logic of commodity exchange; on the contrary, it has always depended on the existence of underlying structures that are not part of this logic. The world of wage labor and commodity exchange depends upon the existence of the world of personal relationships that makes it even possible, no matter whether individual men and women take part in one or both of these worlds.

The result is precisely the split between "work" and "leisure," "production" and "reproduction," "the economy" and "life," and ultimately "male" and "female" realms (and persons) that shapes modern life and anchors the gender binary in almost every aspect of society. The split even runs through individuals themselves, with men socialized into displaying "masculine" and women "feminine" traits at the expense of developing abilities ascribed to the "opposite sex."

A focus on the individual conditions of men and women within capitalist society obscures this much deeper conceptual split. As a result, feminist critiques of the gendered division of labor have largely taken one of two approaches: some feminists saw the exclusion of women from the "male" sphere of wage labor and commodity exchange as the core problem and developed various strategies to enable women to equally participate in it. Others, of a more separatist denomination, condemned capitalism as an inherently male project and called for a "feminization" of the economy by focusing on economic practices that were supposedly oppositional to it. In this latter category, we find, for example, feminist theories of "gift economies" as an alternative to commodity exchange, which, according to these theorists, constitute a "feminine" economy based on nurturing and care rather than competition and violence.

Both traditions, those that want women to fight their way into and those that want them to opt out of the male capitalist project, while offering important insights into the gendered nature of economic practice, do not, however, challenge the very distinction between "male" commodity exchange and "female" economies of giving and the persistent hierarchy between the two. Even though women in the "Western world" have to a degree managed to enter the male world of wage labor, they remain distinctively disadvantaged compared to their male colleagues, while at the same time the emotional work of reproduction still rests mainly on their shoulders.

Although both men and women now have more opportunity than a hundred years ago to escape their assigned economic roles—an option that, for some reason, seems more appealing to women than to men—the gendered distinction between the roles or what could be called "the heterosexual economic matrix" remains firmly in place. The reason for this, I would suggest, is not only the resilience of sexism to struggles for equal opportunities, but also the fact that the heterosexual binary is built into the capitalist economy to such a degree that it is impossible to overcome without overcoming capitalism itself.

In other words, a queer critique of capitalism based on an analysis of commodity fetishism would do the following: it would have to recognize that the heterosexual matrix based on the gendered division of labor is not so much an extension of patriarchy into capitalism but rather a genuine product of it. Capitalism does not only assign men and women different roles within its realm, it also creates the modern notion of 'masculine' and 'feminine.' This is done by splitting the circuit of value production and exchange from the social relations it is embedded in. Deconstructing gender from this perspective means a lot more than the individual subversion of traditional gender roles—it means the collective deconstruction of the heterosexual split that separates the "male" commodity economy from its "female" support system. The task at hand then is not to play one of these realms against the other, as do feminisms that want to either include women in the "male" sphere or emphasize the moral superiority of the "female"; it is to critique and actively subvert the binary as such. Not least in the light of the current and ongoing economic crisis, there are quite a number of attempts at doing precisely that, even if they do not always come from an explicitly queer or feminist background. One example—which I personally am particularly interested in—are the "free shops" that are popping up in an astonishing number of quite different locations. A free shop is a place (mostly DIY or volunteer-run) where people can deposit things they no longer need but that may still be useful for others. These things can then be taken by anyone who needs them, without this person having to give anything themselves. This principle has the potential to subvert the heterosexual economic matrix in a number of ways: it obviously challenges the logic of commodity exchange in its most basic assumption. The basic assumption is that one has first to have something in order to be able to get something. This is effectively addressed by a model that deliberately disconnects individual economic "input" and "output" and gets rid of the accounting in between. It takes the element of competition out of the equation (having to sell something ahead of others to be able to buy things one needs. This creates a system that does not exclude anyone on the basis of their ability to participate in market exchange.

On the other hand, however, this practice ideally avoids the pitfalls of just falling into the other extreme, building social relationships that resemble the split-off "feminine" sphere under-lying the market economy. While the feminine support system rests on the existence of personal relationships and the kind of care and nurturing typical for these, free shops provide a model of polit-ical economy that, extrapolated onto a much larger scale, does not necessarily require the participants to even know or ever meet each other. It therefore potentially provides also for those who do not have a system of personal relations to supplement market partici-pation. In other words, an economy based on this model is neither part of the male nor part of the female realm; although it neces-sarily overlaps with them, it is not fully based on either. The exist-ing overlaps—as for example the current dependence of free shops on the surplus of the commodity economy, or the classification of activists work as "volunteering"—are a consequence of building a new system within the old. It is not yet possible to completely detach any transformative practice entirely from the social condi-tions it is embedded in. As communities of practice grow, however, it may become increasingly possible to think outside the existing boxes and create new concepts and models to speak about social and economic relations.

Free shops—as a practical example of an economic practice that is not fully based in either half of the heterosexual economic binary and thereby challenges its very existence—are embedded in a wide array of practices that can be labeled "freeconomies" and experi-ment with alternatives to commodity exchange and labor. They are places where "undoing gender" becomes synonymous with "undo-ing capitalism." In this, they are one very useful example of what politics at the intersection of queer and anarchism could look like—one that hopefully will be followed by many more.

queering heterosexuality

SANDRA JEPPESEN

In this piece i will be considering the impact that taking on queer politics has had in my life, thinking through ways that queering anarchism might happen in the lives of anarchists and anti-authoritarians who society may identify as heterosexual due to the sex and/or gender of the object of their desire, but who ourselves disidentify with all things straight, perhaps even with the subject-position of heterosexual. what does this mean? this means that we are working on queering straight-seeming spaces, that we are straight-ish allies of queer struggles, challenging heteronormativity in the anarchist movement, as well as in the mainstream spaces we inhabit, from workplaces to families, from classrooms to cultural productions. this piece itself is one intervention that attempts to queer the space of narrative and theory, through non-capitalization[1], on the one hand, and on the other hand, through mobilizing a personal narrative to think through or theorize the queering of heterosexuality and the de-heteronormativizing of 'straight-acting' spaces. through an examination of the queering of hetero-space from an anarchist perspective, a liberatory politics of sexualities and genders emerges that intersects with anarchaqueer liberation[2] in challenging dominant forms of social organization including the state, marriage, capitalism, parenting, love relationships, friendships, families, and other important sites of anarchist politics and struggle.

through a meeting of anarchist and queer politics, we have found alternative positions, actions and relationships that are more profoundly meaningful to us. this is not to stake a claim in queer theory or queer politics for "straight" people—that would be exactly not the point. rather it is to acknowledge an indebtedness to these spaces, places, people and movements, while at the same time acknowledging that, as people who might have partnerships that appear "straight," we can pass as heterosexual, and accrue the privilege that our society accords this category. nonetheless as non-straight-identified heteros, we take on anarchaqueer issues by living as queerly as possible. in other words, queer practices and theories are important for the liberation of heterosexuals from normative standards of intimate relationships from friendships to sexualities. moreover, queering heterosexuality reveals that the categories homosexual and heterosexual are wholly inadequate to describe the vast array of sexualities available to us once we start exploring beyond the heteronormative.

where did this all start for me? i've never been "normal" as far as sexuality goes. but thinking of queerness as relevant to my own life started at a particular identifiable moment for me when i was volunteering at who's emma[3], the anarchist punk infoshop in toronto. a (white gay male) friend took me aside one day and said that, while he admired my anarchafeminist, anticapitalist politics, could i consider the possibility of including gay or queer issues in my conception of anarchism. of course, was my immediate response. i think i must have blushed as well, as i was a bit embarrassed, to be honest, to have to be asked something so obvious. but he didn't criticize me for something i wasn't doing, rather he opened up a space for something new—to move beyond heteronormative conceptions of anarchist politics. this was an incredibly important moment for me, though i did not know it at the time.

i am relating this as a series of narratives about conversations that i have had with many different people over the years, or experiences that i and my friends have had and talked about. as queer and/or anti-heteronormative anarchists i think we value personal experience and interpersonal exchanges as an important site of political knowledge production. in other words, we learn a lot about a wide range of political ideas, about the oppressiveness of language, and about our own position in the world we live in through conversations. through sharing narratives and stories. i want to value and give credit to the people, experiences and collective spaces that have helped me to learn about queer politics. i also want to put together some of these stories in a kind of collection of narratives here, to preserve, at least to some extent, the form in which i encountered them. of course they are filtered through my own perspective, and the lessons i've learned from them. moreover, the things they made me think about may be very different than the things they might bring up for readers, and i want to acknowledge this. my knowledge and my perspective will of course have their limits. at the same time, i did not want to theorize these experiences, putting a kind of intellectual distance between myself and the ideas because that is not how i encountered them. nonetheless i will be engaging many concepts, ideas and theories. our education system teaches us to understand stories one way and ideas another (for example, we study literature or stories differently than we study philosophy or ideas). it is my hope that these narratives will be understood not as cute little stories about my life, but rather as a source of important ideas about sexualities that might be useful to straight people in becoming anti-heterosexist straight allies. and one last hope i have is that many more people will tell their own stories, which will be taken seriously by anarchist and other readers in our struggles toward radical social and political transformation.

friendship, sexuality, polyamory and other intimacies [4]

anarchaqueer theories and practices start with the basics. how do we relate to people emotionally and sexually? how have these types of relationships largely been determined by oppressive systems such as patriarchy, heteronormativity, capitalism, families, culture, and the state, systems that we do not believe in, and which we are constantly rethinking and struggling to dismantle? while i had been a promiscuous feminist who, from a very young age, rejected gendered roles and stereotypes, up to the point when i was volunteering at who's emma, my personal experience of non-monogamy had been pretty rocky. during my undergraduate degree, i struggled against the sexual double standard where women were not supposed to want sex, engaging in casual sex or short-term serial monogamous relationships and taking a lot of flak for it. i then had a few non-monogamous relationships in the punk scene. in one case, when the relationship became long-distance, one of us was poly and one was not. we had bad communication in terms of disclosure and trust. eventually we broke up over it. in another, we both had other partners, and we communicated better at times, but not consistently so. we didn't know anyone else who was having this kind of relationship. eventually we broke up for other reasons.

when i encountered the anarchist scene in toronto, largely at who's emma and the free skool, it seemed like everyone was into polyamory, and people did not really distinguish among partners based on sex, gender, age, or anything else. i had many friends who were having non-monogamous (or non-mono as we called it) relationships at the time, so we were all talking about these things. it was a bit of a free-for-all in terms of hook-ups, which was really fun, and there were also many longer-term relationships that were both fun and serious. we started to think about how the word "non-monogamy" was a reification of the centrality or supposed "normalcy" of monogamy, and we wanted to have a different starting place, a multiplicity of amorous possibilities, so we started to use the word polyamory instead. poly for short. there was an important resource book at the time that we were all reading called *The Ethical Slut*.[5]

also at that time, people said "treat your lovers like friends and your friends like lovers." we have a lot more expectations of lovers, we do a lot more processing about where the relationship is going, negotiating space, articulating needs, setting boundaries, expressing disappointment, etc. and sometimes we forget to have fun and just really enjoy the time we have together. we can be really harsh toward lovers, perhaps because we feel so vulnerable. that's where we need to be better friends to our lovers. with friends we're more likely to cut them some slack, to let things be a little more fluid. no big deal if they're late, or miss a hang-out once in a while, for example. on the positive side, with lovers, we tend to do lots of special little things for them, like cooking their favorite food, making DIY zines or bringing them some little thing when we meet, something that says, i was thinking of you, something that shows we love them. along these lines, we need to be more loving to our friends, do more special things for them, go out on dates with them, make little heartfelt presents for them expressing how much we care. be more attentive to their needs, be supportive in day-to-day ways. treat them more like lovers.

i think around this time, to take one example, a friend and i were both not in any sexual relationship, so for valentine's day, almost satirically, one year she invited me over for a dinner date. she ran me a bath, handed me a glass of wine, and cooked dinner while i relaxed in the tub. the following year i did something similar for her. they were oddly romantic non-romantic, very caring friend-dates.

at this time in toronto there were a few long-term polyamorous "super-couples" who were held up as an example of the potential of polyamory to work. if they can do it, so can we, we all thought. they had good communication, and some interesting strategies that we learned from. one couple, when they were going out to a party, would decide ahead of time if it was a date or not. if not, they were free to hook up with other people. another poly couple i knew lived together, and had the guideline that they couldn't hook up with someone else at their shared apartment. regardless of what the rules were, what was interesting to me was that any two people could make their own rules. you could say what you wanted, and listen to what the other person wanted, and then try it out, and check in with each other afterward and see how they felt about how it went. this for me was super different than heterosexual monogamy which had a bunch of rules, none of which made any sense to me, like the rule about how if you show how jealous you are, it means you really care about the other person. or if you hook up with one person, and then a second person, it means you don't like the first person any-more, whereas in my experience, feelings for one person tended to have little bearing on, or perhaps even augmented, my feelings for another person. being able to incorporate this emotional experience into openly negotiated multiple relationships was awesome.

for me, this openness to building relationships from scratch, not entirely without rules, but negotiating guidelines as needed, makes an appearance in queer theory, in eve sedgwick's first axiom, "people are all different."[6] we all have different bodies, different body parts, different desires; we all want different things from relationships, whether they are intimate, sexual or otherwise. so why shouldn't we negotiate our relationships ourselves instead of following a het-eronormative set of scripts. this was also different for me than my previous open relationships in the punk scene where people some-times practiced dishonesty or coercion and called it non-monogamy. i didn't learn tools for negotiating toward meeting each other's needs in the punk scene. it was more like, i can't be monogamous, so you can either be non-monogamous with me or we can break up. there was no way to say, hey, what you just did hurt me—is there some way we can deal with this by communicating in ways that rebuild trust?

at some point i was lucky to participate in a class at the toronto anarchist free university[7] about polyamory. one of the best things the facilitator said was that, no matter how often or for what reason you have sex with a person, you still need to be honest and respectful with them. even if their motivations are different than yours (e.g., a party night hook-up or one night stand might be one person's motivation, whereas an active polyamorous practice committed to alternative sexual, intimate, and community-based relationships might be the other's). honesty and respect, appropriate establishing of consent among all concerned parties (including sometimes those who are not present, e.g., the other person's other partner/s), setting boundaries, and following through on what you've said are all critical elements of the encounter. to me this seems so far away from what heterosexual relationships are normally like, that it is actually something else. even if your partnerships are "straight."

for me, the polyamory scene and the radical queer scene were connected. we would get all glammed up to go to vazaleen, will munro's radical queer punk anarchist dance party in toronto. people who hung out at vazaleen included trans people, drag queens and kings, and queers of all kinds. some "straight" people went as well, but we were the kind of straight people who disidentified with being straight. we didn't identify with our birth sex/gender, we avoided norms or stereotypes of heterosexuality, we were critical of the objectification of women, we denounced predetermined gender scripts and sexuality scripts which we saw as connected to capitalism and patriarchy. perhaps we identified with queerness, for example, being attracted to people of a particular subculture, such as bears or femmie boys or butch dykes or trannies or whatever. it was a place where lots of gender and sex subversion and play happened. a queer space full of queers of course, some of whom were anarchists, some of whom were non-straight-acting heteros. i loved vazaleen because there was no sense, for me at least, of a normative sexuality. certainly it was not heteronormative. but it was not homonormative either. it did not echo mainstream representations of "gay couples" such as we might see on *The L Word*, or *Queer Eye*, with assimilationist, consumerist norms. instead it felt like a space of many sexual resistances.

non-normative sexualities

non-normative sexuality means, among other things, that people ditch sexual norms, and just hook up with and have long-term relationships with whoever inspires them, doing whatever they are into sexually. for me, sometimes this is women, sometimes it is men.

often it is with people who are not my age. when i was younger i dated older people and now that i'm a bit older i seem to date younger people. these are more or less the people i seem to find myself hanging out with. i don't really see age as an interesting way of dividing people. my friendships have always been across ages and even generations. my current partner is more than ten years younger than me. when we got together we were polyamorous and, although we communicated well and had great sex, we weren't taking the relationship too seriously. it was lots of fun. we both had other partners, but soon that kind of went away, and we made more of an explicit commitment to each other, first to be primary partners, and then to be monogamous. i've always felt a little ambivalent about this decision. recently i moved to another town, and we decided to be poly, although neither of us have acted on it yet.

this relationship is really amazing for me. he's super sexy and we have a red-hot sex life in which we do a lot of non-heteronormative things (whatever that means—i'm not telling you). i feel like this is particular to my own sexuality but also to the way i develop trust and caring or intimacy with a partner. he has the kind of emotional intelligence and empathy that is stereotypically not associated with men, and which is very important in keeping our relationship strong, perhaps because i do not, and so i am learning these things from him. today when someone called they said his voice sounds androgynous, and maybe that is part of the attraction too. he doesn't fit the gender scripts[8] any more than i do. for both of us, the non-normativity of the relationship is at least one of the things that keeps it alive and interesting.

on the other hand, i worry that our age difference means that there is a power imbalance, which we have acknowledged, and we work together to try to compensate and make sure it is more equalized. another thing that concerns me is that maybe in being attracted to younger people, i am somehow replicating ageism—both the ageism in the anarchist scene which is really a youth-oriented scene, and a kind of internalized ageism that mainstream society offers where youth is valued and age is something we are supposed to fight or disavow, rather than accept or even respect (as some cultures do). sometimes i think it is unfortunate that there is not a lot of age diversity in the anarchist "scene." one thing that happens a lot is that when i tell people my age they say i look a lot younger. this is supposed to be a compliment and i don't find it insulting. but at the same time, it sometimes makes me feel like there is something wrong with me being the age that i am. that somehow i would be better if i were younger. or conversely, that i am doing something age-inappropriate that makes people think i am younger. i wonder if this internalized ageism plays a role in partner choice as well, in terms of who i might find attractive. what is considered attractive in older men in mainstream representations makes me a bit nauseous. i think who i am attracted to is more connected, however, to my punk roots and that particular aesthetic.

queer parenting and community

i think another way that anarchism has allowed me to have a more non-heteronormative life is the acceptance of not reproducing children, in a community in which people's choices are accepted. when i chose to be polyamorous, it was accepted. i find being monogamous is also generally accepted because there is the notion of radical monogamy, which interrupts gender and sexuality scripts. some people i know have expressed a hesitation to admit that they have chosen to be monogamous, because there is now, ironically perhaps, an expectation of polyamory among anarchists. not having children is also accepted, whereas mainstream society tends to look askance at women who choose not to have children, or who choose politics over children. for example, when ulrike meinhof, who was part of the red army faction in germany, decided to leave her children behind and become an active urban guerrilla, living underground and working to overthrow the german state, there were many newspaper reports that demonized her for this (not for her political actions in and of themselves), and said she was not just a bad mother but somehow actually insane for leaving her children with their father.[9] for anarchists, though, there seems to be no presumption about anyone's life pattern or direction, in terms of getting married, settling down, having kids, doing political actions, etc. there is a sense that you can do things the way you choose, and people try as much as possible to create new paths for themselves, with the support of other people in our communities.

instead of following a prescriptive path—marriage, kids, house in the suburbs—a long time ago i decided i would rather follow the path of collective living. this was a conscious decision, because i felt that i was unlikely to find, and did not want to succumb to, a happily married suburban life. in fact, that terrified me. it was such a relief to read a book called soft subversions by félix guattari where he talks about growing up in the suburbs and how alienating that was for him, how it made him feel kind of "schizo around the edges."[10] i love that book. so i gave up on that whole dream, it was more of a nightmare for me anyway, growing up in the suburbs among the children of bureaucrats, people who were afraid of an active, gritty life in the city, so they moved to an area of carefully coiffed lawns and polite conversation. dead time, as the situationists say.[11]

when i first wrote this piece, i was living in a crowded four-bedroom apartment in downtown montreal with three other people, one of whom happens to be my partner. it is a queer space and we tend to have queer roommates by intention. our broader community includes the st. henri anarchist punks, student and academic anarchists, the radical queer and trans scene, antiracist activists, and lots of different feminists. these loose groupings extend across canada, into the united states, and to places like korea, france, and germany. our community also includes a lot of people who don't fit into any of these identities, who are nomadic geographically and categorically.

some people in our community have kids, some don't. some people think the current geo-eco-political situation is too unstable to have kids, but some are brave enough to do it anyway. eight years ago, i was living in a collective house in toronto with five other people. three of us wanted to have kids at that point, me and two other women. one of them was part of a super-couple who had been together in a polyamorous relationship for several years, about four years i think. in addition to her cis-gender male partner, the woman was starting to see a person who was a "non-bio-boy" (a term no longer used as it is rooted in biological determinism), a gender queer guy or trans man (in fact, all of these labels are fraught with complex histories and uses, and may also, like "non-bio-boy," fall out of use as we invent new terms that work better). they all three moved together into a big collective house with several other people, and started planning how they would conceive and raise a child together. in the end, though, she broke up with the cis-gender guy, and conceived a baby with a sperm donation from an ex-partner of her trans partner. they are monogamous now and raising the baby together. we had a funny conversation a few years ago when we both confessed to being in monogamous relationships, like it was a dirty secret.

the other woman was strictly monogamous. she started dating a woman and they decided to have a baby together and live together as a couple. interestingly both women decided to have babies with sperm donors whom they knew and had long-term friendships with. the larger community living space becomes smaller when you have a baby, and more intensified. community works itself into your life in other ways.

in my case, on the baby project, i met several times with an ex-partner who has a current partner and two children, living in new york city. we were considering the possibility of having a baby to-gether, and talked about how the future might be, with his current partner and their children. but then he mentioned that he thought it might be better if she didn't know about it. i didn't think that was a very good idea. it seemed like a non-consensual decision, in which all parties' consent would not be obtained. i didn't go through with it. i decided not to have a baby after all.

people make choices about having children in different ways, even people who may be in what appear to be heterosexual rela-tionships. considering the consent of all parties, working around or against the legal sperm donor clinic method of conception (very expensive and medicalized), or even deciding to abstain from breed-ing. interestingly, for me, this decision has meant that i am trying to make deeper connections to people aside from my partner. i feel the need to have closer friendships, and to be more loving to more people, not in a sexual way, but in an intimate friendship way, de-veloping creative collaborative partnerships, finding mutually sup-portive ways of interacting with people, and in fact spending more time, as i grow older, with nieces and nephews who are scattered all over the country, who are unrelated to the anarchist scene, but who are nonetheless of course an important part of my community.

liberation, responsibility and intimacy

in this context, liberation becomes a kind of odd concept. i still like spontaneous walks down by the train tracks, dérives, and nomadic urban wanderings as much as the next anarchist. taking off freight-hopping across the country, or traveling wherever, no apartment, no money, but always finding places to stay, people who will take you places or take you in. this was always liberating for me, on the fringe of capitalism, against the way middle-class people travel, or live generally speaking, tied to house and job.

but then a year or two ago i was at an anarchist workshop where the facilitator had a very interesting take on the notion of responsibility. i feel like mainstream society has inculcated in us the value of irresponsibility, and in anarchism we seem to link this to freedom, to nomadology, to spontaneity, and liberation. whereas really it is a kind of trapping capitalist individualism that seems unsustainable.

for example, i had a conversation with a friend once who had broken up with a partner because he was going traveling. i asked if that was a bit selfish, in that he wasn't really considering her needs or feelings. he countered that he had to put himself first. to me, this is a sentiment that i think a lot of people might agree with, anarchists or not, though by anarchists it might be couched in terms of a liberatory politics. but it seems more like a failure to be responsible to those people with whom we are engaged in intimate relationships.

at the workshop, the facilitator, who was an older indigenous-identified male, said that responsibility tells us where we belong in our lives. i have always been troubled by this notion of belonging, yearning for it in some ways, and yet unable to find it because i was charmed by the notion of spontaneity, freedom, the nomad life, new friendships and relationships everywhere with everyone who came along. at the same time, i was also perplexed by how i loved people who were always roaming, and that made it impossible to have a long-term relationship because we would break up or not see each other for long periods of time, and reconnections were difficult. i think i dreamed of finding a nomadic partner who would travel with me and we could be spontaneous together, and that this would be a sort of traveling set of roots that i could take with me.

now i think of responsibility differently. i think of it as a deep connection to another person, related to intimacy. it means that we think of their feelings and needs as equal to our own, and quite often, more important than our own. we can also think of our responsibility to self as, rather than being in conflict with responsibility to others, being profoundly connected with a responsibility to others, in the very anarchist sense that the liberation of one person is predicated upon the liberation of those around them. to take one example of how this works in everyday practice, this means that a person can ask people in their community for help when they have a health need, because there is an implicit understanding that we each need to take care of ourselves and be taken care of, and that when other people have health needs we will in turn be there for them. so taking care of other people is nurturing ourselves, our community, and the reverse is also true—asking for care is in a way nurturing other people, and developing in our community the capacity for nurturance. this feeds the fostering of intimacies in community with others beyond heteronormative coupled partnerships.

to tie this back to the notion of queering anarchism, what i think queer practices offer to anarchism is a language of intimacy. this language and its concomitant practice of intimacy is crucial for a revolutionary politics. radical queer politics and practices offer to non-normative heterosexual relationships a range of possibilities, including polyamory, intimate friendships, expressive communities, mental and physical and emotional mutual aid health care, and sexualities that are predicated on intimacy, respect, and consent. of course it doesn't always work out as perfectly as this all sounds. but that too is a lesson of queering anarchism. relationships are a life-long process of negotiation and sharing, of putting mutual aid into practice in layers of more intimate and less intimate relationships. what i think anarchism offers to radical queer spaces, groups, networks and communities, is a way of putting consent, respect, non-hierarchical love, emotional nurturance, and collective living into relationships so that those communities can grow and sustain themselves/ourselves, with an anti-statist and anti-capitalist perspective, and bringing in anti-racism, anti-colonialism and other related or intersectional movements and ideas. so in addition to queering anarchist movements, we are anarchizing queer movements. what emerges is a vision of queer and anarchism not as two separate things that are starting to come together (certainly the history of the anarchist movement is full of queers and the history of the queer movement is full of anarchists!) but rather a mutual aid relationship in which the boundaries between the two bleed into one another and they become inextricable.

queering heterosexuality from an anarchist perspective takes place in this context, where relationships are no longer heteronormative, where we are also moving away from homonor-mativity (the capitalist, state-run, white-dominated "gay pride" model, for example), and indeed open up into non-normative sexu-alities, where the labels "homo" and "hetero" are challenged at a basic level. sexuality like gender is thus a narrative, as my roommate said the other day, a fluid series of experiences that we can write and rewrite as we live through them, things we can invent or get rid of, as we see fit, in a kind of multiplicitous, interconnected, nonlin-ear, rhizomatic diversity of sexualities and genders that we engage throughout our lifetimes.

non-heteronormative desires

i had a conversation with a friend of mine last week about our non-heteronormative heterosexual relationships. he is dating someone new, and was having an odd experience, or at least he thought it was odd until he started talking to friends about it. and then it turns out that there are many people having a similar experience. among anar-chist hetero couples, if i may generalize for a moment, it seems that the guys are doing a really good job of being soft and sensitive, of taking direction from women when it comes to intimacy, to sexuality, and friendship. there is a new kind of language where men have had to find ways of expressing desire without being direct or aggressive. a tentative language, a conditional language, a language of questions rather than demands: would it be okay if? what if i told you?

for feminists, for women who want to be respected in friend-ships, in intimate relationships, and in sexualities, this is sweet. it makes relationships wonderful and warm and open and caring and loving. it's fabulous. so where is the odd experience in all of this, you may be wondering?

sometimes, as women, we want to feel passionately desired. we might want to be swept away with passion and desire. we might even want things to get a bit rough, you know, a bite on the neck, an uncomfortable position. sex on the floor under a table, or going at it so hard we almost fall off the bed before we even notice. (and this isn't news to anyone into bdsm or other fetish sex that explores intentional power exchanges in sex). i could go on, but i'll get to the point, which is this—we seem to be creating new norms, and in those norms, there are built-in things like respect and communication, gentleness and sensitivity, and these are all of course great things, and should be a key component in every relationship, from sexual ones to intimacies to friendships to parenting to teaching to work relationships and family. but, as with any set of norms, including polyamory and other forms of anti-heteronormative relationships, the risk is that we become fixed in a certain set of behaviors, and forget that we have the power and agency to say what we want, to negotiate through active listening and honest disclosure, and to achieve very fluid and lively relationships that do not stagnate or conform to previous expectations, or someone else's idea of what is right or wrong for us.

dylan vade is a trans lawyer who has written about the gender galaxy, which is the idea that gender and sex are not configured as a binary (male/female or masculine/feminine) but rather there are thousands of different ways of living out our sex/genders, in a galaxy, where some genders may cluster together into constellations, and sometimes these constellations are perceptible, but sometimes they are not.[12] i'd like to think that sexualities are like this too. rather than the binary homosexual/heterosexual, there are thousands of different ways of living out our sexualities.

this leads me to one last thing that i have recently started having conversations about. we had a houseguest a few weeks ago, a woman who took advantage of the same-sex marriage rights in canada and got married a few years back. as her partner started female-to-male transitioning, their same-sex status became a bit more fluid. she said that now that he has fully transitioned, they are read by others as a heterosexual couple. she enjoys high-femme camp performance in everyday life, particularly when it is queer, and is now unsure how this will be interpreted by others, which is most often as straight. when a queer gender performance is misread as heterosexual, the risk is that the play with signifiers—the feminine dresses, the 1950s style and behavior, etc.—will be misunderstood by both queers and heteros as reinforcing gender role stereotypes rather than subverting them. it is also odd, she said, to suddenly be experiencing heterosexual privilege in her public[13] life, whereas her private relationship is still very queer and does not feel privileged. to put it another way, her narrative of sexuality is not one of privilege, and yet this is how strangers now engage with her and her partner. the narrative thus is becoming uncertain, or what bobby noble calls incoherent.[14]

this is another way in which queering heterosexuality may take place in radical queer milieus and lives.

another FTM trans person has told me how he now struggles to be accepted as queer or trans, since people read him as a straight man, though he lived for nearly forty years as a woman and a lesbian. he almost feels like he can no longer be part of the queer community, unless he is among friends who have known him a long time. for example, he told me that he recently went out to a bar that had a reduced cover charge for trans men, and he had to really insist that he was trans. the door person wouldn't believe him. he repeatedly thanked the person, because they were reaffirming his sex/gender of choice, but in the end, he had to show the dreaded ID that still listed his gender as "F" in order to be accepted as a trans man. oh, the irony. this is not an experience that any trans person wants to go through. it demonstrates how heteronormativity, which causes people to assume everyone is gender-straight and non-queer, seems to permeate even queer scenes that are attempting to privilege trans people. furthermore, it reveals how even in spaces committed to radical queer and trans politics and subjectivities, the notion that someone's own self-identification should be accepted at face value, without having to provide coherent identification, is not always put into practice very well.

this is yet another one of the risks of queering heterosexuality. heterosexuality of course needs to be challenged, to be queered, to be wrested from its place of privilege. at the same time, we need to be very careful not to heterosexualize or heteronormativize queer spaces, subjectivities, identities, ideas, theories, and the like. there is a role here for heterosexual queer allies, even those of us who cringe at the word "heterosexual" and strongly disidentify with it. i believe and hope that we can queer our practices without claiming queer as our own, or appropriating it. in other words, the idea is to support queer struggles, to integrate queer ideas into our practices, to be as queer as possible, in order to work as allies to end queer oppression. the idea certainly is not—and this is another risk—to perform queer identities when it is convenient and then return to our heterosexual privilege unchanged or unchallenged by the experience.

liberation means this. it means we keep writing the narrative of our lives, our desires, our genders, our sexualities. it means that, rather than having the kind of freedom janis joplin sang about (you know, freedom's just another word for nothing left to lose) when my parents were exploring their open relationship (that is another story in itself!) we have liberatory experiences and relationships that are grounded in communities and long-term commitments to exploring what these relationships mean and how they can best be fulfilling to all involved. for me, to get to this openness, the queer and/or anarchist communities that i have encountered over the years have been crucial. crucial to who i am as a person, but more than that—crucial to revolutionary politics. the entire capitalist patriarchal white supremacy that structures our world unequally, and indeed preys on unequal relations of power, requires heteronormative relationships. break down those kinds of relationships, and we are also starting to break down patriarchy, white supremacy, and capitalism. as jamie heckert argues, breaking down micro-fascisms at the level of identities and intimate relationships is at the root of resistance to macro-fascisms at the level of institutions and structures of power.[15] queer practices, relationships, communities, scenes, and intimacies thus are making important contributions toward profoundly liberatory modes of being, doing, thinking, feeling and acting in the world that are intensely political. even for heteros.

1   challenging standard orthography (writing systems) by not using capital letters, by using "improper" grammar such as sentence fragments and the like, has a long history and a complex set of motivations. most importantly, it challenges the phallogocentric domination of textual representation, i.e., the presumed superiority of phallic (masculine) *logos* (use of words, acts of speech) that underlies western traditions of philosophy, theory, literary studies and other logocentric disciplines, and that can lead to semiotic subjugation (Félix Guattari, *Soft Subversions* New York: Semiotext(e), 1996.)—the feeling that we are subjugated to language rather than subjects that can speak through language. second, it challenges the privileging of the written word over oral traditions. third, it challenges pedagogical norms that are imposed upon schoolchildren from a young age, norms called into question by anarchist educational approaches such as free skools. fourth, it disrupts the presumed relationship of the author being dominant over the reader, a binary "other," and instead allows the reader to intervene in the text she reads, to be an equal with the writer. fifth, through this deconstruction of the binary relationships between masculine/

feminine, written/oral, correct/incorrect, writer/reader, etc., non-subjugated orthographies that refuse the use of capital letters and traditional grammar make space for the privileging of the collective, and cooperation in the construction of meaning, decentering the primacy of the individual writer, the supposed (rich, straight, white male) sublime genius who produces texts. this is therefore a radical, feminist, queer, and anarchist strategy that disrupts the way texts are produced, valued, legitimated and circulated. bell hooks drew attention to these debates, for example, by changing her name, disavowing her "slave name," and writing her name without capital letters.

2   Queeruption London, *Queerewind*. London: Queeruption Collective, 2004.

3   O'Connor, Alan. *Who's Emma? Autonomous Zone and Social Anarchism*. Toronto: Confused Editions, 2002.

4   Berlant, Lauren, ed. *Intimacy*. Chicago: University of Chicago Press, 2000.

5   Easton, Dossie. *The Ethical Slut: A Guide to Infinite Sexual Possibilities*. San Francisco: Greenery P, 1997.

6   Sedgwick, Eve Kosofsky. *Epistemology of the Closet*. Berkeley: University of California Press, 1990.

7   Toronto Anarchist Free University. http://www.anarchistu.org/.

8   Butler, Judith. *Gender Trouble*. New York: Routledge, 1990.

9   Bugnon, Fanny. *A propos de la violence politique féminine sous la Troisième République*. unpublished manuscript.

10   Guattari, Félix. *Soft Subversions*. New York: Semiotext(e), 1996.

11   Debord, Guy. *Society of the Spectacle*. 1967. Detroit: Black and Red, 1983.

12   Vade, Dylan. "Expanding Gender and Expanding the Law: Toward a Social and Legal Conceptualization of Gender that Is More Inclusive of Transgender People." In *Michigan Journal of Gender & Law*, 11 (2004–2005): 253–316.

13   Warner, Michael. *Publics and Counterpublics*. New York: Zone Books, 2002.

14   Noble, Jean Bobby. *Masculinities Without Men? Female Masculinity in Twentieth-Century Fictions*. Vancouver: UBC Press, 2004.

15   Heckert, Jamie. "Sexuality/Identity/Politics." In *Changing Anarchism*. Edited by Jonathan Purkis and James Bowen. Manchester: Manchester University Press, 2004.

Polyamory and Queer Anarchism: Infinite Possibilities for Resistance

SUSAN SONG

Queer and Anarchist Intersections

This article discusses queer theory's relevance to anarchist sexual practice and why anarchists might critique *compulsory* monogamy as a relationship form. Queer theory resists heteronormativity and recognizes the limits of identity politics. The term "queer" implies resistance to the "normal," where "normal" is what seems natural and intrinsic. Heteronormativity is a term describing a set of norms based on the assumption that everyone is heterosexual, gendered as male/female and monogamous, along with the assumed and implied permanency and stability of these identities. Queer theory also critiques homonormativity, in which non-heterosexual relationships are expected to resemble heteronormative ones, for instance in being gender-normative, monogamous, and rooted in possession of a partner. In this way, queer theory and practice resists the expectation that everyone should have a monogamous, cisgender,[1] heterosexual relationship form.

In "Anarchism, Poststructuralism and the Future of Radical Politics," Saul Newman distinguishes anarchism from other radical political struggles. Newman conceptualizes emerging anti-capitalist and antiwar movements that are "anti-authoritarian and non-institutional...[as]...anarchist struggles."[2] He describes these movements as those that "resist the centralizing tendencies of many radical struggles that have taken place in the past,...they do not aim at seizing state power as such, or utilizing the mechanisms and institutions of the state."[3] Anarchism is to be understood here as resisting institutionalization, hierarchy, and complete or partial political assimilation into the state.

Newman also cites anarchist thinkers such as "Bakunin and Kropotkin [who] refused to be deceived by social contract theorists, those apologists for the state like Hobbes and Locke, who saw sovereignty as being founded on rational consent and the desire to escape the state of nature. For Bakunin, this was a fiction, an 'unworthy hoax'....In other words, the social contract is merely a mask for the illegitimacy of the state—the fact that sovereignty was imposed violently on people, rather than emerging through their rational consent."[4] He describes resistance to the state by recognizing its illegitimacy as a seemingly chosen form. Similarly, queer theory can act to critique biological discourses about gender and sexuality being "natural," by pointing to its varying forms that are conceptualized in and influenced by historical and social contexts. Queer theory asserts that sexuality as a category and way of identifying, thought to be "biologically natural," is in fact socially constructed.

This is demonstrated by the ways that "homosexual" and "sex" as biological categories came to be created. In the later nineteenth century, the term "homosexual" emerged as a way to *define an identity* for those who engage in same-sex sexual acts. "Homosexuality" as a term arose as a way to define heterosexuality, thus pointing to its socially constructed and unnatural origin. Biological and medical discourses about gender and sexuality shift historically. In *Making Sex*, Thomas Laqueur notes how sex was constructed for political and not medical or scientific reasons "sometime in the eighteenth century."[5] "Organs that had shared a name—ovaries and testicles—were now linguistically distinguished. Organs that had not been distinguished by a name of their own—the vagina, for example—were given one."[6] Female orgasm and its role, if any, in conception were also debated as a contemporary issue. Sexual difference became a way to articulate a hierarchy of gender where women are viewed as inferior to men. This model of sexual difference is, Laqueur writes, "as much the [product] of culture as was, and is, the one-sex model."[7] This transition is demonstrated in instances such as when de Graaf's observations yielded the claim that "'female testicles should rather be called ovaries.'"[8] Eighteenth-century anatomists also "produced detailed illustrations of an explicitly female skeleton to document the fact that sexual difference was more than skin deep."[9] In this one-sex model, the male body is the norm against which other bodies are compared. This model problematically assumes that biological difference creates a "normal" social difference. However, Laqueur destabilizes this idea of sex as a "natural" category that points to significant biological differences, and instead posits that the construction of sex is influenced and shaped by a hierarchy of gender and political impulses.

Class Politics and Beyond

Queer theory denaturalizes hierarchies of gender, sexuality, and political influence, and is a valuable tool for anarchist practice. Queer theory questions what is "normal" and what creates hierarchical differences between us, opening up new sites of struggle outside of class politics alone. From feminist theory emerged the idea that gender is socially and not biologically constructed, and therefore not innate, natural, stable, or "essential" to someone's identity due to their "biology." Instead, gender is a product of social norms, individual behaviors, and institutional power. Gay/lesbian studies added to the discourse around gender and sexuality by introducing homosexuality and LGBT identities as areas to be queried. Following the work of feminist theory and gay/lesbian studies, queer theory understands sexuality and sexual behaviors as similarly socially constructed and historically contingent. Queer theory allows for a multiplicity of sexual practices that challenge heteronormativity, such as non-monogamy, BDSM relationships, and sex work.

Queer theory opens up a space to critique how we relate to each other socially in a distinctly different way than typical anarchist practice. Where classical anarchism is mostly focused on analyzing power relations between people, the economy, and the state, queer theory understands people in relation to the normal and the deviant, creating infinite possibilities for resistance. Queer theory seeks to disrupt the "normal" with the same impulse that anarchists do with relations of hierarchy, exploitation, and oppression. We can use queer theory to conceptualize new relationship forms and social relations that resist patriarchy and other oppressions by creating a distinctly "queer-anarchist" form of social relation. By allowing for multiple and fluid forms of identifying and relating sexually that go beyond a gay/straight binary, a queer anarchist practice allows for challenging the state and capitalism, as well as challenging sexual oppressions and norms that are often embedded in the state and other hierarchical social relations.

Queer Anarchism as a Social Form

A queer rejection of the institution of marriage can be based on an anarchist opposition to hierarchical relationship forms and state assimilation. An anarchist who takes care of someone's children as an alternative way of creating family can be understood as enacting a queer relation. Gustav Landauer in *Revolution and Other Writings* writes, "The state is a social relationship; a certain way of people relating to one another. It can be destroyed by creating new social relationships; i.e., by people relating to one another differently."[10] As anarchists interested and working in areas of sexual politics and in fighting all oppressions, we can create a new "queer-anarchist" form of relating that combines anarchist concepts of mutual aid, solidarity, and voluntary association with a queer analysis of normativity and power. We must strive to create and accept new forms of relating in our anarchist movements that smash the state and that fight oppressions in and outside of our bedrooms.

One way that we can relate socially with a queer anarchist analysis is by practicing alternatives to existing state and heteronormative conceptualizations of sexuality. We can embrace a multiplicity of sexual practices, including BDSM, polyamory, and queer heterosexual practices—not setting them as new norms, but as practices among many varieties that are often marginalized under our normative understandings of sexuality. In polyamorous relationships, the practice of having more than one partner challenges *compulsory* monogamy and state conceptions of what is an appropriate or normal social relation. Polyamory is just one of the practices that arise when we think of relationship forms that can (but do not automatically) embody distinctly queer and anarchist aspects. BDSM allows for the destabilizing of power relations, by performing and deconstructing real-life power relations in a consensual, negotiated setting. Queer heterosexual practices allow for fluidity of gender and sexual practices within heterosexual relationships. Although practicing these relationship forms alone does not make one a revolutionary, we can learn from these practices how to create new conceptualizations of social relations and, importantly, challenge normative indoctrination into our society's constrictive, limited, and hierarchical sexual culture.

Polyamory as a Queer Anarchist Form

Polyamory refers to the practice of openly and honestly having more than one intimate relationship simultaneously with the awareness and knowledge of all participants. This includes relationships like swinging, friends with benefits, and people in open relationships. The open and honest aspect of polyamory points to anarchist conceptions of voluntary association and mutual aid. Polyamory also allows for free love in a way that monogamous state conceptions of sexuality don't allow. Emma Goldman in "Marriage and Love" writes, "Man has bought brains, but all the millions in the world have failed to buy love. Man has subdued bodies, but all the power on earth has been unable to subdue love. Man has conquered whole nations, but all his armies could not conquer love. ...Love has the magic power to make of a beggar a king. Yes, love is free; it can dwell in no other atmosphere. In freedom it gives itself unreservedly, abundantly, completely."[11]

In free love, there reside anarchist notions of mutual aid. Returning to a previous point, polyamory as a form challenges conceptualizing one's partner as possession or property. Instead of having exclusive ownership over a partner, polyamory allows for partners to share love with as many partners as they agree to have. In contrast to compulsory monogamy, polyamory can allow for more than one partner, which can challenge state conceptions of what is a normal/natural relationship and enacts a queer form of relation. *Compulsory* monogamy can refer to relationships that are produced in a context where there is pressure to conform to monogamy. Compulsory monogamy is a concept that's pervasive in our laws and institutions, where the expectation and pressure to conform to monogamy is awarded by material and social gain. This is not to suggest that those who choose monogamous relationships are more restricted than their polyamorous counterparts. A critique of the ways in which monogamy has become *compulsory* is quite different than judging individual romantic/sexual practices.

Polyamory can also challenge state conceptions of possession and property. Marriage as an institution is invested with notions of heterosexual reproduction and patriarchy. Sara Ahmed's work can be used to further help conceptualize polyamory. She writes, "In a way, thinking about the politics of 'lifelines' helps us to rethink the relationship between inheritance (the lines that we are given as our point of arrival into familial and social space) and reproduction (the demand that we return the gift of that line by extending that line). It is not automatic that we reproduce what we inherit, or that we always convert our inheritance into possessions. We must pay attention to the pressure to make such conversions."[12] Her analysis demonstrates how polyamory can challenge ideas of inheritance and possession. Polyamory as a form allows for a multiplicity of partners and isn't necessarily invested in heterosexual reproduction in the same way that marriage as a state institution can be. In this way, polyamory can disrupt practices of reproduction and inheritance by creating new family and relationship forms not invested in sexual ownership and in becoming a part of state-enforced and monitored relations.

A Call to Sexual Freedom

One may ask, how is polyamory relevant to me if I'm not interested in practicing it? What is the point of critiquing monogamy if I'm in a satisfying monogamous relationship? By bringing queer theory into our bedrooms and into the streets, we can begin to expand what may not be thought of as in need of liberating. When folks in fulfilling, monogamous relationships consider this history of sexual repression, they have the tools to understand what it means to become sexually liberated in spite of that history, even while choosing to remain in monogamous relationships. We can liberate ourselves from confining and arbitrary gender norms and expectations in not just our romantic relationships but our everyday lives. Queer theory gives us the spaces to transgress and play with gender and question the limits of identity politics to further consider that sexuality and other identities are not stable and don't have to be. Sexuality can be fluid and come in multiple forms, just as our gender expressions can be.

We want more than class liberation alone. We want to be liberated from the bourgeois expectations that we should be married, that there is only a binary of men and women in rigid normative roles who can date monogamously and express their gender in normative, restrictive ways. We should fight for gender liberation for our gender-transgressive friends and comrades and fight for freedom of consensual sexual expressions and love. This fight isn't just in the streets. It's in our bathrooms where transgender and gender-non-normative folks are policed by people who don't acknowledge trans or other gender-non-normative identities, either by reinforcing a gender binary of cisgendered identities and ignoring a fluidity of gender identities or by otherizing transgender folks as an Other gender. It's in our family structures that create bourgeois order in our lives. It's in our production of discourses around sexuality, where sexuality is seen as something to be studied under a Western, medical, biological model. It's in our meetings and movements where critical voices that don't belong to straight, white, cisgender men are marginalized. We should create new, different ways of living and allow for queerer forms of relating and being.

Sexual liberation looks different for each individual. In my experience, being consensually tied up by a friend and consensually flogged in a negotiated setting is liberating. Kissing or hugging someone who you've carefully negotiated consent with is explosively satisfying. Being in an open, honest, polyamorous relationship for me created one of the most liberating romantic relationships of my life so far. However, sexual liberation is a deeply subjective experience. A problematic binary is set up in conceptualizing polyamory itself as a queer anarchist form and in potentially creating and reinforcing a new "norm" of polyamory as being superior to monogamy and other heteronormative relationships.

Returning to Ahmed, what is significant in considering new relationship forms is the pressure to make conversions and this should be considered as we form new ways of relating that challenge patriarchy,[13] capitalism, and heteronormativity. We must broaden our ideas around what anarchist sexual practice looks like, ensuring that smashing gender norms, accepting that sexuality and gender are fluid, unstable categories, and challenging *pressures* to be monogamous are as part of our anarchist practice as challenging state forms of relating. We should live, organize and work in a way that consciously builds a culture that embodies these norms of being resistant to patriarchy and heteronormativity. This work is fundamental to our shared liberation from capitalism—but also from patriarchy, heteronormativity, and restrictive and coercive sexual expectations of all kinds.

1   "Cisgender" is a term referring to individuals who have a gender identity or gender role that matches their sex assigned at birth. For instance, a cisgender woman is a woman who was assigned female at birth and identifies with female. This term is sometimes thought of as meaning "not transgender."

2   Saul Newman, "Anarchism, Poststructuralism and the Future of Radical Politics." *SubStance* (36)(2) (2007): 4.

3   Ibid.

4   Ibid., 6.

5   Thomas Laqueur, *Making Sex: Body and Gender from the Greeks to Freud* (Cambridge: Harvard University Press, 1990), 27.

6   Ibid.

7   Ibid., 29.

8   Ibid., 44.

9   Ibid., 31.

10   Gustav Landauer, *Revolution and Other Writings: A Political Reader*, edited and translated by Gabriel Kuhn (Oakland: PM Press. 2010), 214.

11   Emma Goldman, *Anarchism and Other Essays*, 3rd ed. (New York: Mother Earth Association, 1917), 93.

12   Sara Ahmed. *Queer Phenomenology: Orientations, Objects, Others* (Durham: Duke University Press, 2006), 17.

13   "Patriarchy" refers to a system of power embedded in institutions and other ways of social organizing that privileges and grants power to men over women and folks who aren't cisgendered.

Sex and the City: Beyond Liberal Politics and toward Holistic Revolutionary Practice[1]

DIANA C. S. BECERRA

I was walking through the streets of downtown New York City to catch the uptown train to Harlem, when I noticed a long line of enthusiastic fans waiting outside a movie theater to catch the latest film: *Sex and the City 2*. It triggered memories of my freshman year at City College, and the nights I spent with friends watching old episodes of *Sex and the City*. A bit tipsy, we talked about our own sexual lives, comparing them to the often-hysterical scenarios of that night's episode. But our experiences in comparison to those of the four glamorous characters were marked by blatant racial and class differences. We were three women of color who ate at family restaurants that blasted *bachata* and salsa—often way too loud—and who drank cheap beer instead of expensive cocktails (unless half off during happy hour).

Sex and the City has been so influential that Natasha Walter, author of *The New Feminism*, felt compelled to say, "I don't think anyone in the future will be able to write about the status of women in the US at the turn of the century without running through some old *Sex and the City* videos, and appreciating how single women bestrode Manhattan."[2] But *which* single women, of what race, class, and sexual orientation, and on what specific streets of Manhattan? Kim Akass of London Metropolitan University argued that the show has provided women with a "language with which to talk about their experiences and their friendships." Pepper Schwartz, a University of Washington sociology professor claimed that *Sex and the City* "was a sea change in how women talked about sexuality."[3] How is the discussion of sex being framed within *Sex and the City*? Just how liberating and inclusive is this sex talk? How does the show set the terms by which we understand our gendered and sexual selves?

It is obvious that most of us could never afford the fabulous lifestyle promoted in the show, especially in this down-spiraling economy: many of us are losing or have lost our jobs and homes and are unable to pay for school, bills, etc. Given the show's blatant glorification of the lives of the rich and its large disdain for working-class culture, some more progressive folks may have the impulse to completely dismiss the show, calling it stupid and irrelevant. Meanwhile the less critical may view the show as pure entertainment and fun, claiming that it has nothing to do with politics. But we must resist the temptation of dismissing popular culture. Popular culture circulates and reinforces many values that are seen as "normal" and "natural." It's a powerful tool for educating the public about which relationships are acceptable, and which are not.

In celebrating the institutionalized social and material privileges of elite women, *Sex and the City* undermines its slightly progressive values. Informed by the basic assumptions of liberal feminism, *Sex and the City* normalizes the oppression of the majority of women and men. Liberal feminism has historically been characterized by its reformist political goals to incorporate racially and economically privileged (cisgender) women within dominant institutions. To take a step in a liberating direction, we need to understand how oppressive relationships are created and enforced in our communities. Given the complex people that we are, we need to understand how different types of privilege and oppression intersect and reinforce one another in both the experiences of others and ourselves. This type of framework can put us in a better position to holistically dismantle a sexuality that oppresses, and to create the conditions for a sexuality that liberates.

From Gucci to Gramsci:

Systems of oppression are maintained through the (often coerced) participation of the oppressed. But how does this happen? How are we compelled to participate within relationships and systems that oppress our communities and ourselves? This is precisely what the Italian revolutionary Antonio Gramsci asked in the early 1920s and 1930s. Gramsci developed the concept of "hegemony" to understand the process by which the working class is socialized to think and act within the dominant framework of class elites. But with the rise of nationalist, feminist, and sexual liberation movements in the latter twentieth century, many revolutionaries expanded the concept of hegemony to racial, gender, and sexual oppression.

While we all have power, clearly some groups have much more power over their own lives, and unfortunately, even more power over the lives (and deaths) of others. The useful concept of hegemony allows us to understand how privileged groups maintain this power. Hegemony is maintained in large part through institutions (marriage, workplace, schools, military, etc) that educate people to accept and identify with the dominant assumptions, values, roles, and consciousness of their society and oppressors. The success of hegemony can often be measured by the inability of the oppressed to envision new alternatives—that somehow our misery is natural or even justified. Luckily, the hegemonic power of privileged groups has its limits. Despite our intense socialization, we still have the ability as human beings to question our circumstances and build alternatives.

Sex (and the City) 101:

It's important to know the show's plot before we analyze the show in relation to hegemony. *Sex and the City* portrays the lives of four single (elite, white, wealthy, heterosexual, thin) women living fabulously in New York City during the late 90s to the early 2000s. The main character, Carrie Bradshaw, (played by Sarah Jessica Parker) writes a witty sex column for the fictional newspaper the New York Star. Carrie uses her personal love life, the experiences, and perspectives of her friends, Samantha Jones, Charlotte York, and Miranda Hobbes, and the dating scene of Manhattan as both her inspiration and writing material. The sex column serves as a space for Carrie to raise questions, and outright doubts about the search for "Mr. Right," marriage, and children. It is through Carrie's confession-style discussion of sex and relationships that the audience is invited to relate to the four characters.

One of the most appealing and controversial aspects of the show was its blatant discussion of sex. As promoted in the show, women have the right to great sex, and also the right to discuss it everywhere! No social space in New York City is off limits. In *Sex and the City*, everything from careers to cunnilingus is discussed over expensive cocktails and cigarettes. And of course sex, all kinds of sex—good sex, bad sex, hit-your-head-against-the-bedpost-sex, mindblowing (I actually orgasmed) sex—is discussed in hysterical detail. While the show mainly focused on heterosexual sex, non-heterosexual sex often made a guest appearance, whether in the form of Samantha's brief relationship with Brazilian artist Maria Diega Reyes, the gay adventures of Stanford Blatch and Anthony Marantino, or more problematically, Samantha's condescending interaction with transgender black sex workers.[4] While *Sex and the City* provided insight into the lives of wealthy gay men and women, the show often promoted a binary of male/female/gay/straight. As Charlotte commented about sexual identities, "I'm all into labels, pick a side and stay there" ("Boy, Girl, Boy, Girl"). This heterosexist statement treats sexuality as fixed and denies people, particularly queer and trans folks, the right to embody an identity that escapes the gender and sexual binary.

Since hegemony is a process of domination, there is space for limited resistance and human agency to reject or question the expectations and roles demanded of certain social groups. Through humor *Sex and the City* challenges the domestic roles assigned to financially privileged women. The show points to a new culture where female friendships, financial independence, female sexual empowerment, individuality, and personal choice are valued. We see this form of questioning in *Sex and the City*. The four female characters ridicule the expectations normally projected onto single women in their thirties; romantic fantasies and notions about love are in a constant process of evaluation. Samantha rejects monogamy, embraces "tri-sexuality" (try anything once), and passionately defends a woman's right to always orgasm during sex. Samantha proudly admits, "I have had to polish myself off once or twice, but yes, when I RSVP to a party, I make it my business to *come*." Samantha is the antithesis to the female stereotype that is desperately in search of a monogamous relationship. Another leading critic is Miranda, who sarcastically questions the double standard for men and women in regards to sex, financial independence, aging, and beauty, to name a few. Miranda is especially critical of romantic fantasies: "Soul mates only exist in the Hallmark aisle of Duane Reade Drugs." Miranda even criticizes her friends for their often-obsessive discussion of men, a subject matter that consumes a large portion of the women's time: "All we talk about anymore is Big [Carrie's love interest], or balls, or small dicks. How does it happen that four such smart women have nothing to talk about but boyfriends? It's like seventh grade with bank accounts. What about us? What we think, we feel, we know. Christ. Does it all have to be about them?"

Miranda expresses her frustration of having to measure her happiness to the extent that her personal relationships with men are "successful" (i.e., long-term and lead to marriage), despite her accomplishments as a corporate lawyer that grant her a sense of worth and financial independence. The constant discussion of men is equated with the stereotypical obsession of inexperienced young girls with boys. Overall, the show tries to highlight the power of female friendship, challenging the idea that women are entirely dependent on men for their emotional needs. It challenges the idea that you're a "nobody till you've found somebody." As Michael Patrick King, the executive producer of *Sex and the City* said, "We get to say what no one would ever say to single people in their thirties, which is 'Maybe your life is better than the married people's.'"[5]

Although Charlotte, a leading character, is eager to get married, *Sex and the City* often suggests that happiness can be found outside marriage, and that not all women want a monogamous relationship or need to have children to feel fulfilled in life. As the radical voices of the LGBTQ movement have suggested, marriage should not be legally, economically, or socially privileged above other relationships.[6] Our vision of society should honor, respect, and materially support the diverse ways that people practice consensual love and build communities beyond relationships of dominance. The majority of people, regardless of their gender and sexual identity, do not live in a traditional nuclear family.[7] This is especially true of queer, people-of-color, and working-class communities who depend on extended families and friends for their well-being; the latter two households are often supported by single mothers.

Confronting Oppression

Through "personal choice" the four characters of *Sex and the City* challenge gender roles. But how is "empowerment" being defined? Charlotte in attempting to rationalize her decision to quit her job and become a housewife says, "The women's movement is supposed to be about choice. And if I choose to quit my job, that is my choice…It's my life and my choice!…I choose my choice! I choose my choice!"[8]

While it is the right of all parents to have the available resources to raise their children, the majority of women are not in the position of power to make Charlotte's choice. Any political project based around "choice" needs to critically question the options available to people, which for the majority are limited and outright oppressive. As we struggle to expand a person's fundamental right to make decisions about their lives, from the bedroom to the doctor's office and workplace, we have to recognize that institutionalized privilege grants some people more choices at the direct or indirect expense of others. Individual choice as the sole means of resistance will always be limited by hierarchical institutions that deny us or others meaningful choice. Although speaking on white privilege, elements of Tim Wise's definition are useful for thinking about gender, sexual, and class privilege:

> White privilege refers to any advantage, opportunity, benefit, head start, or general protection from negative societal mistreatment, which persons deemed white will typically enjoy, but which others will generally not enjoy. These benefits can be material (such as greater opportunity in the labor market, or greater net worth, due to a history in which whites had the ability to accumulate wealth to a greater extent than persons of color), social (such as presumptions of competence, creditworthiness, law-abidingness, intelligence, etc.) or psychological (such as not having to worry about triggering negative stereotypes, rarely having to feel out of place, not having to worry about racial profiling, etc.).[9]

Sex and the City defines social liberation around the privileges of wealthy white cisgender women, meaning women who perform the gender identity assigned to them at birth. Living in a gentrified apartment, buying $495 shoes, getting married, and hiring an immigrant nanny are all presented as the embodiment of feminist liberation. But how does the celebration of white female beauty and femininity, fabulous lifestyles, and wealth reinforce the oppression of working-class women, women of color, and LGBTQ persons? While *Sex and the City* honors the sexually assertive woman and often critiques the sexism that rich women face in the corporate boardroom, the show ultimately points to the accomplishments of wealthy white women as proof of *all* women's gains. Informed by liberal feminism, the show celebrates women who assume powerful positions within dominant institutions. The individual women who enter these elite spaces are presented as the natural champions of women's rights.

Challenging sexism is not simply about breaking gender stereotypes on an individual basis; rather it is about dismantling an institutionalized system of sexism, and by implication other systems of oppression. *Sex and the City* assumes that all women experience sexism in the same manner, although apparently it is only rich, white, predominantly heterosexual women's experiences that are worthy of being presented. Women like Miranda or Samantha can climb the corporate ladder because of their class and racial privilege. So for example, while the show celebrates Miranda's status as a corporate lawyer, it silences the experiences of Magda, a Ukrainian housekeeper whose domestic labor largely contributed to Miranda's success.

The experiences of Miranda and Magda illustrate how a woman's class background and national status greatly impact her gendered experiences. Many wealthy white women can afford to buy themselves out of the gender division of labor within their home. These middle- and upper-class households depend on domestic workers to watch over their kids, clean their homes, and take care of all other domestic chores. The majority of domestic workers are poor women of color (often undocumented immigrants) who are overworked and receive less than minimum wage, while their employers are often white US-born professionals, and economically privileged.[10]

It is worth emphasizing that capitalism, heteropatriarchy, and white supremacy function on the unpaid work and poverty wages of the majority of women; this point is more than relevant in an age of global neoliberalism, where privatization, militarization, and the privileged access of corporations to cheap labor and natural resources is the rule. On a global scale, neoliberal policies that benefit US and foreign elites are enforced through decrees or bullets— from devastating "free-trade" agreements, to US-funded repressive governments and occupations—all which disproportionately affect non-white women and children. The logic and practice of militarization is guided by racism and heterosexism. Proponents of war exploit existing racist and sexist ideas to dehumanize civilians and justify their conquest. Civilians are at best seen as weak and racially inferior peoples in need of patriarchal protection, and at worst the "legitimate" targets of violence, often sexual in nature. On a national scale, we witness expanding tax breaks to millionaires and corporations, funding of billions for war, all while critical social services are severely underfunded. The attacks on social services—such as child care, health care, family planning, maternity leave, public education, and housing, to name a few—displace a societal and state responsibility onto the backs of individual women, thus perpetuating the gender division of labor and impoverishing women and their families. Of course, as the characters of Miranda and Magda suggest, not all women have access to the same resources to lessen the blow. To shift responsibility away from the actual policies and institutions that produce inequality, politicians conveniently scapegoat the "degenerate" identities and relationship practices—such as single parenting, non-monogamy, and non-heterosexual unions—of marginalized communities.

The hierarchies that exist between women demonstrate that race, class, and sexuality are equally important in shaping the oppression of women and the patriarchal privileges of men. In short, patriarchy does not equally oppress all women, and not all men equally benefit from sexism. If we fail to recognize this point, we perpetuate the exploitation of marginalized people. In her classic work, *Feminist Theory: From Margin to Center*, bell hooks says, "White women and black men have it both ways. They can act as oppressor or be oppressed. Black men may be victimized by racism, but sexism allows them to act as exploiters and oppressors of women. White women may be victimized by sexism but racism enables them to act as exploiters and oppressors of black people."[11]

And we might add, that heterosexuals of any color can also perpetuate the oppression of queer and trans folks. To avoid reproducing inequality, social movements must affirm the distinct experiences of oppressed peoples and be guided by the experiences, demands, and visions of those communities.

Revolution: A Struggle That Never Goes Out of Style

The liberal feminism that informs *Sex and the City* cannot successfully address the systemic nature of women's oppression because it expands the privileges of elite women at the expense and continued oppression of others. Radical social movements must challenge one of the most unquestioned assumptions of liberal movements: that inclusion into dominant institutions is in and of itself social liberation. Amidst military and prison scandals of systemic rape and torture, not to mention multiple US wars overseas, the inclusion of women, people of color, LGBTQ folks, and undocumented youth into extremely misogynistic, racist, and capitalist institutions, such as corporations, the military, and police, has life and death consequences. As prison abolitionist Angela Davis warns, inclusion into oppressive institutions offers marginalized peoples the "equal opportunity to perpetuate male dominance and racism," and one might add class oppression, imperialism, and environmental destruction, as well.[12]

Our liberation from heteropatriarchy is intimately tied to the struggle to dismantle racism, capitalism, and an authoritarian state. In other words, our movements need to understand and confront how systems of oppression—capitalism, heteropatriarchy, and white supremacy—intersect, and reproduce one another. A social movement that prioritizes one form of oppression over another fails to address the power of hegemony.[13] Simply put, a reductionist analysis fails to address how privilege and oppression are embodied within existing institutions and identities.

Revolutionary praxis, the relationship between theory and practice, can only be developed through our participation in grass roots movements. Through struggle we build consciousness and leadership; we educate ourselves and others; and we pre-figure the world we want to live in. In short, we build people power and a critical mass to restructure power. While we aim to decenter the authority of the state, we need to utilize state institutions in the now to democratize access to vital social services. In specific contexts, electoral strategies might even be appropriate in order to push forth progressive policies. This has certainly been the case with the rise of popular movements and progressive governments in Latin America. However, as popular movements struggle within existing institutions to win necessary reforms that improve people's everyday lives, the institutions that create miserable conditions in the first place must not go unchallenged. In other words, our struggle does not end with the winning of a particular reform, but rather we must confront the sources of oppression.

Fighting oppression is a collective struggle and an ideological and institutional battle. It requires the cultivation of a new form of consciousness that challenges the legitimacy of existing ideas and practices. We have to unlearn our oppressive roles and beliefs, and learn new ways of valuing, respecting, and loving one another. But sustaining new relationships demands new forms of organizing society. The struggle against sexual and gender oppression is an important component of a larger struggle to transform and establish a new society. A liberatory sexuality and society is only possible with the transformation and creation of alternative institutions that are democratic, decentralized, empowering, and participatory. Alternative institutions that embody a different set of values: love, affirmation, consent, respect, justice, autonomy, and solidarity, to name a few. The project of queering anarchism would possibly not only analyze popular culture but would also redefine it and link together struggles against oppression into a holistic vision of systemic change.

Inspired by the pro-democracy revolutions in the Middle East, and armed only with their values and ideas, New Yorkers who occupied Zuccoti Park in the center of Wall Street have presented a radically different vision of "the City." Occupy Wall Street, the anti-foreclosure movement, the opposition to stop-and-frisk policies, and other struggles, which advance the rights of women, immigrants, working families, the homeless, and trans and queer persons, all bring to light that which media, from *Sex and the City* to news rooms, obscure: the stark and growing inequality that makes New York the most unequal state in the United States.[14] Communities that existed on the margins of *Sex and the City*—communities in Harlem, the Bronx, Queens, Brooklyn, and Staten Island—have taken center stage to hold accountable elites who can profit from the majority behind police barricades, banks, or luxury apartments. Popular struggles also present another vision of "sex" where consent is crucial and celebrated; where gender is fluid and non-hierarchical; where women, trans and queer persons, and sex workers can walk the streets free of fear; where men of color are no longer shot and brutalized in the name of upholding "law and order" and allegedly protecting "us" from racialized thugs and predators; where communities have the necessary resources, including time, space, and goods, to live and maintain their culture. The eruption of global protest movements in 2011, from New York and La Paz to Cairo and Tokyo, all demonstrate that an alternative vision of "sex" and "the city" is not only necessary, but possible, and, in the words of Carrie Bradshow, "well, that's just fabulous."

1   Dedicated to my mother, María Eugenia, and to all *las inmigrantes luchadoras*, whose love and struggles have been the basis of my political consciousness. And a special thank you to Kevin Young and friends for their loving support.

2   *The Guardian*, January 29, 2004.

3   Ibid.

4   See Season Three: "Cock-a-Doodle-Do" and Season Four: "What's Sex Got to Do with It?" Also see Susan Zieger's "Sex and the Citizen in *Sex and the City*'s New York," in *Reading Sex and the City*, edited by Kim Akass and Janet McCabe (New York: St. Martin's Press, 2004), 96–111.

5   Quoted in "Sister Carrie Meets Carrie Bradshaw: Exploring Progress, Politics and the Single Woman in Sex and the City Beyond," in *Reading Sex and the City*, edited by Kim Akass and Janet McCabe (New York: St. Martins Press, 2004), 85.

6   See "Beyond Same Sex Marriage," http://www.beyondmarriage.org/full_statement.html (accessed January 25, 2012).

7   "Nuclear family" often refers to a family composed of man, woman, and children, in which each person conforms to the gender assigned to them at birth. However, the term can also describe relationships of dominance, in which there exists a descending hierarchy: male patriarch, wife, and two dependent children. However, that is not to suggest that families whose members do not reflect nuclear families are inevitably immune to unequal relationships, and in severe cases, domestic violence.

8   "Time and Punishment."

9   "FAQS: What Do You Mean by White Privilege?" http://www.timwise.org/f-a-q-s/ (accessed June 2011).

10 See "Home Is Where the Work Is: Inside New York's Domestic Work Industry," *Domestic Workers United and Datacenter*, July 14, 2006, http://www.domesticworkersunited.org/media/files/266/home-iswheretheworkis.pdf (accessed January 26, 2011). For the wealth divides between women of different race and classes, see Julie Hollar, "Wealth Gap Yawns—and So Do Media: Little Interest in Study of

Massive Race/Gender Disparities," *Extra!* (June 2010), http://www.fair.org/index.php?page=4078. (accessed January 25, 2012).

11 bell hooks, *Feminist Theory: From Margin to Center* (Cambridge, MA: South End Press, 1984), 17.

12 Angela Davis, *Abolition Democracy: Beyond Empire, Prisons, and Torture* (New York: Seven Stories Press, 2005), 66.

13 See Michael Albert, Leslie Cagan, Noam Chomsky, Robin Hahnel, Mel King, Lydia Sargent, and Holy Sklar, *Liberating Theory* (Cambridge: South End Press, 1986).

14 Manhattan is the most unequal county in the most unequal state in the United States. If New York City were a country, its wealth distribution would be on par with Honduras. "Empire State of Inequality: New York's Growing Wealth Divide," *Center for Working Families*, http://www.cwfny.org/wordpress/wp-content/uploads/2011/04/Empire-State-of-Inequality.pdf.

Queering Our Analysis of Sex Work: Laying Capitalism Bare

C. B. DARING

Sex work" is a broad term that encompasses an unimaginably large group of people engaging in diverse labor. For the purposes of this article, the term "sex work" will be used to examine individuals receiving benefit or support from the trading of sex acts. Reproductive labor (housework, child-rearing, etc.) has been argued to be a part of the sex industry; however it is not deeply explored in this piece. Stephanie Grohmann addresses reproductive labor in another article in this collection. This purpose of this piece is not to be a focused argument, so much as it is an exploration of queering an analysis of sex work.

We must include sex work in an anarchist analysis because so often sex work has been treated as an exception to the rule. Every other aspect of labor and social experience has found itself under the anarchist magnifying glass, leaving the issue of sex work to be fought over by feminists, the religious community, and the nongovernmental organization complex. Organizing alongside sex workers cannot simply be an afterthought or a subject too tough to engage. To queer our analysis of sex work, we must move beyond a paternalistic reaction to the thought of sex acts for sale and engage in organizing with sex workers globally. Sex work is a unique intersection between sex and labor, existing entirely neither in the personal nor political realm.

The interconnectedness between economics and society within capitalism is complex. How can we argue that one form of sex is actually outside of capitalism's control? Are sex workers more subservient to capitalism than house-spouses, or any sexual encounter? It's a dangerous path to tread to assume some are more influenced by capitalism than others.[1] Sex is not necessarily "freely" had when money is absent. Patriarchy is pervasive; and while some manifestations may be more visible, they are not necessarily more oppressive. Social structures reflect the dominant narrative of the culture within which they exist. The nuclear family, for example, perpetuates capitalism. Sex work is considered by many to be a primary threat to the nuclear family.

There are generally two major theoretical strains fighting for prostitution abolition. One stems from the religious right seeing sex work as a threat to modesty, chastity, and the moral fabric of society. They are fighting to preserve a heterosexual nuclear family while upholding a firmly heterosexist structure. A queer analysis allows us to envision the sex industry as something other than a threat to marriage and modern fidelity. The anarchist lens allows us to view sex work as something that does not exist within a vacuum, but another sector of capitalist industry.

The second opposition strain tends to originate on the left, but borrows plenty from conservative perspectives. This objection sees sex work as a threat to the overall freedom of women by explicitly putting a price on sex. This assumption also manifests as seeing poor people incapable of immediate agency, unable to consent to sex work because of their economic context.

We will examine both of these strains and their overall effect on the sexual and economic freedom of all people. As a queer, anarchist-communist sex worker, I wish to assist in moving the conversation and action forward without leaving any of my praxis behind. Both the right and left objections to sex work focus the argument about its effect explicitly on women, while either willfully or ignorantly ignoring the experiences of queer people and men.

This article is not intended to explore or argue for the viability of the exchange of sex for other services in a post-revolutionary context. Any form of alienated labor is incompatible within an anarchist-communist society. However, the struggle for the empowerment and self-representation of sex workers does not preclude the fight to end involuntary labor.

I have no intention of speaking for anyone else or their experiences in the industry, but rather to explore what we can learn from this labor. Sex workers must be allowed and supported as individuals to define their own narrative, and not pimped by either the right or the left to further a political agenda.

Scarcity Sexuality and Sacred Sexuality

The underlying tendency to see human sexuality as the most sacred, intrinsic aspect of ourselves is expressed often when speaking of sex work. It is assumed that our genders and sexuality are intrinsically born into us, rather than something that is nurtured and influenced. With these assumptions, a sex act alienated from us as labor becomes a grave infraction against what it means to be a human. There are two aspects to this—to perform a sex act for money somehow diminishes the overall value of our sexuality (considering it a nonrenewable resource) and that other forms of labor alienation aren't really as violent as what is perceived to exist for sex workers. There is a vast difference between a sex act and an individual's sexuality.

The idea that there is a hierarchy of alienation, with sex work ranking as one of the highest, is untrue. This false dichotomy is created by liberal criticisms of capitalism rather than an analysis of anti-capitalism. The implication is that certain alienation is essentially worse than other forms of alienation, that there could be a more *humane* form of alienation and exploitation. A similar mistake is often made to justify small and local businesses as less exploitative or capitalistic, when in fact the volume of a business does not determine if it is capitalistic or not. It is the model of surplus value and labor exploitation that defines a capitalist structure. Creating these hierarchies of alienation is problematic because it drastically alters our ability to discuss labor in any substantive way.

Within capitalism, commodities are affected by the concept of scarcity. In this case, human sexuality is subject to the actual and fabricated ebbs and flows of resources and the overall demand for them. Sexuality is not something that is scarce in the world, and trading sex acts does not suddenly make it true. If scarcity of sex were true, the simple act of having more sex would reduce the overall amount available. It wouldn't matter if sex were sold, simply had for fun, obligation, or pleasure. Scarcity is a myth of capitalism used to manipulate our sense of need toward an object or resource.

Sacred sexuality is the idea that our sexuality is intrinsically connected to something greater than ourselves. This implies the sexual act includes something, or someone, more than the one, two, three, four or more individuals present in body. The most common examples would be a deity or religious figure. Sacred sexuality is a tool used to shame or manipulate people about the sex they have. Sex is this context cannot simply be acts between consenting people but instead an ideal open to moral scrutiny.

This moral scrutiny is ceaselessly subjective and globally reflects a myriad of different social norms. Sacred sexuality is a tool for sexual control hidden under the guise of sexual preservation. Sacred sexuality also greatly contributes to an idealized woman (chaste and heterosexual). This vision of women is ever present in the debate around sex work.

Scarcity sexuality and sacred sexuality are interrelated, as they both serve to control people's bodies. Both of these concepts justify regulation (social and governmental) for a perceived greater good. These regulations may often appear to target only sex workers, but they extend much further.

We should not be surprised that conservative perspectives embrace protecting intimate femininity, but when it happens within the radical left it illustrates a glaring theoretical gap. This is problematic because it perpetuates the fallacy that a woman's (or anyone's really) worth is bound up in their sexuality and capacity for sex. Sex workers are not demeaning themselves on a basic human level anymore than the rest of the working class.

Focusing an argument exclusively on regulating women perceived as straight disregards that significant portions of those working within the sex industry are queer folks, trans folks, and men (of course not mutually exclusive). Women face a unique experience within the industry at the intersection of commerce and patriarchy. However, many other people experience intersectional oppressions within the industry. The narrative that non-trans[2] women have a nearly identical experience to each other, but incomparable to other sex workers, demonstrates a specific agenda by those that peddle it.

Many prostitution abolitionists argue that all those involved in the sex industry were forced to do so by pimps, live in slavery-like conditions, are addicted to drugs, and are riddled with STIs. While sensationally this is appealing, it is not an effective way to view a large group of workers. Statistics on entry into sex work are incredibly hard to come by and tend to be swayed by those that collected them. However, there is fair amount of evidence that pimping (at least in the United States) is not particularly prevalent.[3] Sex workers are not so easily generalized, and while a variety of abuses happen in the sex industry, they are not unique to this industry. The idea that women globally cannot choose to work in the sex industry, but they can choose some other industry within capitalism, is offensive and condescending. It is as if their engagement in the sex industry illustrates some flaw or weakness.

Sex workers are not revolutionary in their labor, but neither are they a threat to the fabric of society. Sex work is another form of exploited labor within capitalism; what makes it unique is what we can learn from seeing how labor is alienated. This process is intimate, but capitalism has mystified it within other sectors.

Choice and Capitalism

Anarchism precludes the belief that there cannot be a more humane form of capitalism. It is fundamentally in opposition to the concept that we can regulate an economic system based on ever-expanding profit and oppression. If we take this as a given, it is necessary to elevate our analysis of sex work.

I have been asked countless times why I chose the sex industry. I answer that I no more chose sex work than I chose retail, tourism or food service. We all have a spectrum of limited options to *choose* from; why does the sex industry imply a personal identity to its workers? The implication is that some labor choices are more political than others.

Another common questions is, "how could someone choose sex work if there were ample options of *meaningful* work?" The reality is that for the working class there are not ample options *of* meaningful work. Seemingly meaningful work may very well be code for non-alienated labor. With a solid analysis of capitalism the term "meaningful work" has no basis within the current capitalism economy. Choice within capitalism is an illusion. These choices are only substantive in that one *may* be able to choose what brand of labor exploitation they prefer. For the vast majority of the working class even that "choice" is nonexistent. It is never an option to choose not to be exploited.

The labor exchange of sex work is no different than that of any other industry. However, the way in which it is presented treats it as uniquely violent.[4] Sex work exposes a significant contradiction within capitalism—we trade the labor in our bodies for a wage while simultaneously supporting the creation of surplus value for the overall economy. This does not mean that it is more intimate than labor alienation in other sectors, but rather it is one of the most transparent. Money exchanged is based on a perceived value of those individuals' services and the value of the benefits for the purchaser.

Sex work illustrates how a capitalist economy values labor and determines the value of the laborers themselves. Workers are only worth the amount that they produce within capitalism. It is this visibility that strips the mysticism of capitalism away.

The State and Sex Workers

Western conceptions of compulsory monogamy propel the idea that a two-person exclusive partnership is the "human universal." Anything that moves individuals away from a two-person monogamous partnership is considered unnatural. This could be applied to either a person providing sexual services or their partner visiting a provider of sexual services. As anarchists we should certainly be able to reject the idea of this "human universal" and clearly see who benefits from the nuclear family. The nuclear family is not the accidental result of urbanization and industrialization, but rather the most efficient way to reproduce labor(ers) and profit.

There is no state that imposes no regulation on the sex industry. State regulation follows the false wisdom that it is for the sex workers' own good. This is not to say that a completely unregulated market favors workers' rights or autonomy, but rather that these regulations must come from the workers themselves. The presumption seems to be that sex workers have no conception of what is good or safe for themselves. A prime example in the United States is the legalized prostitution in Nevada. If prostitutes choose to work at one of the legal brothels, they are required to stay on the compound unless accompanied by a chaperon. They undergo mandatory testing once a month, but if they are off the compound for more than twenty-four hours, they must submit to testing before returning to work. While sex workers spearheaded the movement for mandatory condom use in Nevada, they are still not given access to regulatory advisory board.[5]

What does the state have to gain from the regulation and criminalization of sex work? Regulation justifies further surveillance of poor people, people of color, and queer people (of course these are not mutually exclusive), who are the majority of sex workers globally. The criminalization of the sex industry continues to rationalize incredible violations of human rights around the world, all in the name of protecting sex workers. Many sex workers are placed in rehabilitation camps where they are subjected to sexual assault and beatings by guards and staff.[6] Incarceration seems to be the global universal in the "rehabilitation" of sex workers, for those classified as "voluntary" or "forced" sex workers.

The dichotomy of "forced" vs. "voluntary" sex work is highlighted in most regulation. Providing social and health services for those that are regarded as forced is given tantamount funding and support. However, it is almost impossible to find funding and support for "voluntary" sex workers. In particular the US will not fund any program that they consider to condone prostitution. There is no evidence that regulation is for sex workers' best interests. Regulation serves the purpose of furthering the divide between sex workers and ultimately impedes self-organizing.

Reproductive labor—the labor that is done to produce new laborers and that allows wage earners to continue to work every day—is built into the state apparatus, particularly the unpaid labor of home workers. This labor includes the rearing of children, cooking of meals, and housework, but it also includes the sexual reproduction of the (often male) wage earner within a household. Sexual reproduction—not limited to child producing—remains invisible as labor, but is implicit in the structure.

Sex work fundamentally upsets this balance by requiring money be exchanged for a finite amount of time, as opposed to a housewife (or unwaged home worker) who exchanges unlimited labor for an infinite amount of time without wage. The state relies on this unwaged reproductive labor in order to maintain civil order and the continuation of the nuclear family. Requiring a specific monetary exchange for sexual reproduction socially undermines the concept that it is available without reciprocation, that the sexual availability of women may not be a given.

It has been argued that sex work sets a social precedent that the sexuality of women is always available if the price is right. However, sex work actually undermines the idea women are available for free, or that the purpose of women is labor reproduction. This is dangerous to the state apparatus because it shows the direct benefit to be reaped from free reproductive labor. Having children, reproducing the primary wage earner, and even sex may be done naturally, but these things are work. When the left gets into bed with abolitionists, these are the unintended consequences—the furthering of patriarchy through upholding the nuclear family.

Queer Intersections and Sex Worker Intersections

A queer analysis of sex work frees us from the constraints of viewing it as a threat to marriage and workforce reproduction. This is certainly not meant to imply that fidelity is not important within a queer analysis, but sex work does not threaten an *institution of fidelity*. A queer analysis of sex work allows us to view sex in an unconventional way, where sex is not essentially degrading, private, or for love.

There is huge overlap between sex workers and queer folks. In particular, trans-folks (often ignored by governments, NGOs, and industry abolitionists) make up a tremendous population in the sex industry. Female prostitutes that service male clients are not strictly heterosexual. Many identify as lesbians, bisexual, or queer. Male escorts may service male clients, but may regulate to female partners outside of work. The gender and sexual identity of sex workers is not necessarily reflected by the clients they have.

This fluidity between personal and professional sexuality reflects a certain queerness to the sex industry that may not often be apparent. It is important to remember the difference between what is marketed and what is the reality for those on the inside. This performance may not be reflective of the individual sex worker, but rather a promotion tactic to attract clients.

Socially, both queer folks and sex workers face similar stigma—the people they sleep with determine their entire identity. This is the assumption that gender and sexuality are intrinsic and fundamental, that they are static rather than transitory. As seen in the dominant treatment of other marginalized groups, the defining differences become the rational for exclusion, violence, and discrimination.

Queer, trans, and people of color in the sex industry disproportionately experience violence at the hands of the state and clients.[7] Compounded intersecting oppressions are only drawn in starker contrast by the stigma around sex work. Ultimately it is the stigma that sex workers face that is unique—not the nature of their work.

Organizing with Sex Workers

The goal of organizing with sex workers should be to increase empowerment and self-representation. For many sex workers it is a huge risk to speak publicly for fear of exposure to clients, police, and family. Do not assume that sex workers do not wish to speak for themselves. There are avenues that can limit dangerous exposure.

It is still very controversial to organize with sex workers, especially if the goal is not to get them out of the industry. A movement to improve conditions in the sex industry cannot originate from those that prioritize eliminating the industry over the autonomy of the workers themselves. There is a growing movement of sex workers acting publicly to better conditions within the industry.

In a Western context, sex workers' rights are connected to other prominent anarchist projects, specifically around gentrification, anti-racism, anti-police brutality, and queer rights. Don't assume you know people's history; you may already know plenty of sex workers. Due to the stigma so often attached to this sector of industry, many folks may never disclose (nor feel compelled to) if they have worked in the sex industry.

Individual sex workers should not be expected to be accountable for the discomfort of others' disagreement with the sex industry. Sex workers are often the most vocal about the problems within the industry, and are intimately familiar with possible solutions and strategies. It is a myth that sex workers are the primary apologists for the industry. When the criticisms come from non-sex workers, it should not be surprising that those currently or formerly in the industry may react defensively. It has been our livelihood and regardless of our negative experiences, they are still *our* experiences.

It has been said that there is no room within anarchism for sex work, that to fight for improvement in the industry will only extend its life. There is no room in post-revolutionary society for any alienated labor. That does not mean that we can simply discount the industries we find problematic now. It's all of us or none of us.

Conclusion

We do not live in a world so easily divided by participation or withdrawal from capitalism. Our experiences are intersectional and intertwined. There is no essential sex worker experience, just as there is no essential queer experience. As anarchists and radicals we can begin to critically examine the common intersections. Those who sell sex directly for goods and services are not more entrenched in capitalism than those who sell their labor behind a restaurant counter or in a factory. This is obscured by capitalism in order to maintain a systematic ideal of freedom, sex, and economics. Capitalism's oppression of workers is threatened by the naked truth shown by sex work.

We must not be satiated by these false ideas of freedom and imagined choice. We must continue to push a radical analysis when examining gender and sexuality and reject the convenient moral fallbacks that have plagued the left. Moral fortitudes that limit real freedom serve no greater good. To queer our analysis we must not be satisfied with comfortable or quiet expression, but instead continue to fight loudly for inclusion and self-representation. Not only with the usual suspects, but also with those so often rendered invisible.

1   This is not to imply that certain individuals or groups don't experience relative privilege or disadvantage under capitalism, but rather that *all* members of the working class are subject to labor exploitation.

2   I am using the term "non-trans" in substitution for cisgendered in this piece consciously.

3   "Lost Boys," *Village Voice*, http://www.villagevoice.com/2011-11-02/news/lost-boys/ (accessed January 15, 2012).

4   Capitalism is a system of violence; labor alienation is an act of violence.

5   "Resisting the Sex Panic: Sex Workers Struggle for Evidence-Based Regulation in Nevada," RH Reality Check, http://www.rhreality-check.org/blog/2009/02/10/resisting-sex-panic-sex-workers-struggle-evidencebased-regulation-nevada (accessed January 8, 2012).

6   "Rehabilitation Cuts No Ice with India's Sex Workers," TrustLaw, http://www.trust.org/trustlaw/blogs/the-word-on-women/rehabilitation-cuts-no-ice-with-indias-sex-workers (accessed December 14, 2011).

7   "Stigma and Violence against Transgender Sex Workers," RH Reality Check, http://www.rhrealitycheck.org/blog/2010/12/16/stigma-exclusion-violence-against-trans-workers (accessed December 14, 2011).

Tearing Down the Walls: Queerness, Anarchism and the Prison Industrial Complex

JASON LYDON

With anarchy, the society as a whole not only maintains itself at an equal expense to all, but progresses in a creative process unhindered by any class, caste or party.
—Kuwasi Balagoon[1]

Kuwasi Balagoon was a revolutionary New Afrikan anarchist, closeted queer, freedom fighter who died in prison of AIDS-related illness on December 13, 1986, when I was nearly four years old. His story and struggle is an essential reminder to queer communities that if we do not step up the fight against white supremacy, capitalism, heteropatriarchy, and the prison industrial complex then stories of our revolutionary ancestors will go untold and our capacity to create an intersectional movement for today will be minimal. This essay works to bring together the interlocking aspects of the movements for queer liberation, abolition of the prison industrial complex, and anarchism.

It is vital to have a common understanding of language to most effectively have a conversation that is movement building. The prison industrial complex is a multifaceted construction of control and domination, most commonly seen as the US prison and jail system, the concrete and steel buildings that warehouse individuals. While prisons and jails are a pivotal aspect, the prison industrial complex includes an entire culture of state and corporate collusion to control, discipline, and torture poor/low-income communities and communities of color. The tactics range from police forces to cameras mounted in communities; from the (in)justice system to corporate profiteering off prison phone-calls; from immigration enforcement to media depictions of "criminals," and so on. The prison industrial complex builds its strength from the myth that it is solving the problems of "crime" and "violence."

Marilyn Buck, a white anti-racist revolutionary political prisoner, speaks of prison as "a relationship with an abuser who controls your every move, keeps you locked in the house. There's the ever-present threat of violence or further repression, if you don't toe the line."[2] While Buck is specifically referring to her experience within a particular prison, the metaphor of an abusive relationship is significant when one considers the prison industrial complex as the abuser and marginalized communities as the survivor. The Network/La Red, a lesbian, bisexual, gay, transgender, and queer domestic violence organization based in Boston, Massachusetts, defines partner abuse as "a systematic pattern of control where one person tries to control the thoughts, beliefs, and/or actions of their partner, someone they are dating or someone they had an intimate relationship with."[3] The prison industrial complex is this ever-present force in the daily lives of those most marginalized in our society, continuously constricting the borders of what is considered right, legal, and appropriate while constantly limiting access to loved ones and support structures.

Throughout this essay I will use the terms "racism" and "white supremacy" interchangeably. Racism is commonly understood, now, as a combination of institutional power and prejudice that creates systems to privilege white people at the expense of people of color. Ruth Wilson Gilmore defines racism in *Golden Gulag: Prisons, Surplus, Crisis and Opposition in Globalizing California* as, "the state-sanctioned and/or extralegal production and exploitation of group-differentiated vulnerability to premature death. Prison expansion is a new iteration of this theme."[4] White supremacy is one of the foundational building blocks of the US prison system. In order to understand the complexity of the penal system in the United States one must also understand the complexity of white supremacy. Andrea Smith offers a framework for understanding these deep complexities in the "Three Pillars of White Supremacy." This framework does not assume that racism and white supremacy are enacted in a singular fashion; rather, white supremacy is constituted by separate and distinct, but still interrelated, logics. Envision three pillars, one labeled Slavery/Capitalism, another labeled Genocide/Capitalism, and the last one labeled Orientalism/War, as well as arrows connecting each of the pillars together.[5] The prison industrial complex has the capacity to operate within each of these pillars of white supremacy, creating intraracial struggles and perpetuating divisions.

Queerness is challenging to fit into a box of definition; in some ways that is one of its strengths; in other ways it complicates the conversation. Other writers in this anthology will more aptly divulge the multitude of queer theories open to interpretation. For the purpose of this essay, I look at queerness as not only the identity of those violently targeted by the prison industrial complex, but also as a sexual/political/social tool for deconstructing the borders of power. Queerness is not only about fiercer sex, truer gender expression, and theoretical masturbation; it has the potential to expand the possibilities available to intersectional movements for liberation.

Abolition of the prison industrial complex is not some ridiculous pipe dream, but rather what queer theorist José Esteban Muñoz would call a concrete utopia. Muñoz suggests, "Concrete utopias...are the hopes of a collective, an emergent group, or even the solitary oddball who is the one who dreams for many. Concrete utopias are the realm of educated hope."[6] Conceptions of abolition come out of communities most impacted by the prison industrial complex and are told through stories of survival; in mediocre to amazing prisoner poetry; within resistance chants outside of police stations; and through the actions of thieves, sex-workers, saboteurs, and others considered criminal by the state.

Abolition is not only the goal of eliminating all forms of state control, corporate profit of exploited labor, police surveillance, and destruction of prison walls, but also the strategy for getting us there. Abolition and anarchism hold the same strategies and goals of collective liberation and community autonomy. As Peggy Kornegger writes, "[T]o separate the process from the goals of revolution is to insure the perpetuation of oppressive structure and style."[7] As mainstream/assimilationist gay and lesbian organizations push for the passage of hate crimes legislation, such as the Matthew Shepard Act, they directly perpetuate the power of the prison industrial complex by relying on its violence while stating that they wish to protect our communities from hateful attacks and murder. Anarchists and abolitionists together have a responsibility to publicly oppose these types of legislation and must offer concrete alternatives that authentically strive to make our communities safer from interpersonal violence as well as systemic violence. Mainstream gay and lesbian organizations have a tendency to exploit our sadness, pain, and suffering after losing people we love and care about to give rise to their campaigns for hate crimes legislation. Organizations such as the Sylvia Rivera Law Project, Communities United Against Violence, Audre Lorde Project, and multiple chapters of INCITE! Women of Color Against Violence have all actively supported survivors of violence while also opposing hate crimes legislation, work that must be understood as part of our anarchist and abolitionist struggle.

The need to consistently challenge GLBT/queer groups' involvement with the prison industrial complex is not new work for our movements. Kuwasi Balagoon wrote on May 31, 1983, "When a gay group protests lack of police protection, by making an alliance with police to form a gay task force, they ain't making a stand against the system they are joining it."[8] Many police forces in major cities around the United States have "gay and lesbian community liaison" and pride marches often have some kind of gay police force fraternity parading along with corporations next to drag queens and community organizations. These types of hypocrisy are exactly why anarchism and abolition are needed at queer celebrations and in queer movements.

When it is operating at its best, anarchism is tearing down the borders of nation states, smashing the borders of capitalist control, and transgressing all borders of oppression and authoritarianism. When queer(ness) is operating at its best it is tearing down the borders of gender, smashing the confines of compulsory monogamy, and transgressing the moralism of sex and sexuality. When abolition is at its best it is tearing down the prison walls, smashing the police state, and transgressing the power of punishment while instituting new forms of transformative justice. I recognize that all of this destruction and abolition can appear to be placed strictly in the negative and oppositional—without a positive vision for society. However, all of this border destruction and wall crumbling provides a beautiful opportunity for creativity and new visions that are already being articulated and acted upon throughout the world. Not only is abolition a concrete utopia, queer(ness) and anarchism flourish in the growing space. And yet we understand that this concrete utopia has not yet arrived. INCITE! Women of Color Against Violence and Critical Resistance wrote a much-needed critique and demand of the abolitionist movement: do not pretend we have already reached some utopian community alternative that is actually supporting survivors of violence and be sure to actually create and facilitate alternatives to the prison industrial complex that keep people safe and accountable for the suffering and trauma that exists and is perpetuated on the left and throughout the entirety of our culture.[9] I think it is when queerness, abolition, and anarchism are in relationship with each other that we have the greatest creative power to actually create a project and culture that celebrates the possibilities of our humanness.

How do we move forward? It takes more than articles, hand holding, or hand jobs to build these relationships and to create effective strategies for winning. When strategizing to abolish the prison industrial complex, many more voices are needed at the table. Transgender women of color, working-class faggots, and anarchist dykes, who are all directly targeted by police surveillance and criminalization of their lives, need to be prioritized as experts on the violence of the prison industrial complex. The policing of public sex must get on the agenda of abolitionists. The pervasiveness of sexual violence in prison and the particular targeting of queer and transgender people need to be addressed with community programs and group therapy or processing opportunities in anarchist spaces. Many anarchists need to reconsider their repulsion of identity politics and learn some of their history. Alexander Berkman's *Prison Memoirs of an Anarchist* was "one of the most important political texts dealing with homosexuality to have been written by an American before the 1950s."[10] However, while reading Berkman anarchists should be critical of his "gay" sex-negativity/fear and question how his own internalized homophobia impacted his understanding of his own same-gender sexual desires. Queer organizations need to be more vocal in opposition to hate crimes legislation and look at models of community accountability programs and see what can meet the needs of their organizing efforts. These same groups should also host self-defense classes. In Boston, Queers with Guns takes a group of queers to a shooting range to learn how to shoot handguns, revolvers, and assault weapons. There need to be more groups that are actually protecting queer and transgender people. The Audre Lorde Project has developed the Safe Outside the System project that works to address community issues without relying on the police. These projects must not be isolated and they need to communicate with other queer organizations to foster growth and development of even more programs like these in many other communities and cities.

Strategizing must be both long-term and short-term. Any good strategy is shaped by history. Stories must be told and articles must be read about the Out of Control Lesbian Committee to Support Women Political Prisoners, which was founded in 1986 for the purpose of resisting the Lexington Control Unit for women in Kentucky. Stories must be told about the Pink Panthers, who established themselves in multiple cities around the United States to defend queer and transgender people who were on the streets, living or walking home. Queers need to learn about Men Against Sexism in Walla Walla prison, the George Jackson Brigade, and other 1960s and 1970s revolutionary queer movements and campaigns. As Mumia Abu-Jamal continues to be locked behind the walls, we need to remember the role queers have played in his support campaigns, especially Rainbow Flags for Mumia. The actions of ACT UP, including their creative political confrontations and advocacy for compassionate release for prisoners living with HIV/AIDS, must be shared while picking each other up on the dance floor. We need to hear these stories and tell these stories to our lovers, friends, and anyone who will be our comrades in our growing movements. We need to listen for the explicit anarchist aspects and the implicit anarchist forms of organizing. In our experience of inspiration we have the potential to continue living in the hope for our struggles to succeed. When we tell our history, it is given new life as it breathes new life into us.

Support for queer and transgender people who are in prison or being attacked by other arms of the prison industrial complex is not only something of the past. In Montreal the Prisoner Correspondence Project connects queer and transgender prisoners with "free world" people for pen pal friendships, and their website acts as an extensive resource for "free-world" pen pals. The Transgender, Gender Variant and Intersex Justice Project in San Francisco, headed up by Miss Major, works to support transgender, gender variant, and intersex people who are incarcerated in California prisons and beyond. TGIJP also works with people as they get out of prison and is run by formerly incarcerated transgender women, specifically transgender women of color. They were among a large coordinating effort that brought together Transforming Justice, a conference and ongoing national project that works to bring attention to the impact the prison industrial complex has on transgender people, particularly transgender people of color and low-income/poor transgender people. Chicago has the Write to Win Collective which is a "penpal project for transgender, transsexual, queer, gender self-determining, and gender-variant people who are living and surviving inside Illinois prisons."[11]

In Boston I am part of the outside leadership circle of Black and Pink; there is also a leadership circle of currently incarcerated people. We produce a monthly newsletter of queer and transgender prisoner-written stories, political articles, and poetry that we send to approximately 1,300 queer and transgender prisoners. We also maintain a list of incarcerated people looking for pen pals that is available on the Black and Pink website. As we continue to grow, we are able to do more direct support for prisoners, community outreach, and trainings about the impact of the prison industrial complex on queer communities. Our statement of purpose describes our work, "Black & Pink is an open family of LGBTQ prisoners and 'free world' allies who support each other. Our work toward the abolition of the prison industrial complex is rooted in the experience of currently and formerly incarcerated people. We are outraged by the specific violence of the prison industrial complex against LGBTQ people, and respond through advocacy, education, direct service, and organizing." We chose to call ourselves a family after all the letters we received writing to us as their Black and Pink family, so often the families queer and trans people come from can be so harmful and we have the potential to help queer the notion of family and provide real care and attention too often denied.

Black and Pink and all of these other projects have anarchist leanings, if they are not explicitly anarchist. They are all abolitionist projects and strive to be accountable to those most impacted by the violence of the prison industrial complex. New history of queer involvement in abolition and anarchism is being created daily.

More projects and new strategies are always needed. Cop Watch is a strategy used in multiple cities that has a strong anarchist analysis and abolitionist approach. There are multiple Cop Watch groups around the United States–Chicago, Portland, the Bay Area, and New York City have the strongest and most successful Cop Watch organizations. Massachusetts has a functional Cop Watch in western Massachusetts and a sporadic chapter in Boston. The Portland Cop Watch list their goals as: "To empower victims of police misconduct to pursue their grievances, with the goal of resolving individual cases and preventing future occurrences; to educate the general public and, in particular, 'target groups' of police abuse on their rights and responsibilities; and to promote and monitor an effective system for civilian oversight of police."[12] Cop Watches regularly patrol the streets and monitor police activity with video cameras and still photo cameras as a form of deterrence of police brutality and to document any misconduct that does occur. Cop Watch is completely legal and can provide a vital organizing tool in communities most impacted by policing. During the New York City Gay Pride march a coalition of queer people of color organizations formed a Cop Watch Patrol because of the long history of police targeting queers of color during the parade and the lack of support by parade organizers and mainstream gay and lesbian organizations. The Boston Cop Watch did outreach in "the Fens," a highly policed public sex spot. Queers and queer analyses are needed within Cop Watch groups to best serve the needs of highly policed queer and transgender people.

Another strategy for organizing is called the attrition model, "the rubbing away or wearing down by friction...the *persistent* and *continuing* strategy necessary to diminish the function and power of prisons in our society."[13] This strategy specifically targets the prison and incarceration aspects of the prison industrial complex. It begins with moratorium on all prison, jail, detention center growth, development, research, and building. The moratorium process forces the government and corporations to examine alternatives to incarcerating people. Moratoriums have a measurable impact in prohibiting the further development of the physical confinement institutions of the prison industrial complex. While we fight for a moratorium on all expansion of the punishment industry, the next step in the strategy is decarceration. Decarceration is the struggle to get as many people as possible out of prison. While the strategy of a neo-underground railroad should certainly be attempted and advocated for, the repercussions for those caught will certainly be severe. Other strategies include "a prisoner release timeline: at least 80 percent immediately; 15 percent gradually; the remaining 5 percent within ten years."[14] To accomplish that, first, eighty percent of all prisoners convicted of nonviolent offenses should be released. Next, we should ensure the compassionate release of all prisoners with terminal diseases, all prisoners over the age of 65, all prisoners convicted of sex work, all prisoners convicted of killing/injuring their abusive partners, and all prisoners who have served ten years or more on a sentence. Certainly all of these individuals getting out of prison will need support structures to acclimate into society. Programs to serve formerly incarcerated people will need to be individualized. In 2006, $68,747,203,000 was spent on corrections. "The average annual operating cost per state inmate in 2001 was $22,650, or $62.05 per day; among facilities operated by the Federal Bureau of Prisons, it was $22,632 per inmate, or $62.01 per day."[15] If the United States is able to spend that amount on incarcerating people every year, then it should be able to spend half that amount to care for people in their process of returning to society with money that should be given directly to community-based organizations, not state-controlled programs.

The next step in the struggle for abolition is excarceration, the act of *not* putting people in prison. This is where the transformative justice practices come in. Decriminalization must also be included in this process. In the United States one in thirty-one adults are either on probation, parole, or incarcerated.[16] Tactics to excarcerate include, "Abolish categories of crime. Start by decriminalizing crimes without victims; abolish bail and pretrial detention [let people out]; create community dispute and mediation centers; utilize suspended sentences, fines and restitution; establish community probation; and create legislative standards and procedures for alternative sentencing."[17] These are by no means exhaustive lists of possibilities, but rather a spotlight on particular strategies as suggested by abolitionists. At all levels there is a need for a queer and anarchist analysis in order to keep the goal, our concrete utopia, at the forefront of the organizing. It is far too easy for liberals to co-opt abolitionist campaigns; queer anarchists have a vital role to play in holding everyone accountable to the larger vision.

As we tear down the walls of the prison industrial complex, let us continue to build and create revolutionary communities at the same time. These communities will be anarcha/o queer spaces that affirm the great potentiality of our humanness. We must live the alternatives even as we work to deconstruct the systems that we are forced to operate within. As we are queering anarchism and queering the abolitionist movement, we will find ourselves in spaces where we have to address the problem of sexual violence within our communities. We will have to address concerns about the continued forms of oppression that we perpetuate. With attentiveness to our complexities as human beings we will be able to truly engage one another in movement building as we bring together the intersections of movements and tactics that too often exist within their own spaces. The walls and borders we must tear down are not only those belonging to the state or to capitalism but also those that keep our movements from working together and informing one another. Our potential is in our capacity to fight oppression on all of its fronts, and these queer anarchist abolitionist tools are going to be needed if we intend to win.

1   Kuwasi Balagoon, *A Soldier's Story* (Montreal: Kersplebedeb Publishing, 2003), 75.

2   Joy James, *The New Abolitionists: (Neo)Slave Narratives and Contemporary Prison Writings* (New York: State University of New York Press, 2005), 262.

3   The Network/La Red, "What Is Partner Abuse," http://www.thenetworklared.org/partnerabuse.htm (accessed May 28, 2010).

4   Ruth Wilson Gilmore, *Golden Gulag: Prisons, Surplus, Crisis, and Opposition in Globalizing California* (Berkeley: University of California Press, 2007), 247.

5   Andrea Smith, "Heteropatriarchy and the Three Pillars of White Supremacy," in *Color of Violence Anthology*, edited by Incite! Women of Color Against Violence (Cambridge: South End Press, 2006), 67

6   José Esteban Muñoz, *Cruising Utopia: The Then and There of Queer Futurity* (New York: NYU Press, 2009), 3.

7   Peggy Kornegger, "Anarchism: The Feminist Connection," in *Reinventing Anarchy, Again*, edited by Howard J. Ehrlich (San Francisco: AK Press, 1996), 156.

8   Kuwasi Balagoon, *A Soldier's Story*, 105.

9   See "Critical Resistance—Incite! Statement on Gender Violence and the Prison Industrial Complex," in *Color of Violence Anthology*, edited by Incite! Women of Color Against Violence (Cambridge: South End Press, 2006).

10 Terence Kissack, *Free Comrades: Anarchism and Homosexuality in the*

United States, 1895–1917 (San Francisco: AK Press, 2008), 102.

11 The Write to Win Collective, http://writetowin.wordpress.com/about/ (accessed June 3, 2010).

12 "About Portland Copwatch (PCW)," http://www.portlandcopwatch.org/whois.html#Goals (accessed May 22, 2010).

13 Prison Research Education Action Project, *Instead of Prisons: A Handbook for Abolitionists* (Boston: PREAP, 1976), 62.

14 Ibid., 63.

15 Bureau of Justice Statistics, "Inmate Expenditures," http://bjs.ojp.usdoj.gov/index.cfm?ty=tp&tid=16 (accessed June 2, 2010).

16 Pew Foundation, "1 in 31 U.S. Adults are Behind Bars, on Parole or Probation," http://www.pewcenteronthestates.org/news_room_detail.aspx?id=49398#factsheets (accessed May 18, 2010).

17 PREAP, *Instead of Prisons*, 63.

Queer-Cripping Anarchism: Intersections and Reflections on Anarchism, Queerness, and Dis-ability

LIAT BEN-MOSHE, ANTHONY J. NOCELLA, II, AND A.J. WITHERS

Introduction

Anarchism, like feminism, is not a monolithic field; it has many branches, articulations and frames of thought. However, a few tenets can be identified that are shared by most anarchist thought and practice. These include opposition to any socio-political, economic, or religious hierarchy, domination, and authoritarianism, and support for decentralization and emphasis on freedom and autonomy. Some anarchists also have strong opposition to vanguardism, and challenge the intellectual and experiential elitism that is entrenched in academia and in some collectives because of their claim to authority. Throughout this chapter we aim to demonstrate the relation of disability, as formulated by critical disability studies frameworks,[1] or disability pedagogy rooted in critical pedagogy,[2] to these and other tenants of anarchist thought and practice. We will therefore queer-crip anarchism by providing an analysis that takes disability critically as its analytical tool and asks what would a just queer-crip world look like.

Queerness and dis/ability

The history of an oppressive medical model for homosexuality and disability and the threat of eugenic extermination (by selective abortion, isolations of genes for specific disabilities or a "gay" gene) offer additional areas of potential common ground between queer activism and disability activism.[3] The tools of such activism have been quite similar as well, as both queer and disabled activists often use anger, humor, and parody as tools for social change.[4] Another activist connection is a strong debate among activists in both communities of the impetus to assimilate, as opposed to creating their own identity, vocabulary, and ("safe"/accessible) spaces.[5]

Ableism and heteronormativity are both oppressive ideologies and cultural constructs that hinder the full potential of realizing the scope of human sexuality and modes of being in the world. Ableism is the idea that disability is not just a form of difference, but is an inferior trait, a deficit, an undesirable entity. An ableist society is one that constructs itself (in infrastructure such as buildings, curricula, media representations) as if disability does not exist, is repugnant, or needs to be modified in order to fit in the existing order. Heteronormative societies, similarly, structure themselves as if heterosexuality is not only preferred, but indeed the only mode of living, desiring, and being with others. It is important to emphasize that ableism and heteronormativity are not just analogous but also intersecting. Not realizing how they work as interlocking oppressions would deny the lived reality of disabled queers who feel marginalized, at times in both communities. One explanation for the exclusion of disability from queer theory and existence, as well as the lack of any effective coalition politics, could be the similar history of medicalization. Queer theory takes back a negative term and articulates gender as a social construction, while understanding the complexity of individual sexual desires. Science and the medical world identified those who are gay or lesbian as disabled and as having a smaller brain, and attempted to prove this through eugenics and other pseudoscientific theories.

The historical conceptualization of homosexuality as pathological led to an attempt to normalize it, largely beginning in the 1960s. In 1965, one prominent mainstream gay rights activist, Frank Kameny, said "the entire homophile movement...is going to stand or fall" on the issue of the medicalization of homosexuality.[6] The lengthy campaign to remove homosexuality as a psychiatric illness was finally successful in 1973, with homosexuality being removed from the Diagnostic and Statistical Manual of Mental Disorders. Many LGBTQ folks today may want to distance themselves from any community that has been medicalized in similar ways, in order to cut off the historical ties to notions of pathology and abnormality.[7] This process has been well described by Baynton, who demonstrates how, throughout history, disability has been used not only as a justification for excluding disabled people but also to exclude other marginal groups (people of color, immigrants) by attributing disability to them.[8] The marked groups usually do not question the assumption that underpin disability as inferior, but instead try to distance themselves from the disability label, by scientific means if possible.

This resistance to allying queer communities with disabled ones is not only cumbersome to the realization of shared ideals and coalition politics, but it is also detrimental to the lives of disabled queers. Because disabled people are perceived as asexual and/or sexually inferior to nondisabled (except in fetishized communities, like amputee-devotee or dwarf fetish), being queer may seem like a logical step, since being gay is also regarded as an inferior sexual form by heterosexual people and heteronormative cultures.[9]

Not only are the lived experiences of queerness and disability parallel, but their theorizations are as well; disability studies and queer theory can be regarded as critical and liberating discourses. Critical of the social constructions of heteronormativity and normalcy, the 4 "D"s of disability criminology—demonizing, delinquency, deviance, and dissent[10]—similarly critique how these labels stigmatize marginalized groups, including queers and those with disabilities.

Queer-cripping

Of course, queerness and disability are not just similar, as identities and theories, but also are inextricably interconnected. Queer theory's subject of interrogation has been the compulsory nature of heteronormativity. Scholars in disability studies, such as Robert McRuer[11] and Lennard Davis,[12] suggest that disability studies should be "normalcy studies" instead. McRuer's crip theory's aim is to "continuously invoke, in order to further the crisis, the inadequate resolutions that compulsory heterosexuality and compulsory able bodiedness offer us."[13] "Crip" is used here as a reclaimed word (used both as a verb and as an identity of those who embody it) that resists the negative connotations of disability that have been bestowed upon it by an abelist culture.

Crip theory, McRuer argues, will "draw attention to critically queer, severely disabled possibilities in order to bring to the fore the crip actors who…will exacerbate in more productive ways, the crisis of authority that currently besets heterosexual/able-bodied norms."[14] By "severely disabled" McRuer is not referring to the level of impairment a person is presumed to have, but rather as a queer position. By reclaiming "severe" as "fierce" or "defiant," McRuer reverses able-bodied standards that view severe disabilities as ones that will never be integrated to the circuit (the adage of "everyone should be included, except for…"). From their marginal state, "severe disabilities" and queer subjects are positioned to re-enter the margins and point to the inadequacies of straight and nondisabled assumptions.

McRuer not only claims that the norms and the subjects they produce are connected or interlocking, but also they are dependent on each other. Each normative framework cannot function, i.e., is disabled, without the other. Compulsory heterosexuality only operates as it does because of presumed able-bodiedness of its subjects, and vice versa. For instance, heterosexuality is not assumed for disabled/crip folks as they are often perceived as asexual. In the same token, queerness is perceived as a disability from a heteronormative framework. Such an analysis goes beyond understanding the connections between queerness and disability as identities (i.e., the lived experience of queer crips) in a move that both de-essentializes these identities (as "queering" and "cripping" are used as verbs, not mere identities) and tries to grapple with their full existence, materially and imaginarily.

Carrie Sandahl further suggests that "both queering and cripping expose the arbitrary delineation between normal and defective and the negative social ramifications of attempts to homogenize humanity"—hence the term "queercrip" or "queercripping."[15] Both "queer" and "crip" open up areas for conversation and imagination that are closed off by the cultural imperialism of the idea of normalcy. According to Robert McRuer and Abby Wilkerson, "a queercrip consciousness is about desiring more, about developing and defending public cultures in which we do not necessarily 'stand' united. …A queercrip consciousness resists containment and imagines other, more inventive, expansive, and just communities."[16] Because queercrips cannot live in the world as is, a queer-crip consciousness imagines a new world order.

At its very core, disability destabilizes identity and escapes any neat categorizations. Disability is fluid and contextual rather than biological. This does not mean that biology does not play out on our minds and bodies, but that the definition of disability is imposed upon certain kinds of minds and bodies. Those of you who are reading this chapter with your glasses on perhaps do not identify with disability (or crip) culture, but you would be quite disabled without your visual aids. It is also a truism that we will all experience some kind of disability if we live long enough. But more than that, disability, if understood as constructed through historical and cultural processes, should be seen not as a binary but as a continuum. One is always dis/abled in relation to the context in which one is put. A person has a learning disability if put in a scholarly setting; using a wheelchair becomes a disability and a disadvantage when the environment is inaccessible; someone who wears glasses may be disabled without them when attempting to read written language or see far away, but this can change depending on the context that they are seeing and being seen within. The definition of dis/ability shifts depending on what the needs of those at the top of hierarchical structures dictate. The state commonly defines disability loosely when that definition is used to marginalize people, and more rigidly when it is used to determine access to resources.[17]

As a fluid state, disability, much like queerness, should be perceived as a normal state of affairs. Imagining the world through a crip-queer lens then, aids in challenges to forms of hierarchy and domination by challenging the very idea of normalcy. A queer-cripped anarchism would resist the hierarchies that permit the imposition of disabled identities on minds and bodies that are considered deviant as an integral component to resisting domination and achieving autonomy. This differs from Marxist thought, which is centered more on resistance to exploitation and appropriation.

Construction of Normalcy

Normalcy is a relatively new concept, which arose as part of the modernity project in 1800–1850 in western Europe and its North American colonized spaces. The word "normal" did not enter the English language until around 1840.[18] Prior to the concept of normalcy there was the concept of the ideal (and its corollary—the grotesque). In Roman-Greek culture it was understood that everyone falls beneath this standard. The ideal was perceived as unachievable and imperfection was on a continuum (like a Greek statue). Imperfection was seen as being on various degrees from the ideal and was not penalized as such.[19]

In the nineteenth century the concept of the norm entered European culture, as related to the concept of the average. Normalcy began with the creation of measurements and statistics. Qualities are represented on a bell curve, and the extremes of the curve are abnormal. Statistics were created as state tools (hence their etymology as state-istics) with the advent of modernity, as "political arithmetic."[20] It is hard to imagine that before 1820, political bodies did not make decisions solely based on crime, poverty, birth, death, and unemployment rates.[21] This new form of governance is what Foucault characterized as biopolitics, the newfound ability to measure performances of individuals and groups that makes them governable.

Davis states that there is a difference between normalcy and normality, in which normality is the actual state of being normal or being regarded as normal, and normalcy is the structural realm that controls and normalized bodies.[22] It is the ideology behind normality. This ideology is embedded with bourgeois (and of course white heterosexual and male) norms, in which the middle class is seen as the "mean." "This ideology," claims Davis, "can be seen as developing the kind of science that would then justify the notions of the norm."[23] These norms also centered on the body and its performance.

The key argument Davis makes is that ableism and normalization are not unusual practices that we must denounce but are part of the modernist project by definition (the creation of modern nation-states, democracy, measurement and science, capitalism). There are several paradoxes associated with modernism: representational democracy vs. individual representation, capitalism vs. equality, etc. Normalcy as an ideology seemingly resolves these conflicts. In regards to wealth—on a curve it is clear that not all can be wealthy. Some have to be in the margins of the curve for capitalism to be sustained. Equality under these parameters is not morally or ethically defined, but rather scientifically. So, many people fight for equality, but what we should be fighting for is diversity and respect of differences.

The concept of the norm, unlike the ideal, implies that the majority of the population must somehow be around the mean. Everyone has to work hard to conform to norms but people with disabilities, and other marginalized groups, are scapegoated for not being able to fit these standards, while in fact they are needed to create these standards and maintain them. There is a need for people at the margin, but they are punished for being placed there. As an example for such punitive ideology, Davis analyzes the interesting fact that almost all the early statisticians (Galton, Pearson, and others) were also known eugenicists. It is not surprising perhaps since the notion of the norm and the average divided the populace into standard and substandard populations. Difference is thus projected onto stigmatized populations so all others can strive for the illusive normalcy.

Disability is not based on a binary, but a multinary. It is an understanding that all are different. Queer-cripping is thus a premier lens through which to fight against normalcy, average, standardization, and conformity. Queer-cripping, as an analytical lens as well as a lived experience, can offer insights into the ways historical and cultural formations, such as labor, productivity, and dependence, can be interrogated. It offers a radical critique of work, as a practice and a concept, which goes well beyond labor politics. Global capitalism is forcing us to become as efficient as possible. Marx and subsequent traditions identified people based on class rather than other particular identities such as race, gender, sex, age, ability, etc., and were only interested in the concept of class struggle and no other modes of power beyond an economic influence. An anarchist framework that centers on the rejection of domination will do well by going beyond a class based analysis into an interrogation of all forms of power that subjugate us and simultaneously separate us from each other.

Queer-Crip Resistance to Capitalism

Capitalist ideology creates and reproduces a disciplinary world in which people conform to a particular hegemonic set of values and patterns of thought. "Shallow equality" (as contrasted with "radical equality" as identified by Ben-Moshe, Hill, Nocella, and Templer[24]), normality, and being "average" seem so ingrained that most people take them as neutral terms that have always guided our ways of living and thinking, and as a taken-for-granted way of creating social hierarchies.

Under a neo-Marxist analysis, disability is an ideology upon which the capitalist system rests. A disability ideology can regulate and control the unequal distribution of surplus by invoking biological difference as the "natural" cause of inequality.[25] Charlton sees disabled people as surplus population,[26] those who don't even serve as part of what Marx termed the "reserve army of labor," a resource tapped into during economic expansion or crisis. They are essentially the underclass. The definition of unemployment itself historically excludes disabled people, undocumented immigrants, retired people (who often wish to work), and women (who do unpaid labor). One strategy used by post-industrial nations to maintain certain rates of unemployment is to categorize people to be clients of the human service industry, such as therapists, social workers, nurses, case managers, paid assistants, evaluators, special educators, etc., and thus to keep them out of the labor force (by creating and maintaining the jobs of service providers at the same time).

Work is central to industrial societies, not only as means of obtaining life's necessities, but also to establish certain kind or relations with others.[27] Industrialization not only posed a problem for disabled people to participate in the work force (which now required greater speed, stamina, and rigid production norms), but also excluded disability as a culture. Disabled people had increasingly found themselves marginalized within segregated settings such as institutions and "special" education.[28] Disabled people mark, with their different bodies and minds, the boundaries of normalcy. They serve as an ideological reminder of the fate of those who do not participate in the capitalist production. The notion of disability is so intertwined with perceived inability to work that if a person is able to work, they cannot be regarded as disabled (according to Social Security, for instance).

All societies function through principles that distribute goods and services amongst the entire population. Stone argues that in capitalist societies the major mechanism of distribution is work done, but that not all are willing or able to work.[29] Therefore a second distributive mechanism is established, which is based on need. With the rise of capitalism, disability became the category through which people are measured as need-based or work-based. Such analyses, which emphasize a political economy lens, dispel the common belief that people with disabilities are not productive under the capitalist system, since they do not hold jobs. Many (including policy makers) believe that disabled people are a strain on the economy, especially under neoliberal ideology. But political economists argue that disability supports a whole industry of professionals that keeps the economy afloat, such as service providers, case managers, medical professionals, health care specialists, etc. The human service industry and health care professionals have to keep people in need of their services, and keep them dependent upon these services.

Beginning in the 1980s, "health-care consumer" became interchangeable with "consumer." Nancy Tomes argues that the use of the term "consumer" is a "violation" and it imposes "the base language of the marketplace to the sacred realm of the doctor-patient relationship."[30] According to Tomes, patients initiated the use of the consumer language in the 1960s and 1970s because they viewed it as "a liberating alternative to the traditional doctor-patient relationship they believed to be hopelessly mired in paternalism."[31]

The adoption of the term "consumer" has, however, not eliminated medical paternalism. The concept of disabled people as consumers (mental health consumer, Consumer Advocacy and Advisory Committee for Persons with Disabilities, etc.) remains predominant. With respect to disability organizations self-labeling as consumer organizations, this is generally done to have business and industry recognize disabled people as an important market. The name and the organizational approach exclude many poor disabled people who do not have the funds to *vote with their dollars*. It is highly problematic to call individuals who are forced into "treatment" by the state "consumers." Many psychiatrized people are forced to take medication, undergo electroshock "therapy," or to reside in institutions. For many, forced psychiatric treatment is not a service that people consume; it is a violation of their autonomy and it is abuse.

DeJong,[32] who is known as one of the formulators of the independent living movement, accused that movement of being entrenched in ideals of "radical consumerism," as they relate to people with disabilities. The movement is deeply wedded to capitalist ideals such as self-reliance, political freedom, and consumer sovereignty. In the same vein as critics heard in the LGBT movement, from self-identified queers for instance, the conceptualization of the "movement" as consumer-driven is beneficial to a small section of its constituency—mainly middle-class white American men.

A Hope for an Inter/dependent Collaborative Mutual Aid

This article, written by three authors, is disability anarchism in action, stressing interdependency on assisting each other on editing, concepts, theory, and writing. Collaboration is interdependency in action, while the concept of mutual aid is more of a macro-socio-political and economic system to build community and relationships. Mutual aid is a core tenet of anarchism. Much of the anarchist tradition rejects the ideology of individualism and focuses on mutual aid, or, in queer-crip language, interdependence.

Within some anarchist communities mutual aid has been put into practice specifically to support their disabled members. In Toronto, where A.J. lives and participates in care collectives both as a recipient and a supporter, a number of care collectives have been established to support disabled people. The longest running of these collectives has been operating for about six years and has provided three to four half-hour to hour-long shifts a day. None of these shifts are paid and none of them were established out of charity. They were created and continue to function with the acknowledgement of the contributions that the disabled people make to community and the desire to build mutual support.

The notion of radical access as proposed by some disabled activists also calls on the ideas of mutual aid. Griffin Epstein explains that "access means paying attention to the actual needs of actual people, keeping in mind histories and legacies of oppression."[33] Radical access calls for a collective negotiation of needs within communities (including sign language interpretation, attendant care, physical barriers, emotional support, financial support, child care, etc.) as well as fundamental social changes that would lead to the fair and just distribution of resources.

If disability studies and activism could offer a corrective to the anarchist practice of mutual reliance, it will be to the concept of DIY, including anarcho-primivitism, which is DIY culture taken to an extreme. There seems to be a growing literature, especially in what has become to be called "green anarchism," which focuses on self-reliance and a "return to nature." This politic requires a non-disabled body for its ideal society. Chellis Glendinning writes of "lean hunter-gatherer women" who endure "strenuous demands of walking long distances while carrying equipment, mounds of plant food, and children—physical conditions that are reproduced among today's female athletes."[34] Such calls will have devastating effects on the lives of disabled people who truly embody a spirit of mutual aid everyday by relying on personal assistants, friends, and family members to achieve independence and autonomy, which are also core practices of anarchism. Through a queer-crip lens we should perhaps focus more on DIT—do it together. The focus on independence, we would argue, is an adoption of capitalist values. Capitalism asserts an ideology of independence and emphasizes relationships and interactions for which there are economic transactions. This ideology, however, is a lie as all of us are interdependent and rely on each other not only for our food, shelter, and clothing, but also for our emotional, physical, and intellectual needs. Shifting focus from DIY to DIT reasserts our collectivity and interdependence and rejects the focus on rugged individualism, a value that negates many people's needs for care.

Enabling Politics

Engaging in prefigurative politics in relation to a queer-crip existence entails (re)thinking inclusivity. The knee-jerk types of anarchist organizing and activism are often quite exclusive spaces and enterprises. For instance, many radical conferences and actions lack attention to basic accessibility such as interpreters, note-takers, and accessible bathrooms and entranceways. For example, one Anarchist Bookfair in Toronto was held up a long narrow flight of stairs. The argument for it being inaccessible was that it had to be in an "anarchist friendly space"; their definition of anarchist friendly excluded people who could not scale a flight of stairs. It is also becoming a kind of ironic truism that whenever there is resistance, there is a march. Although a march or an organized protest may yield some visibility to the cause and create solidarity amongst its participants, it is also a quite exclusionary resistance strategy for many disabled activists. As such it can be as polarizing as it is galvanizing around a particular issue.

Queer-cripping political organizing requires recognition of the intersectionality of marginalized identities and a shift toward coalitional politics and inclusive strategies and tactics. An example is the anti-G20 organizing in Toronto in 2010. As the organizing for the protests got under way, an accessibility strategy was implemented that required every aspect of the organizing to make things as accessible as possible and to report on progress to the broader organization. It worked to supply attendant care, accessible housing, and accessible transportation throughout the days of protest.[35]

In conclusion, social justice cannot be achieved without proper representation by and inclusion of queer/disabled communities, but the contributions of a queer-crip analysis and queer-crip communities are not solely about inclusion. Queer-crip perspectives work to push anarchist politics forward in directions that anarchism has failed to go historically. Queercripping anarchism works to fill some of the gaps of anarchist history, to address its omissions, and to undo its ableist assumptions. We recognize that the work in transforming anarchism is and will continue to be slow. However, for those of us concerned with social justice, it is our responsibility to do this work.

1 A. J. Withers, "Defining Disability," (2009). From *If I Can't Dance Is It Still My Revolution?*, http://still.my.revolution.tao.ca (accessed May 2, 2010).

2 See A. J. Nocella, II, "Emergence of disability pedagogy," *Journal for Critical Education Policy Studies* (6)(2) (2008).

3 See Mark Sherry, "Overlaps and Contradictions Between Queer Theory and Disability Studies," *Disability and Society* (19)(7) (2004); and Ellen Samuels, "My Body, My Closet: Invisible Disability and the Limits of Coming-Out Discourse," *GLQ: A Journal of Lesbian and Gay Studies* (9) (1–2), 233–255.

4 See Sherry, "Overlaps and Contradictions."

5 Ibid.

6 Franklin E. Kameny, "Civil Liberties: A Progress Report," New York Mattachine Newsletter, July, 1965, http://www.rainbowhistory.org/kameny75b.pdf (accessed April 2, 2010), 12.

7 See D. Atkins and K Marston, "Creating Accessible Queer Community," *Journal of Gay, Lesbian and Bisexual Identity* (4)(1) (1999).

8 See Douglas Baynton, "Disability and the Justification of Inequality in American History," in *The New Disability History: American Perspectives* edited by P. Longmore and L. Umansky, (New York: University Press, 2001).

9 See Atkins and Marston, "Creating."

10 See A. J. Nocella, II, "Anarcho-Disability Criminology," in *Anarchist Criminology*, edited by J. Ferrell, A. Brisman, and A. J. Nocella, II, (Forthcoming).

11 Robert McRuer, *Crip Theory: Cultural Signs of Queerness and Disability* (New York: NYU Press, 2006).

12 Lennard Davis, "The Rule of Normalcy: Politics and Disability in the

U.S.A. [United States of Ability]." In *Bending Over Backwards: Disability, Dismodernism, and Other Difficult Positions* edited by L. Davis. (New York: New York University Press).

13 McRuer, *Crip Theory*, 31.

14 Ibid.

15 Carrie Sandahal, "Queering the Crip or Crippling the Queer?: Intersections of Queer and Crip Identities in Solo Autobiographical Performance," *GLQ: A Journal of Lesbian and Gay Studies* (9) (2003), 25–56.

16 Robert McRuer and Abby L. Wilkerson, ed., "Desiring Disability: Queer Theory Meets Disability Studies," *GLQ: A Journal of Lesbian and Gay Studies* (9) (2003), 7.

17 A. J. Withers, "Definitions and Divisions: Naming Disability," PsychOut: A Conference for Organizing Critical Resistance against Psychiatry, May 7, 2010, OISE, University of Toronto, Toronto, Ontario.

18 See L. J. Davis, *Enforcing Normalcy: Disability, Deafness, and the Body* (London and New York: Verso, 1995); and R. Reiser, "Disability Equality: Confronting the Oppression of the Past," in *Education, Equality and Human Rights* edited by M. Cole, (London: Routledge, 2006).

19 Davis, *Enforcing Normalcy*.

20 T. M. Porter, *Trust in Numbers: The Pursuit of Objectivity in Science and Public Life* (Princeton: Princeton University Press, 1995).

21 Ibid.

22 See L. Davis, "The Rule of Normalcy: Politics and Disability in the U.S.A. [United States of Ability]," in *Bending over Backwards: Disability, Dismodernism, and Other Difficult Positions*, edited by L. Davis, (New York: New York University Press, 2002).

23 Davis, *Enforcing Normalcy*, 27.

24 L. Ben-Moshe, D. Hill, A. J. Nocella II, and B. Templer, "Dis-Abling Capitalism and an Anarchism of 'Radical Equality' in Resistance to Ideologies of Normalcy," in *Contemporary Anarchist Studies*, edited by Randall Amster, Abraham DeLeon, Luis Fernandez, Anthony J. Nocella, II, and Deric Shannon (NYC, New York: Routledge Press, 2009).

25 See N. Erevelles, "Disability and the Dialectics of Difference," *Disability and Society* (11)(4) (1996); Marta Russell, *Beyond Ramps: Disability at the End of the Social Contract: A Warning from an Uppity Crip*

(Monroe, Me.: Common Courage Press, 1998); Marta Russell, "The New Reserve Army of Labor?" *Review of Radical Political Economics* (33) (2) (2001): 224–234; and D. Stone, *The Disabled State* (Philadelphia: Temple University Press, 1984).

26　See James Charlton, *Nothing About Us Without Us: Disability Oppression and Empowerment* (Berkeley, CA: University of California Press, 2000).

27　See Mike Oliver, *The Politics of Disablement* (London: Macmillan, 1991).

28　Ibid.

29　See Stone, *The Disabled State*.

30　Nancy Tomes, "Patients or Health-Care Consumers?: Why the History of Contested Terms Matters," in *History and Health Policy in the United States: Putting the Past Back in*, edited by Rosemary Stevens, Charles E. Rosenberg, and Lawton R. Burns (New Brunswick, NJ: Rutgers University Press, 2006), 83.

31　Ibid.

32　Quoted in Barnes "The Social Model of Disability: A Sociological Phenomenon Ignored by Sociologists?" in *The Disability Reader: Social Science Perspectives*, edited by Tom Shakespeare (London: Cassell Publishing, 1998).

33　Griffin Epstein, "Extension: Towards a Genealogical Accountability (The Critical [E]Race[ing] of Mad Jewish Identity," Master's Thesis, University of Toronto, 2009), 7.

34　Chellis Glendinning, "A Lesson in Earth Civics," http://www.eco-action.org/dt/civics.html (accessed February 10, 2012).

35　Toronto Community Mobilization Network, "Accessibility Policy," http://g20.torontomobilize.org/accessibility (accessed June 25, 2010).

Straightness Must Be Destroyed

SAFFO PAPANTONOPOULOU

It's a Body!

A baby is born. The doctor slaps a gender onto the body—"it's a boy!" or "it's a girl!" For those whose bodies do not seem to fit easily into the categories "male" or "female," the doctor—almost invariably—will treat this as a medical emergency. The parents will be intimidated into forcing invasive surgery: mutilating the baby's genitalia so they will appear to fit easily into these categories. For all bodies regardless, the category "it's a boy!" or "it's a girl!" must be applied onto the baby. From the very moment of birth, our bodies fit into a social system in which there are two genders, built upon the myth that the two sexes are "natural." Our heteronormative society considers it urgent that every*body* be labeled "boy" or "girl"—to the point that it will not shy away from using violence against intersex bodies in order to apply these labels.

For some reason, the vast majority of people identify with the gender label that was applied to them at birth without their consent. (This majority of people we call "cisgender." The rest of us are transgender, genderqueer, gender-nonconforming, etc.). But then again, the vast majority of people seem to be content to go along with most things. After this we grow up and we learn all sorts of other roles that stem from the label "boy" or "girl." This label determines everything from what sort of toys we are supposed to play with, to what sorts of expectations are to be placed upon us in social situations, to what kind of sexual desires we are supposed to have. We cannot escape these assumptions; they are everywhere. Daring to transgress these norms can result in violent punishment. These norms, and the threats that back them up, are all a part of straightness.

Straightness is not an orientation, or even really an identity, but a system of social relations. In that regard, straightness is very much like capitalism. Straightness is a multifaceted set of social rules that police our bodies, our minds, our desires, and the ways we interact with others. Straightness tells us that people with certain bodies have to be "men" and others have to be "women." It tells us that men have to act in certain ways, and women have to act in other ways. It tells us that we have to have certain kinds of desires, and not others. It tells us that we have to fuck certain kinds of people, in certain positions, for certain reasons. We can change certain aspects of straightness—for instance, the fight for gay marriage, which seeks to allow privileges for certain monogamous, normative gay couples, without challenging the state institution of marriage altogether—but ultimately we need to destroy this system that polices every aspect of our existence—from the deeply intimate to the highly public.

Like any system of social relations, straightness is both something that is "out there," in the larger world we call "society," or "the system," as well as something that is "inside"—in our heads, our hearts, our minds. It is something that we do to other people as we have had done to ourselves. For people who call themselves straight, it is something that one is constantly proving and reifying. Part of this is because straightness is an impossibility. The ideal man and the ideal woman—these are impossible ideals. Nobody ever quite fits. Part of straightness as a social system is the collective effort of those who subscribe to force themselves and others around them to meet this definition—to kill the inner queer in order to fit oneself into the straight mold. These are the internal contradictions of straightness.

The destruction of straightness would not mean the destruction of heterosexuality. "Women" and "men" would still exist. "Women" and "men" would still fuck each other. The destruction of straightness, however, would mean the destruction of a set of norms, of assumptions, of hierarchical social relations that are forcibly imposed upon all of us. The destruction of straightness would mean we no longer take it as self-evident that being born with a certain kind of body makes someone a "man" or a "woman." The destruction of straightness would mean we no longer take it as self-evident that people with certain bodies will desire certain types of other bodies. The destruction of straightness would mean the destruction of the "ideal" woman and the "ideal" man. The destruction of straightness would mean a world in which all of our bodies, all of our desires, all of our genders, all of our consensual sexualities, would be honored and viable.

Queering Shit Up

Queerness is, by definition, the antithesis of straightness. Queerness is the total of every desire, every body, every way of relating, that is prohibited by straightness. Queerness includes gender nonconformity, transness, homoeroticism, BDSM, or even the radical notion that two hetero men who are friends can hold hands in public. Queerness is everything that straightness is not. Queerness is every desire, every way of being, that is forbidden under this regime. Queer liberation seeks to liberate all these forms of expression—as long as they are consensual. Queer liberation is the destruction of straightness. Queer liberation is the abolition of gender hierarchies, as well as hierarchies based on sexual desire. Straightness, by contrast, *is* hierarchy. Part of anarchist struggle is to create spaces outside of these hierarchies within the shadows of this world. Therefore, the destruction of straightness (and the building of alternatives within its shadows) is *inseparable* from anarchist revolution.

There are people in my life who are predominantly heterosexual, who identify with the gender they were assigned at birth, who live in monogamous relationships, but whom I would consider queer. What do I mean by this? There is a world of difference between those who have accepted the dominant order of things because that is what they have been told and they have never questioned it, and those who have actually challenged themselves. If you have searched within your soul and challenged yourself and come to the conclusion that you feel yourself to be the gender you were assigned at birth, that you are sexually attracted to people of the "opposite" gender, etc., then that is completely different from someone who calls themselves "straight" because they have never challenged the social norms of straightness. Not questioning these norms—within yourself and your relationships with others around you—is to play into the dominant order of straightness. Questioning them—regardless of the conclusions you may reach—is a revolutionary act.

Straightness Doesn't Make Any Sense:
The Internal Contradictions

I want to look at a few concrete examples of how straightness functions in our society. I want to preface this with the recognition that there is tremendous diversity across cultures in terms of gender and sexual norms. In case you were wondering about my own background, I am a queer, transgender, thirdgender anarchist. My family is Greek-Egyptian and my mother was a war refugee. I was born in the United States. I write this based on my own experience of being queer in the United States, and I do not mean to generalize this across all cultures. However, I hope and I believe that these ideas will prove relevant in a variety of contexts. All of these examples are imagined as taking place in the United States, but could perhaps be translated and transformed to represent gender and sexual regimes in other cultures and other contexts.

A working-class, heterosexual, cisgender man wants to marry his girlfriend. His girlfriend is a heterosexual, cisgender woman who comes from a middle-class background, but is currently broke. She feels entitled to a very expensive diamond engagement ring. He feels slightly jilted by this—"why should I have to pay for something so expensive for *her*," he thinks. She feels hurt by this and feels that he doesn't love her enough. They get into a fight about it. Finally, he takes out loans and maxes out all his credit cards to buy her the ring. The money that he borrows from the credit card industry—and which will cause him to be enslaved in debt for years to come in order to pay back—goes to support the blood diamond trade in southern, central, and western Africa. There, people have been massacred, societies torn to shreds, to fuel Westerners' hunger for shiny objects.

This is one way in which straightness as a system of social relations feeds into and is fed by capitalism—particularly capitalist economic (neo)colonialism and its quest to ravage the people and the lands of the global south. Both members of the couple are oppressed and wounded by a set of social norms—which exists outside the two of them—which has dictated the right and wrong ways for them to express their feelings for each other. She feels entitled to a diamond and feels hurt if he doesn't provide. He is expected to provide and feels his masculinity called into question if he doesn't. Finally, he ends up enslaved in debt to the banks and credit card companies that make tremendous profit off the two of them. Their straightness is integral to a capitalist set of social relations that is built off of environmental destruction and genocide against people in the global south, while feeding them into an institution of debt slavery.

Two straight-identified, cisgender men are best friends and feel a deep love for each other. They go out of their way to express this affection for each other without challenging their privilege as straight men—subconsciously creating excuses to touch each other. Fortunately for them, there are a plethora of such forms of expression available in straight society—wrestling, for instance. Straight society is full of supposedly desexualized excuses for two male bodies to touch. But the two of them will never simply hold each other. We can see, it is not simply a matter of them being straight people—we are looking beyond straightness as an identity—rather, straightness is an internalized set of social relations that dictates the acceptable and unacceptable ways in which the two of them may physically interact. Wrestling, moshing, various form of hazing, and real physical violence…these are all contexts through which the internal contradictions of straightness may be literally hammered out.

A cisgender man identifies as straight, and is very homophobic. He meets a woman he is attracted to and they go somewhere to have sex. In the process, he finds that she has male genitalia. He flips out and reacts violently against her. This is a fear that many trans women, such as her, must constantly deal with. He beats her and calls her "it" and "faggot" and other dehumanizing things. All the mean time, in the back of his mind, he is really trying to beat back a part of himself—a part of himself that maybe knew she was trans and sought her out, a part of himself that he is very uncomfortable with. She has been made into a target from the outset—first as a target for his frustrated desires, second as a target for his fears of himself as a result of those desires. Her marginalized status—as a woman in general, and as a trans woman in particular—allows him to dehumanize her and use her as a vessel to project everything that he despises about himself—everything about *him* that does not match *his* own internalized straightness—onto her. She is an escape hatch for the internal contradictions of straightness—and she may be killed for it.

A young cisgender boy first learns about anarchism by going to punk shows. He feels naïve but doesn't want to show it. He hears from his friends about how "real" punks and "real" anarchists do things—it's all tremendously macho. He feels pressured to perform a certain form of anarchism because he feels his masculinity threatened if he doesn't. Some older (straight, cis male) anarchists pressure him to take part in an action involving property destruction. He doesn't totally feel comfortable doing it, but feels the need to prove himself, and prove his straight masculinity. He gets arrested and it turns out that the older anarchists who pressured him were government agents who set him up. They took advantage of his vulnerability—particularly his need to perform a certain type of anarchist straight masculinity—in order to entrap him. He ends up spending a long time in prison. Regardless of the forms of desire this young person may feel, queer liberation for him would have meant having the strength to be vulnerable—the strength to say no, and not be masculinity-baited by the cops. The irony is that this form of straight masculinity is an enormous vulnerability for straight males—and those who associate with them. In other words, straightness is a threat to security culture.[1]

Various forms of queerness exist inside everyone. People who identify as straight are people who have, to varying degrees, suppressed this queerness. But that doesn't mean it doesn't pop up sometimes. These are the contradictions of straightness. The ways in which straight-identified people police their own straightness and then (sometimes violently) project that woundedness onto others (particularly queer and trans people) are all forms of violence (both psychological and physical) that are inherent to the social institution that is straightness. This straightness predominantly and primarily oppresses queer people—for instance the woman who was subjected to transphobic violence. But it also confines straight people. It forces straight people to take out loans to assimilate to a particular model for showing affection. It forces straight people to kill a little part of them—sometimes endangering themselves and those around them. This struggle to abolish straightness is a struggle that plays out within anarchist and anti-capitalist communities as well as in capitalist society at large.

Queer Liberation Is for Everyone: Queering Anarchism

What does this all mean? For one thing, if you are scratching your head now and wondering if there is such a thing as a straight person anymore—good. If your concept of normal is feeling a little less secure—good. Everyone is, in some way or another, alienated, confined, or oppressed by rigid gender roles and sexual mores. In other words, the moral of this story is not just that straightness must be destroyed but also that *queer liberation is for everyone*. There are certainly people with a great deal of *straight privilege*; we can't forget about that. But what matters the most is, do you act in a way that reinforces straightness as an oppressive social institution? (For example, do you make gender assumptions about people, assume people are heterosexual, make insensitive assumptions about peoples' pronoun preferences, judge people whom you view as gender nonconforming, etc.?) If you challenge the ways you have internalized straight forms of social relations, and listen to people with less straight privilege than you, then you will become, in a ways, less straight. You will become part of the solution—creating a better world for queer and trans folks and queer experiences of gender and sexuality within the shadows of this world.

When we talk about queerness as something separate from identity, something beyond just queer *people*, we see it as a set of desires, relationships, ways of being, ways of acting, and forms of gender and sexuality that are violently repressed, through various means, by straightness. In other words, it is straightness that insists all bodies must be either male or female. It is straightness that dictates those whose bodies don't fit the binary model of sex/gender must be mutilated at birth. It is straightness that says male-bodied people must identify as "men" and act as "men." It is straightness that says female-bodied people must identify as "women" and act as "women." It is straightness that confines us to certain limited numbers of acceptable ways to express our desires. Everyone who dares to defy these prescriptions, and all the desires we feel that fall outside of them—this is queerness.

Those of us who live the most visibly outside of these straight norms are often subjected to violence. Trans women, drag queens, and effeminate gay men along with bull dykes and trans men, are the most common target of straight men's projecting of their own traumas around gender and sexuality. Straight people, especially straight men, as the people with the most privilege in our society when it comes to gender and sexuality, have an obligation, as part of an anarchist movement, to unlearn their own gender and sexual assumptions. All of us have an obligation to unlearn straightness—to unlearn the ways we have been socialized into straightness, much like the ways in which we have been socialized into capitalism.

There is an old Situationist slogan that calls to "Kill the Cop Inside Your Head." Killing your inner cop means abolishing capitalist ways of thinking, abolishing the messages the state has fed us and we have internalized. This is a hard, painful process, and it is never fully complete. Part of killing your inner cop and dismantling internalized hierarchies is deconstructing forms of oppression you have internalized: class society, racism/white supremacy, patriarchy, ableism, ageism. All of these forms of oppression are part of systematic hierarchies we internalize. Everyone who is an anarchist and wants to work to create better worlds needs to work on all of these struggles within themselves as part of a larger anti-capitalist, anti-statist struggle. Part of killing the cop inside our head means addressing internalized straightness.

The struggle for liberation is one that extends from the small-scale to the large-scale and back again. From the small-scale, intimate world of our own personal relationships, deep down to our minds and our bodies and our souls, to the large-scale world of globalized capitalism, the struggle for queer liberation, and the struggle to abolish straightness; these are inseparable from anti-capitalist and anti-statist struggle. The collective effort to abolish straightness is one that serves to benefit all in the long run. The collective effort to abolish straightness, to allow for queer forms of gender, sexuality, identity, and performance out of the closet and into our own anti-capitalist struggle—this is a kind of liberation for all. Taking the time to reevaluate the language we use to communicate about gender and sexuality, and the assumptions we make about people's bodies and desires (including our own), is not only absolutely essential for the inclusion of queer *people* in our struggles, it is essential for the inclusion of the queer*ness* that is present inside all of us. This kind of queer praxis, and the radical inclusion that it allows, is absolutely essential to any kind of genuine anti-hierarchical, anti-capitalist, anti-statist struggle.

1   Please note, I am not arguing that there is anything inherently "straight" about property destruction. There are plenty of anarchists out there who practice various forms of direct action—including property destruction and other forms of action—in ways that are conscious of inter-group power dynamics. What I am concerned with is not which particular forms of anarchist politics are used, but rather the

cult of machismo within many anarchist communities, and the ways in which these forms of machismo make straight men and those around them vulnerable.

Anarchy, BDSM, and Consent-based Culture

HEXE

I want to talk about anarchy, and I want to talk about BDSM and kinky sex. They are both incredibly controversial subjects. So let's start slowly, with some lube. As if we were going to attempt anal sex.

Let's do some defining. Defining is great; it makes sense of previously confusing subjects. BDSM is an acronym that has several interpretations; indeed, it is a compound acronym! It is derived from the terms bondage and discipline (B&D or B/D), dominance and submission (D&S or D/s), and sadism and masochism (S&M or S/M). BDSM includes a wide spectrum of activities, interpersonal relationships, and distinct subcultures. Participants usually take on complementary but unequal roles within a BDSM context. The idea of consent of both the partners becomes essential. Of- ten participants who are active (applying the activity or exercising some from of control over others) are known as tops or dominants. Those participants who are recipients of the activities, or who are controlled by their partners, are typically known as bottoms or submissives. Individuals who assume either top/dominant or bottom/submissive roles (whether from relationship to relationship or within a specific relationship only) are known as switches. I should also mention that tops and dominants are different roles, and bottoms and submissives are also different roles. The differences are not immediately apparent to the outside observer, but very important to the people who identify with them. There are also people who enjoy aspects of BDSM that are not explicitly sexual. BDSM is based on sexual practices but also incorporates our daily interactions and experiences with power. So that is the very, very tip of the iceberg. Inevitably, no matter what, someone somewhere will find offense with any definition and start a heated discussion about it.

The diverse rainbow of anarchy, henceforth referred to as the Anarchy-Bow, can be a confusing mess. It is comprised of bickering theorists, insurrectionists, primitivists, armchair radicals, and the occasional right-wing jerk all struggling to be correct about the next tactic or developing analysis. There is often disagreement within the Anarchy-Bow. This disagreement is particularly rabid due to a basic consensus. The Anarchy-Bow disagrees with itself with the rabid intensity of people who share similar ethics debating how to change the current world order from a hierarchy based on abuse and exploitation to a system without someone at the top of the oppression pyramid scheme. (And without the entire pyramid scheme). What we want is a system that benefits everyone and eliminates prejudice and racism and the inequalities of capitalism; and then we'll all have our own unicorn to ride along shining streams. Because you know you want your own unicorn. To ride into battle. Against capitalism.

In an attempt to simplify the Anarchy-Bow, I have divined what is to me the First Unwritten Rule of Anarchy. The First Unwritten Rule of Anarchy is "Don't Be A Douchebag." All of the fancy theories, all of the discussion about tactics and support and building a new world by tearing down the old and whatnot all come down to the fact that in this world people are often douchebags. They are douchebags to one another; they are douchebags to the planet; they are douchebags to animals. There are whole systems of indoctrination that teach us to be douchebags to one another from the time we are children. Many people have spent lots and lots of time explaining the ways that people are douchebags and how the structure of society teaches us to be douchebags. The goal of anarchy is to change that, not just a little, but entirely.

All of our wonderful systems of organization and activism that work so well are often undermined by the brokenness of the system we are raised in. The way that even in a non-hierarchical organization there are often people who call the shots, or the person who is always getting their way and not allowing others to speak. We are the result of hundreds of years of oppression, colonization, capitalism, genocide, racism, and sexism. We can't help but have internalized some of that, even if we are dedicated to changing the system. Often this happens on the traditional lines of gender and race oppressions, but other times it is subtler. In attempting to dismantle a busted system, we all bring our own baggage and prejudices. What we can do is learn from it and work to make our practice of anarchy as equal as possible.

"Revolution" is a funny word. It has been assigned to many things, and according to the cultural history of the United States of America there has already been a sexual revolution. A lot of people in the last century did a lot of work around sexuality and freedom and we are benefiting from it today, but there were radicals before the hippies who were doing and saying the same things about sexual freedom. The sexual revolution has been happening for a long time and continues to do so. Some people even go so far as to say anarchy is love. Which sounds like we're all a bunch of hippies with fancy analyses of politics and anti-oppression and whatnot, but I'm sure Emma Goldman had no fucking clue what a hippie was going to be and she was all about love. Emma Goldman was a really huge badass. Sadly there are no surviving pictures of her riding a unicorn.

I believe there are hundreds of sexual revolutions happening every day. Every day people accept themselves and their sexuality and support one another to subvert the heterosexist idea that the only valid sexual relationships are between one man and one woman. The dominant narrative says they must both be cisgendered—having a match between the gender they were assigned at birth, their bodies, and their personal identity. This oppression hurts all of us. Sex can be very personally revolutionary. It can be healthy and it can be a form of self-care and it can be medicine, but only if it is done with full consent and participation of all parties. Historically anarchists have been very vocal about supporting sexual freedom and queer rights. Emma Goldman spoke out against marriage and for the right of women to have access to birth control; her lover and compatriot Alexander Berkman wrote about being queer and supporting queer rights. Anarchy has always been a little queer, and anarchists have always been nerds for sexual freedom and choice. Why not BDSM as well?

You might have noticed I used the word "queer" in several different ways. Originally "queer" was used to describe something odd or abnormal. It is also used in reference to a group of people. Traditionally "queers" have been folk who engage in sexy times with people of a similar gender, transgender folk, and the word extends to include those who engage in relationships outside the heteronormative monogamous party line. The label "queer" was reclaimed from being a slur, an insult. That's how tough we are; we can take language intended to hurt us and turn it into a something completely different. The definition has fluctuated and is often in debate. To queer something, used as a verb is to subvert it, change it subtly or radically. Like we did with the use and definition of the word itself. The Anarchy-Bow both loves and hates queerness.

Like in the anarchist community, again in the BDSM community there is the problem of people coming to it as a sexual practice with the same amount of baggage as when people come to anarchy. I have sometimes heard people speak of their personal practice of BDSM as if it cures all things. In those experiences, I felt like I was witnessing a personal spiritual moment. I am not a proponent of choosing anything as your shining light, though as a human race we have a tendency to do so. The mainstream BDSM community has been called out in many, many instances for sexism, heterosexism, racism, ableism, and not being accessible to people who are not middle class or financially liquid. Sexism, the act of gender discrimination, is a problem in almost every part of this society and hence carries over into BDSM spaces. Heterosexism is interesting in the context of the current incarnation of the mainstream BDSM community, which often identifies itself as a pansexual, open to all sexualities and genders, space. The history of BDSM in the United States comes directly from queer spaces, particularly the gay male leather and fisting community, quickly taking hold in lesbian spaces as well. At a certain point, some called BDSM the practice of "radical sex." One thing the BDSM community adheres to with a passion is the idea of consensual power exchange. A scene can look non-consensual, can be playing with non-consent, but it is still just playing.

One's experience with BDSM, like any sexual practice, is personal. For some it's not something they will be interested in for various reasons. Some people just aren't wired kinky; some people need time to work out their feelings about it. There's a lot of guilt around sexuality in general, and around non-normative sexuality specifically. It's a hard journey for a lot of us to a place where we are comfortable with all aspects of our selves and our sexuality. Another thing folks have come up against is just plain bad experiences with BDSM. Maybe the person they played with was a jerk and didn't respect their boundaries. Maybe they had a bad experience with the community they joined to experience BDSM. Maybe they just felt alienated by some of the monetary barriers to the BDSM scene; play parties cost a lot of money; conventions cost hundreds of dollars, and that's before you add in lodging and food. Or perhaps the overwhelming lack of people of color in many kinky communities was a barrier. There is value in BDSM as a fun thing, as a human need, as a fulfilling practice, as a way to play with power, and just as a way to play as an adult. We can't take off our skin color or gender easily or switch up our privileges at the drop of a hat in the real world, but we can play with power and control or the lack of it in a BDSM scene. And it ends when you are done. Not when the intersections of oppressions and privilege stop doing their various screwy things, because that might take a while. We're chipping steadily away at them, but the leviathan of inequality is massive. The ability to play with power can teach us new ways to understand how we have internalized different parts of the abusive dominant culture, and new ways to think about resistance.

Doing anarchy might not include practicing BDSM, but doesn't exclude it either. BDSM and anarchy have more than their share of differences, but if anything, there is one fetish both anarchists and BDSM folk share and that is a fetish for consent and organizing people. Both communities are consent-based cultures. Consent is the act of agreeing to an act, situation, or circumstance by various means, generally verbal or written. Occasionally implied consent is used in medical situations so caregivers can administer medical attention while someone is unconscious. However, administering a life-saving protocol and having sex with someone are too drastically different to fall under the same guidelines of consent. By consent-based cultures I mean they talk about consent, they discuss ways to gain and give consent. As a community and as individuals they write things about consent, what it means to them, and how to implement it

The dominant culture is terrible at consent; capitalism doesn't ask if you want to be exploited; patriarchy doesn't ask if you want to be considered a second-class citizen based on what's between your legs, or, inversely, be taught to be an oppressor based on what's between your legs. We are all constantly learning how to give and obtain consent, and not everyone is good at it…yet. Everyone has a story about a creepy anarchist or a messed up kinky person not respecting folks. Through applying active principles of consent to our lives and our sex lives and taking that into every relationship we have, sexual and nonsexual, more and more people will be able to use those skills, and we will always be improving our own use of consent as well.

Everything and anything can be revolutionary. The most insignificant tool can begin an insurrection. Anything that is fulfilling, healthy and doesn't harm anyone else can be medicine. As a community and as individuals it is a revolutionary act to be dedicated to consent. Doing anarchy and doing BDSM are not things that intersect often except in the lives of people who practice both. However, if there is something that both the Anarchy-Bow and ethical BDSM practices can give to the struggle for a just society, it is the skill of active consent.

And everyone gets a unicorn.

Acknowledgments

C. B. Daring:

I want to thank my co-editors Abbey Volcano, Deric Shannon, J. Rogue, all the authors included in this collection, Martha Ackelsberg, Kate Khatib, and Dustin Shannon for all their work. Rogue, you're an amazing friend and have constantly challenged me to develop my analysis. Deric, you have pushed me to be more thoughtful and deliberate in my writing. Abbey, your humor and intellectual innovation is inspiring. I also want to thank my best friend and partner James Hannon for tirelessly editing and encouraging me. This book would not have been possible without the years of work you all have dedicated to it. I am so grateful to all of the people who have influenced and helped shape me politically and personally, and to all of the sex workers who have helped me see the embodiment of the economy. I believe that the work we have all done here will serve to further a movement of beauty, freedom, creativity, justice and intersectionality.

J. Rogue:

There are so many people to thank, I can't possibly name them all, but here are a few: Deric, for encouraging and challenging me. I am so glad to know you and work with you. C. B. Daring, for being an amazing comrade, friend, confidante and conversationalist. I love you. Abbey, for being incredibly smart and fun, making me think, and doing awesome work. Andi, Del, Katie and Tyrone, for processing with me and being smart and awesome. My brother Travis and my father, for their support and encouragement in my writing and organizing, for teaching me critical thinking, and for great conversations. My mom, from whom I learned a lot in the time we had. Dr. Sheppard for all her inspiration and help. My WSA people for all the incredible work y'all do. All of our authors, their amazing writing and great organizing, and AK Press for putting it out in the world. It has been a pleasure to work with you all. All of my comrades and friends that I have worked with over the years and across the country. Thanks for challenging me to learn and grow as a person and an anarchist. For struggling alongside me and refusing to give up. When I am overwhelmed by all that we are fighting against, thank you for reminding me what we are fighting for.

Deric Shannon:

First, I'd like to thank my friends and fellow editors, Abbey, J. Rogue, and C. B. Daring. It's been a wonderful few years of a project—particularly Rogue since we've been in this thing since the beginning and because Rogue originally helped come up with the idea and plan. Secondly, I'd like to thank our copyeditor extraordinaire, Dustin Shannon, my brother and friend. My friends and comrades from Queers Without Borders deserve a special thank you—particularly Richard, Jerimarie, Frank, Paul, Alvin, Sarah, Alice, and M. Bernardo McLaughlin for helping shape a lot of my ideas around politics generally, but specifically around gender and sexuality, often through long and intense conversations—sometimes through writing, and other times through actions. Special thanks are also due to Abbey V, my teacher when it comes to queer theory and my translator of Judith Butler texts and my near-constant companion over the last few years. Some other friends who have helped shape my ideas around the intersections of desire, sexual freedom, gender, sex, and the complicated mess of daily life through conversations, editing, collective writing, and loving also deserve much gratitude: Jamie Heckert, Maria Yates, Virgil Carstens, Davita Silfen Glasberg, Benjamin Shepard, Martha Ackelsberg, Nancy Naples, Mary Burke, Brooke Hammond, Gayge Operaista, Saffo, and Amney Harper. Much love and respect to each and every one of you. I'd like to thank AK Press, and particularly Kate Khatib, Suzanne Shaffer, and Zach Blue, all of whom have been awesome to work with. Finally, I'd like to thank every person alive struggling to smash the structures, cultures, and concepts that oppress, repress, and exploit us and fill our daily lives with violence, banality, boredom, misery, and loss. Let's build many different futures by negating those social relations! Negate negate negate!

Abbey Volcano:

I'd like to thank J. Rogue, C. B. Daring, and Deric Shannon for being incredibly patient people to work with. And mostly for being lovely friends. I love y'all. I'd also like to thank all contributing authors, Martha Ackelsberg, Dustin Shannon, and Kate, Suzanne, and Zach at AK for all the effort they have put into this project. The folks at Queers Without Borders have helped me think through much of the content in my chapter and I am grateful to have them as friends and comrades. Ella, Lauren, Joe, and Mom have all been an incredibly supportive family and have continuously made me feel like I am awesome even when I make really bad decisions. Deric has consistently pushed me to speak, write, and think in ways that I never would've done without him as a loving friend, comrade, and mentor. I want to thank him for making my life way more hilarious, complex, and interesting than ever. I'd like to thank my friends and mentors who have challenged me to think more complexly about gender, sexuality, desire, and practice: Charles Weigl, Flint Arthur, Saffo, Mary Burke, Joshua Stephens, Maria Yates, Naitha Bellissis, Fleury Rose, Mary Bernstein, Nancy Naples, Grace Hart, Angie Mejia, Margaret Breen, Brenna Harvey, Andrej Grubacic, Mike Jackson, Jerimarie Liesegang, Carrie Elliott, Katie Gregory, Jamie Heckert, Meredith Arcari, David Hays, Gayge Operaista, Chris Spannos, Lauren Lo Bue, Chris Wohlers, and Jason Lydon. RIP Boomer. I hope this volume helps to spark seeds of understanding, connection, destruction, creation, and struggle toward a less fucked-up world.

J. ROGUE is an intersectional anarchist-communist who has been organizing in anarchist, feminist and radical queer movements for over ten years. Much of that work has centered around HIV/AIDS, prisons, and militarism, and making connections between systems of oppression and exploitation, in particular through the lens of media analysis. Rogue is a member of the Workers Solidarity Alliance and currently lives and works in Austin, Texas.

DERIC SHANNON is a radical currently living on the West Coast in the United States. He is co-author and co-editor of *Political Sociology: Oppression, Resistance, and the State* (Pine Forge Press 2010) and *The Accumulation of Freedom: Writings on Anarchist Economics* (AK Press 2012) respectively. He is also the author of many book chapters, journal articles, and reviews typically on social movements, political economy, culture, sexuality, and their intersections with radical politics. He is a believer in radically different presents and futures.

ABBEY VOLCANO is an anarchist militant currently living in eastern Connecticut, typically organizing around sexuality, gender, and struggles for reproductive freedom. When she's not reading graphic novels and watching sci-fi, she's trying to subvert the dominant paradigm, typically writing on identity, sexuality, gender, and political economy. She's a member of the Workers Solidarity Alliance, Queers Without Borders, the IWW, and a constant critic of the violence and boredom inherent in institutionalized hierarchies of all kinds. Her latest essay is co-authored with J. Rogue and can be found in the new edition of *Quiet Rumours* just republished this season by AK Press.

C. B. DARING is an intersectional, anarchist-communist, queer sex worker. They have spent many years organizing within the radical queer, sex worker rights, anarchist, and labor movements nationally and regionally. They have been published in various magazines, newspapers and blogs. They are a member of the Workers Solidarity Alliance, a collective member at Red Emma's Bookstore and Coffeehouse and a popular education facilitator. C. B. heartily believes that practice makes progress.

SANDRA JEPPESEN has been active in anti-authoritarian collective grassroots organizing for fifteen years. She has written about the use of autonomous media by the Ontario Coalition Against Poverty, Les Panthères Roses, a radical queer anarchist group in Montreal, and the Elaho Valley Anarchist Horde, an ecoanarchist group in British Columbia. She is assistant professor in the Department of Communication Studies, Concordia University, Montreal (for now).

HEXE is a genderqueer adventurer (a bit more on the boy edge these days) with the alignment of Chaotic Good and a love for for harm reduction, sex workers, horizontal organizing, sexual freedom, and radical politics. With a deep reverence for medicine in all its forms, Hexe tries to channel the spirit (but not always the word) of André Breton as a doctor (he totally was) and also the spirits of all other creatures dedicated to or inspired by surrealism or Dadaism in the art and medicine and adventures they/he practices.

A.J. WITHERS is a disabled, queer/trans organizer with the Ontario Coalition Against Poverty and a co-founder of DAMN, a radical cross disability organization in Toronto. He is the author of *Disability Politics and Theory* (Fernwood Publishing) and the popular web and zine series "If I Can't Dance Is It Still My Revolution?," which can be found at still.my.revolution.tao.ca.

ANTHONY J. NOCELLA, II, Ph.D., is a visiting professor in the School of Education at Hamline University. Nocella focuses his attention on critical urban education, peace and conflict studies, inclusive social justice education, environmental education, disability pedagogy, queer pedagogy, feminist pedagogy, critical pedagogy, anarchist studies, critical animal studies, and hip-hop pedagogy. He has written in more than two dozen publications, co-founded more than ten active sociopolitical organizations and five academic journals, and is working on his fifteenth book.

LIAT BEN-MOSHE is a scholar/activist who had written on such topics as inclusive pedagogy; disability studies in higher education; academic repression; disability, anti-capitalism and anarchism; disability in Israel; representations of disability; the International Symbol of Access; deinstitutionalization and incarceration; activism and the politics of abolition. Her dissertation, "Genealogies of Resistance to Incarceration: Abolition Politics in Anti-prison and Deinstitutionalization Activism in the U.S.," looked at demands to close down repressive institutions that house those labeled as "criminals," mentally disabled and "mentally ill." Liat is currently a postdoctoral research associate at the Department of Disability and Human Development at the University of Illinois at Chicago and earned her PhD in sociology, disability studies and women and gender studies from Syracuse University.

GAYGE OPERAISTA is an autonomist Marxist and Italian@ butch deep lezzing it up in New England. They are a street medic, herbalist, W-EMT, health care educator, and nursing student, as well as a spoken word artist, writer, and an organizer, having been involved in some form of organizing or another for well over a decade. They are a member of the IWW, a former TransFix NorCal organizer, and a former Camp Trans organizer. The major focuses of their work are nursing student and nurse organizing, organizing around caregiving, disseminating knowledge to enable members of their community to better provide care and support to each other, helping those mutual aid networks form, and linking trans community struggles for survival to workplace struggles.

FARHANG ROUHANI is an associate professor of cultural and political geography at the University of Mary Washington in Fredericksburg, Virginia. His academic and activist interests include globalization and state formation in Iran, migration rights, queer liberation, and anarchist theory and practice.

BENJAMIN HEIM SHEPARD, PhD, is an assistant professor of human services at New York City College of Technology. He is the author of six books, including *Queer Political Performance and Protest: Play, Pleasure and Social Movement* and *Play, Creativity, and Social Movements*, and *The Beach Beneath the Streets*, with Greg Smithsimon. Correspondence to: benshepard@mindspring.com www.benjaminheimshepard.com.

JERIMARIE LIESEGANG is a genderqueer anarchist and long-time Connecticut trans activist and advocate. Jerimarie started the transgender grass roots advocacy organization It's Time Connecticut over a decade ago that has evolved into the current Connecticut TransAdvocacy

Coalition. Jerimarie is also a co-founder of Queers Without Borders and has authored numerous published articles, spoken on many panels and presented workshops around social justice and gender-noncon-forming issues. Jerimarie is a strong advocate of multi-issue organizing in the spirit of Audre Lorde's vision that "there is no such thing as a single-issue struggle because we do not live single-issue lives."

JASON LYDON is a Unitarian Universalist minister, radical queer anarchist committed to the movement to abolish the prison industrial complex. Jason is the founder of Black and Pink—an organization that advocates for and supports queer and trans prisoners across the United States. If you are searching for fun things to do with Jason, outside of organizing the revolution, you may find him riding bicycles, eating cupcakes, or watching obnoxious blockbuster movies on opening night.

RYAN CONRAD is an outlaw artist, terrorist academic, petty thief, and sassy anarchist faggot from a small mill town in Maine. He works through visual culture and performance to rupture the queer here and now in hopes of making time and space to imagine the most fantastic queer futures. His visual work is archived at faggotz.org and he is a member of the editorial collective for the digital archive Against Equal-ity (againstequality.org). He can be reached at rconrad@meca.edu.

COLLECTIF DE RECHERCHE SUR L'AUTONOMIE COLLEC-TIVE (CRAC) is an anti-authoritarian feminist queer anti-racist anti-colonialist research collective in Montreal that engages in Participatory-Action Research of Montreal anti-authoritarian groups and networks.

STEPHANIE GROHMANN was born in Vienna, Austria, and after doing her undergraduate degree in social work moved to the UK in 2009 to do a MSc in gender studies. Currently she is in the first year of my PhD course in Goldsmiths College, University of London. She has been an activist in anarchist and related contexts for the last de-cade, focusing mostly on alternative economic practices, the critique of work and exchange, and various feminist contexts. She currently live in London.

STACY/SALLYDARITY is the creator and editor of anarchalibrary. blogspot.com, formerly the "resources" section of anarcha.org, which provides a vast archive of items of interest to anarcha-feminists. She also blogs at chaparralrespectsnoborders.blogspot.com about the situation around the border and immigration enforcement. She has been involved in various activities such as copwatch, indymedia, indigenous solidarity, political prisoner support, etc. She also dabbles in music, herbalism, nutrition, and gardening.

SUSAN SONG is a queer, kinky, Chinese anarchist. She recently graduated from the University of Illinois at Urbana-Champaign with a bachelors' in psychology and was involved in an anarchist reading group and Really Really Free Market. She currently resides in Chicago.

SAFFO PAPANTONOPOULOU is a queer, third-gender, fabulous femme, anticapitalist blogger, academic, and community (dis)organizer. She is the daughter of a war refugee. Her family is Greek-Egyptian. She is passionate about queer liberation, decolonization, anti-Zionism and anti-imperialism. She is currently pursuing an MA in anthropology, and hopes to someday actually get paid for her ideas. You can read more of her writing at saffosmash.blogspot.com.

DIANA C. S. BECERRA has organized within various movements, from immigrant and domestic workers' rights, to the struggle for accessible public education. She is an aspiring historian and journalist.

JAMIE HECKERT is an interdependent scholar and founding member of the Anarchist Studies Network. Editor of two collections of writing on anarchism and sexuality, *Sexualities* 13(4) and *Anarchism & Sexuality: Ethics, Relationships and Power* (co-edited with Richard Cleminson), his writings on ethics, erotics, and ecology have also appeared in various books, zines, magazines and websites. Jamie is continuing to queer anarchism with a forthcoming book based on his PhD thesis and in his everyday life. He currently lives on the south coast of England.

Index

Support AK Press!

AK Press is one of the world's largest and most productive

anarchist publishing houses. We're entirely worker-run and democratically managed. We operate without a corporate structure—no boss, no managers, no bullshit. We publish close to twenty books every year, and distribute thousands of other titles published by other like-minded independent presses from around the globe.

The Friends of AK program is a way that you can directly contribute to the continued existence of AK Press, and ensure that we're able to keep publishing great books just like this one! Friends pay a minimum of $25 per month, for a minimum three month period, into our publishing account. In return, Friends automatically receive (for the duration of their membership), as they appear, one free copy of every new AK Press title. They're also entitled to a 20% discount on everything featured in the AK Press Distribution catalog and on the website, on any and every order. You or your organization can even sponsor an entire book if you should so choose!

There's great stuff in the works—so sign up now to become a Friend of AK Press, and let the presses roll!

Won't you be our friend? Email friendsofak@akpress.org for more info, or visit the Friends of AK Press website: http://www.akpress.org/programs/friendsofak